James McC

THE KING OF DOWN FOOTBALL

with
Seamus McRory

BLACKWATER PRESS

Edited by: Adam Brophy
Design and Layout: Liz White Designs

ISBN 978-0-9566612-2-7
© James McCartan, 2010
BWP Ltd., 1-5 North Frederick Street, Dublin 1
Printed in the Republic of Ireland.
jloconnor@eircom.net

All rights reserved. No part of this publication may be reproduced, stored in a retrieval system, or transmitted in any form, or by any means, electronic, mechanical, photocopying, recording, or otherwise, without the prior written permission of the publisher.

This book is sold subject to the conditions that it shall not, by way of trade or otherwise, be lent, resold, hired out or otherwise circulated without the publisher's prior consent in any form of binding or cover other than that in which it is published and without a similar condition including this condition being imposed on the subsequent purchaser.

Dedication

To Marie, Brian, James, Delia, Charlie Pat, Maria, Daniel and Eoin.

With sincere thanks for your constant help and support over the years.

Acknowledgments

As well as the people and the publications that helped me in the research for this book, there are many others to whom I will always be deeply indebted. My wife Marie and all my family take pride of place. Their constant encouragement and consistent support was very much appreciated. My sister Gay Glynn and Ulster Council GAA Secretary Danny Murphy receive special plaudits for their regular "hands-on" advice and extremely valuable input. Their incredible and combined photographic memories enhanced the entire process.

I would especially like to thank Olive, Mairéad and Diarmuid McRory for their many and varied contributions to the preparation of the final script. To three of my former and very formidable opponents and now good friends – James Brady (Cavan), Paddy McCormack (Offaly) and Mick O'Dwyer (Kerry) – my deepest appreciation for your generous written tributes in this book.

Managing Director John O'Connor and all the staff at Blackwater Press deserve my sincere thanks for being so enthusiastic and professional about the whole project. Editor Adam Brophy, in particular, was exceptionally helpful in so many different ways as the book gradually unfolded. I would particularly like to thank Joe Hunt from Legan in County Longford for the highly efficient manner in which he undertook the arduous task of proofing. Being a native of Offaly I know that Joe took great delight in checking the accuracy of what I had to say about the intriguing contests between our two counties in 1960 and 1961!

When Derryman Seamus McRory, who lives in Longford, approached me several years ago with the concept of an autobiography I was at first very reluctant to participate in such an ambitious idea. However, after his continual persistence, endless research and numerous journeys from Longford to conduct interviews, what initially appeared to be a fanciful notion has now become a reality. To Seamus go my greatest thanks.

James McCartan
September 2010

The Co-Author

Seamus McRory was born in the parish of Lissan in south Derry. A former chairman of his native club, with whom he played football in the 1960s and 1970s, he currently represents his adopted club, Longford Slashers, on the Longford County Board.

Over the past number of years, Seamus, a retired primary school principal, has contributed many articles to various GAA publications. He is also the author of *The Voice from the Sideline: Famous GAA Managers* (1997), *The Road to Croke Park: Great GAA Personalities* (1999) and *The All-Ireland Dream* (2005).

Educated at his local primary school and St Patrick's College, Armagh, Seamus continued his studies at St Joseph's College of Education and Queen's University, Belfast. He lives in Abbeycartron just outside Longford town with his wife Olive and family Mairéad and Diarmuid.

Contents

Foreword .... *viii*

Introduction .... *x*

1. "I'll Bring Home the Sam Maguire Cup, Even If I Have To Steal It" 1
2. My Native Place – Donacloney 12
3. St Colman's College – Where It All Began 19
4. Early Career 27
5. Our Time Has Come 36
6. A Good Team Becomes Great 52
7. America Here We Come 67
8. The Last Goodbye 76
9. The Stars of the County Down 85
10. Dr Maurice Hayes – The Visionary 100
11. My Clubs – Glenn and Tullylish 109
12. The Glory Days Revisited 117
13. A Voice From The Sideline 123
14. A New Generation of Heroes 135
15. Red And Black Come Again 144
16. Going To The Dogs 153
17. Loyalist Intimidation and Extreme Republicanism 158
18. A GAA Family Dynasty 173
19. The Cream of the Crop 181
20. Past Memories, Future Hopes 188

    Epilogue *201*

    Index *204*

Foreword

I write this foreword in the belief that it is virtually impossible to totally encapsulate the person that James McCartan really is. He is a legendary figure within the Gaelic Athletic Association who will always be remembered as the unstoppable dynamo of the developing Down team of the 1950s and the talismanic figure of the vastly talented sides of the 1960s. James was a central part of those wonderful teams that consisted of magnificent footballers who had a combined vision of what could be achieved. They were a group of highly motivated people who put their individual and collective ambitions into red and black jerseys and accepted that nothing short of victory would suffice. They had a common goal and it was the cause of Down. Who were these heroes and why did they achieve what previous generations had failed to do despite their valiant efforts? In essence these were all great men whose phenomenal commitment and marvellous ability left a permanent legacy to the GAA and to their county that is truly immeasurable.

This book tells the story of James McCartan in every facet of his existence. It is a remarkable life that is both outstanding and outspoken. Throughout, the whole person of James is there to be seen. It is there in the young boy who was defiant to the extent that his grandfather rewarded him for his determination. It is there in his trials and tribulations as a student at famed St Colman's College. But these are cameos of James' overall personality. The lifelong affair with the GAA, the development of friendships, the constant emphasis on teamwork and, of course, the many disagreements are all part of this fascinating personal history. His and the Down team's setback against Galway in 1959 and his clear statement to his father that the Sam Maguire Cup would be in Donacloney in 1960, even if he had to steal it, reflect his unstinted support for his native county. The McCartan family's service to the GAA and to Down, the input and achievements of his brother Dan and also his sons, especially "Wee" James, are all part of this GAA narrative, as are the teams he managed. The good days and bad days, the great days and the sad days are all recalled with both honesty and feeling.

Then there is the family, his parents, the sisters and brother, his wife Marie and their family and the grandchildren. The home in Donacloney, the difficult days of the Troubles and the decision to leave the family home are all given prominence, as are the people who worked in the bar and at Tullyraine Quarries. The greyhounds and friends are all integrated into the memory of James McCartan and provide an incisive insight into his unique personality as well as his separate roles as a player and as a family man. He is still passionate about Gaelic football, the games and the adversaries on opposing teams. His historical involvement and interactions with administration simply make this book compulsory reading.

The publication is a testament, in his own words, to the progress of the GAA not only in Down but nationwide. More importantly, it provides an overdue opportunity for an amazing footballing talent, an astute greyhound aficionado and a forthright and honest man to tell the real account of one of Ireland's greatest sporting icons. This is the story of James McCartan that revisits the milestones, records the total dedication and commitment to the things that are important in his life: his wife, family, Gaelic football, hard work and a tremendous sense of fun. This is a book about a hero I supported in the 1960s, worked with in the seventies and eighties, travelled to games throughout Ireland with in the intervening years and who I am proud to call a friend.

Danny Murphy
(Secretary to Ulster GAA Council)

Introduction

I have been honoured to have had the privilege of sharing with a GAA legend his innermost thoughts, views and memories of the most important occasions that defined his sporting, working and social lives. As we compiled the story of his life I came to know and appreciate the totality of a great family man and a caring and honest human being.

James McCartan was a magnificent footballer and a dedicated and successful greyhound owner with an entrepreneurial flair for farming and business activities. There were many exceptional features to his football ability but it was his penchant for not only creating but also scoring decisive and match-winning goals that set him apart. Three, in particular, come to mind. Undoubtedly his goal in the 1960 All-Ireland senior football final was the catalyst for launching a brilliant all-round Down side into footballing immortality. Down's creative and impressive style of play endeared them to a rapidly increasing number of GAA followers. As a consequence the sport quickly developed a more widespread, positive and infectious impetus of its own. This novel national achievement effectively changed the course of Gaelic football history. Thus a new football force was established for posterity.

James scored many terrific goals in his illustrious career and none more opportune than the one in the 1961 Ulster final against Armagh. Unable to field because of a shoulder injury sustained in the provincial semi-final against Derry, Down supporters burst into a spontaneous roar of approval when he was drafted into the team at the beginning of the second half. As Down were trailing by five points the selectors felt they had no choice but to bring on the unfit star at full forward. Thanks to his clever promptings the Armagh lead was whittled down to two points within the first seven minutes of the second half. Shortly afterwards James gained possession to score a wonderful goal to put the Mourne men on course for their third successive provincial title. Though physically curtailed, his inspirational style of play and goalpoaching skill had turned a possible defeat into a great victory.

In that year's All-Ireland final with Offaly, the midlanders led Down by six points after only six minutes of play. Over 20 minutes later the northerners were still five points behind. In 1984, at the Down Centenary Banquet, former GAA President Paddy Buggy eloquently recalled what happened next:

> *I was standing with a group of fellow Kilkenny people and I can remember to this day James McCartan's goal – the greatest that I have ever seen scored in Croke Park. With his back to the goals James went up to the clouds to field the ball. Having safely grasped it, he pivoted in mid-air and before he touched the ground he hit a left-footed screamer to the back of the net. The green flag was waving long before the goalkeeper knew where the ball was.*

In a lifetime of watching Gaelic games I have never known of a player to create such a buzz of excitement amongst his supporters whenever he got the ball and at the same time generate incredible, outright panic between playing opponents and opposing fans. The reason for this was quite simple. James McCartan was a dynamic talisman whose electrifying runs led inevitably to the raising of a flag – usually green. That was what made him so special in the eyes of Down supporters.

During the 30 years of the Troubles, James, his wife Marie and their family displayed tremendous personal courage and self-sacrifice. In what must have been an especially difficult and challenging period in their lives they showed fantastic forbearance and marvellous dignity despite the many huge obstacles being continually placed in front of them.

In 1960 I was a young secondary school student at St Patrick's College in Armagh. The college was a real bastion of Gaelic football; they were the first winners of the Hogan cup in 1946. On entering the college we were happily indoctrinated into the GAA by being shown an old recording of that historic match on an end-to-end film reel and we were really impressed by the outstanding contributions of the incomparable Iggy Jones and the Devlin brothers, Jim and Eddie, in that game. Of course all three went on to star for Tyrone in the 1956 and 1957 All-Ireland semi-finals. I remember well how excited we all were as the whole student body assembled in the study hall to listen to the 1960 All-Ireland final match commentary by Micheal O'Hehir on the radio. For us the most important question was would Down be the first team to bring the Sam Maguire cup across the border. Thankfully we were not to be disappointed. I have recalled my personal reminiscences of that famous red-letter day in the following prose poem, which I dedicate to all who avidly follow the Games of the Gael.

MAGICAL MEMORIES OF A SEPTEMBER SUNDAY

Sitting in the study hall
Of an old, grey college building,
Spending a lonely boarding school Sunday afternoon,
Listening to the golden voice emanating from a
Battered brown radio in the corner;
Our minds wandered back in time as our
Thoughts dovetailed perfectly into feelings
Of isolation and hopelessness.

For years we had felt disillusioned,
Almost totally abandoned,
Though patronised by some with
"You are great for keeping the GAA alive."
Yet we knew there was no real ambition,
No chance of progress or success;
Just loosely attached antennae on the
Periphery of where we wanted to be.

Our games were really for the Kerrys and Kilkennys,
The Corks and Dublins of this world.
Sometimes the Louths, Roscommons, Waterfords
And Armaghs would suddenly appear on the horizon,
Only to disappear rapidly into the abyss where
The rest of us permanently resided;
Often eliminated in the first round,
Rarely going any further than the second.

Along came a man of clear vision, a person
Of definite purpose, of real substance.
Different structures were laid, visionary strategies planned
And the best footballers in the Mournes
Perfectly positioned.
The ethic of team play, on and off the field,
Became paramount;
Everyone singularly focused on the same specific goal.

Introduction

That day of days, that moment of truth had now arrived.
The footballers of Down were ready
For whatever was placed in front of them.
Running out to an almighty roar
And a huge unfurling of the red and black,
Kevin Mussen led his warriors
To the cauldron of their destiny;
Kerry in their twenty-ninth – Down in their first.

The first half ebbed and flowed as first
David and then Goliath exchanged leading roles,
Before the short whistle sounded.
With the northern stars in front by two.
At half time the excitement was palpable, almost unbearable,
As that dream of dreams became more attainable
For every man, woman and child
Who had travelled southwards from early morn.

In the second half a long James McCartan lob
Was the defining catalyst for each Down player
To be released from the shackles of history and mediocrity.
When a Paddy Doherty penalty special put them six ahead,
The whole arena spontaneously erupted
Into a cacophony of joy and anticipated glory.
Kerry supporters stunned into silence;
Down fans praying for the remaining minutes to pass quickly and easily.

They need not have worried.
The Mourne workrate increased immensely.
New heights of skill were scaled.
The full repertoire of their collective artistry
Was displayed with exquisite panache and exhilarating beauty.
The Ballykinlar bricklayer, in particular,
Nonchalantly executing unprecedented levels of scoring excellence;
To seal a momentous occasion.

When the final whistle sounded
Down had not just won a marvellous football match,

They had captured the hearts of a national and admiring audience.
Down were the All-Ireland football champions,
The voice on the radio said.
A great football team had accomplished
What others ignored.
We really were a nation once again.

Leaving the study hall excited, exuberant;
Momentarily forgetting the chores of books and learning
And the boring repetition of a secondary school routine.
A freshly found freedom permeated our minds.
People of similarity, of aspiration,
With realistic hopes for a future of distinction.
Those magical words "Down are 1960 All-Ireland football champions"
Eliminated the insecurities of the past and fostered togetherness for the future.

To Kevin Mussen and his side of heroes,
We say no team anywhere will ever surpass
What you did for us.
More emphatically – you were the best because you were the first
To remove the iron curtain of suspicion and division.
And bring supporter – friendly, player-friendly Gaelic football
Across the four provinces of Ireland and
To future generations of all our people.

And Maurice Hayes we are glad
That you "Let Go Your Anchor"
On Sweet Killough Bay!
And opened your heart and mind
To a better way of doing things
For the Gaelic footballers of Down and, by extension, every other county.
With your calculated planning and prophetic perception
You have become the real Star of the County Down.

Seamus McRory
25 September 2010

1

"I'll Bring Home the Sam Maguire Cup, Even If I Have To Steal It"

There is one date and one occasion that I will never forget. It was over fifty years ago, Sunday, 23 August 1959, to be precise. For the first time ever Down had arrived in Croke Park as Ulster senior football champions. They were playing Connacht champions Galway in the Mourne County's first All-Ireland senior football semi-final. For me what made everything so special was the fact that I had the honour of being the team's centre half back. Until then the whole year had been a wonderful rollercoaster experience for us but that semi-final turned out to be a complete disaster, or so we thought in the immediate aftermath of the encounter. Galway were a very good, experienced side that had won the 1956 All-Ireland final against Cork. They possessed many fine footballers including the late Jack Mahon at centre half back and the tall, high-fielding Frank Evers at centrefield. In the forward line they had, in Sean Purcell, the greatest all-round footballer that I had ever seen. Full forward Frankie Stockwell was another household name. In the 1956 final he had practically destroyed Cork on his own with a personal tally of 2-5. Despite this we felt that we had enough quality within our own ranks to really put it up to the westerners.

We travelled on the Saturday before the game and stayed overnight in the chalets in Butlin's holiday camp near Gormanston in County Meath. On the morning of the match we drove to Dublin, excited and anticipating if not a good result, at least a first-class performance. Waiting in the dressing room before that game or any game was, for me, always the worst part. With all due respect to our mentors and officials, their words of advice on what to do or not to do tended to fall on deaf ears as far as I was concerned. I just wanted to get out on the pitch and start the game. When we left the darkness of the tunnel and emerged onto the field the roar from our many supporters was deafening. As our colours of red and black were deemed to clash with Galway's maroon and white, both sides were in provincial jerseys. We wore the saffron of Ulster and Galway wore the white of Connacht.

Directly from the throw-in Down's Jarlath Carey gained possession in the half forward line and passed the ball to Brian Morgan in his customary corner forward position. Brian shot brilliantly but his goalbound effort hit the bottom of an upright and rebounded into the waiting hands of Galway defender Sean Meade who was penalised for charging with the ball. The youngest player on the field, Down's Sean O'Neill, pointed the resulting free. Patsy O'Hagan scored a fantastic left-footed point and twice Tony Hadden was unlucky not to find the net. I was happy enough. This was the way I thought we would play.

Then, just as quickly, our normal coolness and ball-winning ability seemed to desert us. By the end of the first quarter Galway had drawn level. Our management then tried many switches but all to no avail. Galway had taken complete control of the game. At half time they went in three points to the good on a 0-5 to 0-2 scoreline.

At half time we were convinced that because we were only three points behind we could and would turn things around. However, Galway began the second half as they ended the first, on top in every sector of the field. Thanks to a Sean Purcell penalty and another point they led 1-6 to 0-2 with only ten minutes of the half gone.

With our backs now to the wall we played with renewed spirit. I managed to catch the ball and passed it out to Sean O'Neill in his right half forward position. He cleverly evaded two Galway tackles and found the overlapping Jarlath Carey with an intelligent pass. Carey sidestepped Jack Mahon and returned the compliment and the ball to O'Neill. Sean soloed goalwards and planted the ball in the net for a really marvellous goal.

For the following five minutes we had a purple patch and when the impressive Carey landed another point we were only three points behind with 15 minutes left to play. Unfortunately for us we then seemed to disappear from the game. Galway upped their performance considerably and we appeared to lack any penetration in that final quarter. Galway eventually ran out deserving and convincing winners by 1-11 to 1-4. Very few of us played well. Leo Murphy, Pat Rice and team captain Kevin Mussen were our best defenders while Sean O'Neill was the only forward to perform to his potential. The papers the next day were complimentary on my own game at centre half back stating I "was here, there and everywhere". That may have been true but I could not get the ball often enough. I was not at all satisfied with my display.

This was a far cry from the optimism that we had all shared in the county at the beginning of the year. Thanks to the foresight of county secretary Maurice Hayes it was agreed at the annual convention in January to reorganise how county teams would be selected. As opposed to the old unwieldy system of the whole county board selecting sides, a new method whereby only three people would be responsible for team selection was adopted. Barney Carr, Brian Denvir and Maurice Hayes were appointed selectors with Barney to act as manager. Danny Flynn, the principal of Saint Malachy's secondary school in Castlewellan, was made team trainer and Dr Martin Walsh from Banbridge became medical advisor to the side.

Our competitive season began when we beat Derry in a play-off for the honour of representing Ulster at the Wembley tournament at the Whit weekend in London in May. This was a competition where the finalists of the previous year's Ulster and Connacht senior football championships played each other again for the right to qualify for the final at the famous soccer stadium. Similarly, the finalists of the Munster and Leinster senior hurling championships played off to qualify for a double header at the same venue.

To indicate the forward thinking of our management team, a challenge game was arranged against Mayo. I will never forget that Mayo match. In those days one had to have a travel pass to cross the border after a certain time. When we reached it, on our way home, we were late as well as having no passes. The very officious official would not let us through. After a prolonged argument he still would not let us cross. By this time many of us were afraid we would not arrive home in time for work the next morning. Eventually, after much hassle, we were permitted to enter Fermanagh. Everyone breathed a collective sigh of relief. Suddenly a player, who shall remain nameless, whispered excitedly. "We'll be home before that so and so." "Why?" asked 20 voices instantly. "Well let us say there is not much air left in the four tyres of his car!" the innocent looking prankster replied.

The Wembley final was arranged for Saturday, 10 May and the county board chartered a plane to bring the team and our growing band of supporters to England. For many of us this was our first experience of flying and everyone was very excited. On the Friday evening we set off from Belfast airport, then known as Nutt's Corner. A communications mix-up meant that our full back Leo

Murphy's seat had been allocated to a stand-by passenger and he was unable to board the flight. However, everything was quickly resolved. Leo got a later flight and eventually joined us at the Russell Hotel in London.

On the morning of the game we could not wait to get on our coach to Wembley Stadium. The moment we first spotted Wembley's famous Twin Towers the whole coachload of us cheered loudly. The English are great people for rules, regulations and protocol but, oblivious to the increasingly frantic instructions of the Wembley officials, we dashed up the tunnel leading onto the pitch. We wanted to see who would have the honour of first setting foot on the sacred sod.

With equal haste we then sped into our dressing rooms, togged out and ran back again into the famous arena. A crowd of over 32,000 made a tremendous din around the ground as Galway and ourselves waited impatiently for the throw-in. Playing in that game was one of my most outstanding memories during all the years that I played Gaelic football. The weather was glorious and when the contest began it was played at a fast and furious pace. More importantly, we as a team really played well. One of that team's great characteristics was its teamwork. The forwards never stopped running even when the ball was in our defence. A player was always available to take a pass when you had possession of the ball. Despite a good start in terms of our ball-winning ability, we soon became wayward in our shooting and as a result we lost our way. Galway took over completely and by the twelfth minute they led by 2-1 to 0-2. Our points were excellent efforts by Paddy Doherty who was the one player who kept his nerve during that initial bad spell. Then, showing maturity beyond his years, Sean O'Neill notched an opportunist goal to leave only two points between the teams.

A few minutes later came one of the greatest goals that I have ever seen. Our full forward Patsy O'Hagan raced towards a ball that appeared to be going wide. He expertly caught it on the end line and, in the same movement, turned and sent a rasping angular shot to the Galway net. Miraculously, we were now in front by a point. From that moment until half time we played superbly as a unit. Three terrific frees from the accurate boot of Paddy Doherty sent us into the interval, leading 2-5 to 2-1.

Not to be outdone, Galway started the second half at a blistering pace with that brilliant footballer Sean Purcell dominating proceedings. Two goals, one by Purcell and one by Mick Garrett, put the westerners ahead. Doherty and Purcell swapped points before two further Galway scores had the Tribesmen leading by two points with ten minutes to go.

It was during this last period that I finally realised that there was something special about this Down team. Everyone had great spirit and determination to succeed no matter how difficult the circumstances. This is easy to achieve when you are winning comfortably but it is when a team is behind that its true mettle is really tested. During those last ten minutes we fought for every ball as if our lives depended on winning it. Patsy O'Hagan – one of the most versatile footballers of that Down team – scored a beauty of a goal. A point followed this from centre half forward Joe Lennon. There was no reply from Galway and we had won. The final score was Down 3-9, Galway 4-4. From a personal viewpoint I was happy with my own performance at centre half back but it was the quality of our teamwork that impressed me most.

Shortly afterwards Down again beat Derry in the semi-final of the McKenna Cup before going on to defeat Monaghan in the final. After that double success I was eagerly awaiting our first round Ulster championship clash with Antrim. It was scheduled for Newcastle on 14 June. Even without our emerging star Sean O'Neill and, in spite of the fact that Antrim recorded a large number of wides, I felt we were good value for a comprehensive 4-9 to 1-3 victory.

As part of the management's strategy to play higher quality sides from outside Ulster we played a challenge game against the then All-Ireland Champions Dublin on 7 July. On that Tuesday evening a huge crowd of 9,000 turned up in Croke Park to see us making our debut in every Gaelic footballer's theatre of dreams. It was an hour of top class football with both sets of supporters showing their appreciation of the fare by applauding the teams off the field both at half time and at full time. I was particularly satisfied after this game because Down continued to show that they could really play with the best sides in the country. It was only in the closing minutes that Dublin scored the equalising goal and that was achieved in very controversial circumstances. Three of the Dublin forwards fouled our goalkeeper Eddie McKay as he attempted to field the ball. Tony Hadden at midfield gave an outstanding performance, as indeed did our whole half forward line of Sean O'Neill, Jarlath Carey and Paddy Doherty. At that time both Paddy Doherty and Joe Lennon were based in England and, to illustrate the serious intent of our selectors, both were flown in for the match. This would have been unheard of at that time, especially when one considers it was only a challenge match. The game itself bore no resemblance whatsoever to the modern concept of these games which are usually played at a leisurely pace with substitutes continually being introduced.

Five days later (there did not appear to be the same need for rest periods or fear of injuries in those days) we played Tyrone in the semi-final of the Ulster Championship at Casement Park. The big question amongst the radio and newspaper pundits centred on one issue. Would the brilliant Down team that were so fantastic against Galway and Dublin turn up, or would we see the mediocre side that struggled to beat an average Monaghan team in the McKenna Cup final appear? To make both statements even more relevant, Tyrone had already beaten Monaghan in the first round of the Ulster Championship.

Played on a very wet and windy day, Tyrone started like a whirlwind, scoring 1-2 before Paddy Doherty opened Down's account with a point. Only several marvellous saves from Eddie McKay prevented Tyrone from dominating the first half on the scoreboard. As it was, they led at half time, 1-4 to 0-2. For the first ten minutes of the second period we were inept. Then I caught the ball from a Joe Lennon free in the middle third of the field, soloed up to the 21-yard line and kicked the ball as low and as hard as I could. Luckily for me (the selectors were always shouting at me about the dangers of leaving my then normal centre half position) the ball went into the net. That score seemed to spur all of us into action. It was nip and tuck for the remainder of the game with the lead alternating several times. Only a magical display by Tyrone's goalkeeper, Thady Turbett, kept our forwards from driving home our territorial advantage. Still, after our abysmal first half display we were happy to settle for a 1-6 draw.

For the drawn encounter we were missing our promising young full back Leo Murphy even though normal left half back Kevin O'Neill had been an able deputy. In the first match my brother Dan had deputised at left half back and had been one of our best defenders despite the fact that he was barely 20 years of age. With Leo now available for the replay the selectors had a dilemma. A late injury to regular midfielder Tony Hadden solved the problem. Patsy O'Hagan was brought from full forward to midfield and Dan was relocated to the number 14 jersey. Kieran Denvir and Brian Morgan occupied the corner forward positions. The weather conditions were as bad as the first day, making the Casement Park pitch even more slippery. Nevertheless that inner resolve in the face of adversity that we had developed stood to us. I mention this because that is what kept us from losing the first game. More importantly that is why we won the second game. Tyrone scored the first two points in the replay but then our brilliant forward line, aided by the magnificence of Patsy O'Hagan and Joe Lennon, tore their defence to shreds. At half time, mainly thanks to the devastating combination play and accuracy of Doherty and Morgan, Down led 1-5 to 0-3. The whole second half was a repeat of the second quarter and Down ran out easy winners on a 1-12 to 0-4 scoreline. The genius of Sean O'Neill, the accuracy and opportunism of Paddy Doherty and Brian Morgan and the sheer hard work of Jarlath Carey on the 40 were a joy to behold. Very often when a team wins, only the forwards get the credit. Our forwards that day were truly outstanding but so was our full back line. To win any game you must at least achieve parity at midfield. Not only did Joe Lennon and Patsy O'Hagan break even, they dominated the sector.

Our manager Barney Carr summed up their performance in his other role as sports journalist. Writing under the pseudonym 'Linesman' in the *Frontier Sentinel*, Barney stated: "Some of O'Hagan's blocking bordered on the heroic and one sequence when he twice blocked Jody O'Neill and then came out with the ball himself had the crowd roaring. Joe Lennon played himself to a standstill and some of his carrying was a delight to watch."

Now for the second year in succession we were in an Ulster final. This time we would be meeting the mighty men of Cavan. They had beaten Down in previous Ulster finals in 1940 and 1942. We hoped that the experience gained in the past 12 months would help us to overcome this bogey team of ours.

Even though many of the leading sportswriters had us as favourites, I realised that this meant nothing if we did not perform to our potential on the day. After all Cavan had a proud and successful record in Ulster finals. Furthermore they possessed many talented players. Men such as Noel O'Reilly, Gabriel Kelly, Captain Tom Maguire and Jim McDonnell were very able defenders. Brian Gallagher was a classy half forward. James Brady, whether at full or corner forward, was an excellent target man. Charlie Gallagher was a very elusive player who could score from any angle. Physically Cavan were big and strong. On the other hand we may have conceded some inches in the height department but overall we liked to play open, fast football. At the same time we all had the ability not to shirk any hard challenges.

When Ulster final day arrived on Sunday, 9 August, the sun shone brilliantly. A huge crowd of Down supporters greeted us when we arrived in Clones. As always I felt impatient as we paraded around the field before the match began. I know supporters love the excitement before a game. They definitely increased the tempo as the whole arena echoed to the cheering and continuous noise. It seemed an eternity before referee Michael McArdle of Louth threw in the ball. We began well and within 20 seconds Tony Hadden had given us the lead with a superb point. Almost immediately Brian Gallagher equalised for Cavan. Briefly,

I wondered was this the way it was going to be for the remainder of the game. Then our midfield assumed complete control.

Within the next five minutes Paddy Doherty scored two points, and Kevin Mussen came up from the half back line to add another well-taken point. Though Charlie Gallagher scored another point soon afterwards, the Cavan side faded from the game for the rest of the half. Our midfielders remained on top; our defence was tight and always alert to the broken ball. I was happy enough with my own display as well. It was the movement and accuracy of our forwards, however, that stood out most. Their skill and pace ripped the Cavan defence asunder with the result that they resorted to conceding a lot of frees. Consequently, our free taker Paddy Doherty scored two points. Kieran Denvir then added another from play. The excellent Tony Hadden made a terrific catch near the end line before curling the ball over the bar for a spectacular point. Doherty, who was having a field day, then raced through the heart of the Cavan rearguard before parting to Brian Morgan in the left corner who duly blasted the ball to the net. Two more fouls by the Cavan defence meant two more frees for Paddy Doherty who coolly slotted both over the bar to leave the half time score reading Down 1-10, Cavan 0-2.

Our dressing room at half time was a very enjoyable place. We were very pleased with the way the whole team was playing and could not wait to get out onto the field for the second half. Cavan began well but our defenders were equal to the task. Then, showing terrific acceleration, Sean O'Neill danced through the whole Cavan backline and passed the ball to Jarlath Carey. The Dundrum man flicked the ball first time over Tom Maguire's head to Tony Hadden who blasted the ball to the net. Only two minutes of the second half had elapsed and we were leading 2-10 to 0-2. Our goalkeeper Eddie McKay then showed his fantastic agility when he stopped a piledriver from James Brady. A brilliant interception and a lengthy clearance from Leo Murphy prevented another Cavan score. Kieran Denvir and Charlie Gallagher exchanged points to leave the score 2-11 to 0-3 in our favour.

When Sean O'Neill got injured, after a very heavy challenge from a Cavan defender, my brother Dan came on at full forward and Tony Hadden switched to right half forward. Immediately O'Hagan got a point before the Gallagher brothers notched 0-3 between them. It was now 2-12 to 0-6 with fifteen minutes to go. Recovered from his injury, Sean O'Neill returned at the expense of Kieran Denvir. He showed no ill effects when he too scored a point just after Cavan had scored their seventh and last score. At this stage we were all playing with great confidence and flair. The whole side was showing fast, combination football at its best with a man always available to support the player in possession of the ball. A Joe Lennon free, plus two from play by Tony Hadden, put the icing on the cake.

At the end we scored 2-16 to Cavan's 0-7. When the full time whistle sounded it seemed that the whole of County Down descended onto the pitch. We were Ulster senior football champions for the first time and what a wonderful feeling it was. What made the victory all the more special was the fact that we had defeated Cavan-the acknowledged masters of Ulster football. When Kevin Mussen raised aloft the Anglo Celt Cup it seemed that a whole weight of years of failure had at last been removed. To see countless numbers of previous Down players congratulating us made me feel that we were truly unique.

For the next few days the media coverage was lavish in its praise of our achievement. In the *Irish Independent* John D. Hickey hailed the significance of the occasion and the splendid quality of our performance:

> *The Breffni men were beaten by a Down side of striking power and zeal. The Down forwards were an attack of rare splendour. The manner in which they changed the direction of their attacks was at times baffling.*
>
> *James McCartan is a man who will surely become a "great" of the game if his utter exuberance did not at times cause him to become incautious as he seeks new worlds to conquer having already beaten his man.*

These last lines highlighted what was a weakness in my game, particularly as a central defender. I loved to get the ball and solo upfield for 30 to 40 yards before parting to a colleague in a scoring position. I must admit that I liked doing this because the whole team seemed to become livelier at the prospect of one or more of them scoring a vital point or goal increased. The downside of that type of play was the danger of losing possession of the ball when out of my centre half position. It could afford the opposition the chance to counter attack and score rather easily. I would be to blame because I was not doing my primary duty which was to prevent my man from getting the ball and clear downfield. The management kept reminding me about what my first priority was but I found it very difficult to ignore my natural instincts. This was a problem in my method of play that would be addressed sooner rather than later.

Ignoring his own input, team manager Barney Carr, writing in the *Frontier Sentinel*, praised the dedication of team trainer Danny Flynn. He also lauded all the clubs, schools and colleges that had perfected the skills of the Down players. Barney singled one man out for special praise, Bobby Langan who had joined the team on the victory platform back in Newry after the final: "Bobby hopped on board and took his rightful place among the heroes. How he had earned that moment of glory, constant, faithful Bobby, who had worked so hard over long and frustrating years to see this happy day." Of the many fulfilling moments in my GAA career, observing the joy in Bobby's face has to rank with the very best.

After that Sunday in Clones, band parades and civic receptions were held throughout every town and village in the footballing parts of the county. Supporters, so long starved of success, celebrated for days and nights and understandably so. I, on the other hand, did not celebrate too much. I could not wait for our date, a fortnight later, with Galway in the All-Ireland semi-final. The omens for a terrific Croke Park performance were good. Hopefully we would play to our highest standards and do the county and ourselves proud.

So it was against that background of hope and expectation of future glory that we met Galway. When we trudged off the pitch, disappointed and dejected after such an abysmal display, we entered the losers' dressing room. To a man, the whole team and management made a promise to each other. Though we had let down our supporters and ourselves we resolved to come back the following year and go the whole way to the final. As I left the dressing room I knew instantly that there was another huge problem I had to confront.

My father had always been a passionate supporter of the Down football team ever since he played for them in the twenties and thirties. Popularly known as Briney McCartan he dreamed the dream of so many Down followers that the Mourne County would one day grace Croke Park in a major championship match. When he followed our progress, especially since I joined the team in 1956, he was convinced that we had the talent and the determination to achieve national honours. When he witnessed how we steadily improved and played such magical football during that 1959 season he was satisfied, like the rest of us, that we were on the threshold of greatness. Now I was destined to travel home with him in his car. Like myself he was blunt and straight and would not hold back if he thought my teammates and myself should be criticised for a poor performance. During that whole car journey he continually gave out about the team and myself and how pathetically we had played. It was not nastiness on his part. It was a summary of his sheer frustration at how we failed to realise our full potential. As he kept scolding, I tried at the same time, in my mind, to find a realistic reason for our wretched display. Then slowly I retraced how we had spent the 24 hours preceding the game and what we had done differently from our normal preparations.

Usually before a big game I went to first mass at home and then returned to have a good steak breakfast. On this occasion, we left to go to Butlin's holiday camp on the previous Saturday evening. We had a tea that consisted of beans and toast at around six o'clock. We hadn't any supper and as a result I went to bed ravenous with hunger. To make matters worse, the chalets were uncomfortable because of the intense heat. Unfortunately it had been one of the hottest nights of the year and I could not sleep.

The next morning we went to second mass having been told in advance we could have our breakfast when we returned. Unfortunately, however, breakfast was over when we got back. Several of us, including myself, had missed out. After we complained vigorously, the staff relented and gave me an egg in a cup. Then we packed our gear, stopped for a very light lunch in a hotel in Dublin and headed for Croke Park. As my father kept scolding I thought I knew why we played so poorly. No wonder our mental energy and physical strength was so awful, particularly during the last quarter of the game. I knew that I was weak from the hunger and that surely was a proper explanation for my terrible display. I also had no doubt that the discomfort experienced by the whole team in the chalets was the dominant reason for the overall inept performance.

As we neared home I had sorted out my own thoughts and had become more optimistic for the future. I also knew it was not the time to explain my analysis to my father. Only time and a lot of hard work would prove whether or not I was correct. There was no way, in the mood he was in, that my Dad could be consoled. So when we arrived in our yard at home I jumped out of the car and shouted at him: "Daddy, I will bring home the Sam Maguire Cup next year even if I have to steal it!"

In the meantime I would do what most disappointed people do. I would do my utmost to make sure that what I perceived were the mistakes of 1959 would not be repeated in 1960. I hoped that all of us together, the team and the management, would keep the promise we made in that Croke Park dressing room. Even though I was only 21 years of age, I would also reflect on all that happened to me since I first entered the world in my native parish of Tullylish. Perhaps both those personal and team decisions would lead Down and myself to the promised land. Only time would tell.

2

My Native Place – Donacloney

My home parish of Tullylish, where I spent my childhood and most of my adult life, is situated in the north west of County Down. It is basically a rural parish that also includes the small urban areas of Gilford, Laurencetown and Donacloney.

The McCartans have been living in the general mid-Down and east Down areas for the past eight hundred years. After King James II was defeated at the Battle of the Boyne in 1690 a lot of McCartan families were dispossessed. Many were forced to escape from Ireland and they joined the armies of France and Austria. The most famous descendant of them was Marie Angelique McCartan who was the great grandmother of the late president of France, General Charles de Gaulle.

Even though the total Catholic population of Tullylish parish is now about 2250, the part of the parish in which I lived was and is predominantly Protestant. This fact was to have a major influence in my life.

I was born on 19 November 1937 in the townland of Tonnaghmore. I was the third eldest of five children born to Brian and Delia McCartan. My two older sisters were Eileen and Delia. My brother Dan came after me and my sister Gay was the youngest of the family. My mother was formerly Delia Murphy from Hilltown in the south of the county. In the mid-forties my father bought my grandfather's farm and public house on the outskirts of Donacloney village. Though sad to leave my birthplace, I really enjoyed having a new home and the opportunity to meet more people. My father, my uncle Charlie and the family of my uncle Jimmy were joint shareholders in a quarry business. Unfortunately, my uncle Jimmy was tragically killed due to a fall from a horse before I was born. The other co-owners were a family by the name of Moore. They had two quarries, one in Newtownhamilton in County Armagh and one in Tullyraine near Banbridge. Eventually, by mutual consent, both families decided to restructure their joint ownership of the quarries. The Moores took over sole control of the Newtownhamilton enterprise and the

McCartans did likewise with Tullyraine. So began a life-long association with an independently owned family concern that has expanded enormously over the years and is still very much a thriving operation today.

My earliest memories date back to when I was about three or four years old. My father used to go to Donacloney to help my grandfather in the bar. He always took me with him. I remember one time I got into trouble. When my Dad went into the bar I dashed into the back kitchen where there was a new tabletop. Seeing a hammer and a bag of nails I did what all innocent and curious children would do. I started to hammer the nails into the top of the worktop, rather successfully I might add! When I had six or seven nails firmly implanted on the top, the excessive noise alerted my grandfather. He came running in and shouted at me to get out immediately as I had done enough damage already. I ignored him. Half in fear, and not knowing what to do, I ran underneath the bench. He kept poking at me with a stick but I refused to budge. My friends now would tell me that it was perhaps an example of a certain stubborn streak that I still possess.

When he got fed up remonstrating with me, he went away back to the bar. I slowly crept outside and sat on a stone step. Then my grandfather returned and in a friendly voice he said, "Come here Curly." As I looked at him fearfully, he stood and stared at me and uttered in a proud voice, "You are a McCartan alright." With that he pushed a crisp white five pound note into my surprised hand. My carpentry skills had really paid off.

During my primary school days of the 1940s there were three dominant influences. They were my growing love of farm life, my attendance at the local Protestant primary school and the impact of World War II on the ordinary lives of all the people in our area. The whole concept of farming itself and the farming way of life has always held pleasant memories for me. All the summer days seemed to be long and filled with excitement and sunshine. The highlight of every year was when our first cousins Sean and Kevin O'Neill (my mother was their aunt) came to stay with us. Little did we then know that Sean, Kevin, Dan and myself would share many fantastic and exciting days together in several greener, larger and noisier fields throughout Ireland. For us then the satisfaction of sitting down in the midst of a hayfield surpassed all other earthly pleasures. On deeper reflection, however, I do recall the utter misery we sometimes felt when after several days of hard physical work in getting the hay ready to be put up, the skies would suddenly open. Rain and maybe thunder and lightning would undo everything.

During our teenage years the O'Neills and the McCartans had many wonderful times. Bringing in the hay was an especially enjoyable experience. One day I remember Kevin O'Neill and I had two tractors and two hay floats. Before the entrance to the haggard, where the hay was to be stacked, there was only room for one tractor to pass through at a time. So, on this particular occasion, the big challenge for both of us was to see who would reach the entrance first. As we raced towards our target our respective siblings were aboard the floats. I managed to win the race. Poor Kevin, in his attempt to overtake me, hit a wall and damaged the tractor. Luckily his passengers, spotting that danger was imminent, jumped off before the impact. Our workmen, who were very loyal to us, never revealed the true facts. They brought the damaged vehicle to the quarry where my father was working and told him that the hay was all safely in. Then they added that the tractor had accidentally broken down and needed repairing. The fact that it had been a bad summer and that the hay was safe meant more to Dad, at that moment, than the small issue of a tractor requiring repair.

We also grew potatoes, vegetables and corn. Watching my father ploughing the ground with horse and plough and seeing the shine of the upturned sod made a lasting impression on me. Spreading the farmyard manure, planting the potatoes and, most of all, weeding them were chores that I never relished. To prevent potato blight, potatoes had to be sprayed at least three times, at ten-day intervals. A chemical substance called bluestone was mixed with water and lime in a thirty-gallon wooden barrel. When it was stirred, the mixture would be put into a knapsack copper sprayer. My father would then put it on his back and spray the green, growing potato tubers. Watching the birth of newborn calves and the excitement of the mother cows as they watched their offspring take their first tentative steps were just some of the other joys that I remember.

Electricity as we know it today simply did not feature in the days of my youth. In our house we used paraffin oil lamps for light before the days of the more sophisticated Tilley lamp arrived. When we were waiting for cows to calve during the late winter, we had a hurricane or storm lamp for yard use at night. This was a strong iron-bottomed lamp with a very thick globe. Calves were fed with milk in the bucket. I was a very proud boy the first day that I was allowed to feed the calves. I graduated with first class honours when my mother announced to my father that I had fed them without spilling a drop of milk. Being considered capable of milking the cows was another important stepping stone in developing all round farming skills. Harvesting time was particularly exciting.

In those days there was no public water supply. Many houses had no running water of any kind. We were lucky in this regard. Some time prior to this, a water diviner had pinpointed a spot in our yard. A well was duly sunk and a pump erected. This was the source of our water both for household and farm use. Many people then had to rely on a local river or stream to provide water, especially at potato spraying time. People presently do not appreciate how hard access to such basic necessities was back in the 1940s or before. Still, overall I loved the freedom and variety of the work. To see the stack of corn, a field full of potato pits and a barn full of hay at the end of the year made life really fulfilling.

Between 1939 and 1945 World War II took place. As Northern Ireland was under the political jurisdiction of Britain we were constantly aware of the possibility of the bombing of our major areas of population, particularly Belfast. The city of Belfast, which was relatively close to Donacloney, was centrally involved in the war effort. It was against this background that the daily talk in all homes, newspapers and radio was summed up on one stark sentence: What will happen us if the Germans launch one of their infamous bombing raids?

Many people from both unionist and nationalist traditions enlisted for the British armed services. A lot of my neighbours in Donacloney and surrounding areas took up this challenge. Sadly, several of them never returned home as they were killed in the battlefields of France or elsewhere. When Belfast was bombed in 1941, accommodation had to be found for 100,000 people. Many of these people, or evacuees as they were called, came to the village of Donacloney and were welcomed with open arms. The children went to the local school and integrated into the community so well that some of them never returned to Belfast, even when the war ended.

As we lived in a predominantly Protestant part of the parish, there was no Catholic school nearby. Also, in those days we had no car so we had no option but to go to the local Protestant primary school about a mile and a half away. In the parish itself there were three Catholic churches at Clare, Gilford and Tullylish. The latter was adjacent to the village of Laurencetown. Like the Catholic schools, these churches were a long distance from my home. Therefore we went to Drumnavaddy Catholic Church, which was only two miles away, for mass and devotions.

Fr Joe O'Hagan used to say mass in Drumnavaddy when we were at primary school. After mass, he and his two altar boys would come to our house for the breakfast. The boys were always very neatly dressed. My mother kept praising them, saying that she wished Dan and I could imitate their sense of tidiness and cleanliness. We were not really amused by this. Once, when breakfast was over, my mother told all of us to go and play. Now we had two donkeys at this time. They were in a mucky part of an adjacent field. When we tried to put our two visitors up on the donkeys backs the donkeys did what donkeys do. They knelt down and tossed the pair of boys into the muck. It would be true to say that Dan and I secretly enjoyed letting our mother see how the stubborn donkeys had transformed the two lovely clean altar boys.

The primary school that we attended had five teachers and catered for our local area, which was almost exclusively Protestant in religious terms and mainly unionist in political affiliation. Even though there were very few Catholic families attending the school, I have many fond memories of it. Teachers such as Miss Smyth, Mrs Graham, Mr Wright and the principal, Master Crothers, were all talented, fair-minded and decent people. It was in school that I had my first experience of winning. The teacher said, one day, that a prize would be given to the child who could recite by heart a very good poem. So I stood up and recited a poem that my father used to say every morning when he was shaving.

> *There was an old man called Phelan,*
> *Who walked upside down on the ceiling,*
> *He fell on his neck,*
> *And wondered the heck,*
> *Wasn't that a funny feeling?*

After I came home with a gleaming silver new sixpence my father was delighted with my success, though not particularly enamoured with the specific poem I had chosen.

I made many friends in that school. Indeed I still often meet many of them and we love to reminisce about our happy school days. Sammy Hughes, Roy Copeland and John Sydney Hyland were my main friends. When it came to preparation for the sacraments of First Confession, First Holy Communion and Confirmation my mother did all the work. She was a very kind, helpful, religious person who prepared us as well as any Catholic teacher or priest could have done.

The teachers in the school treated us very fairly and never made us conscious that we belonged to a different religion than the rest of the pupils. However, that did not prevent us from being ostracised occasionally in the schoolyard by the other children. This occurred mainly when we were playing football and very often they prevented us from taking part at all. They called us 'papishes' and we often went home and asked our parents what that meant. They politely ignored us and told us to pay no attention to such unkind comments. Funnily enough, even to this day, I never blamed those children who teased us. People who have since come to know me so well over all of my adult life find this tolerant behaviour of mine hard to believe. However, that schoolyard in Donacloney was no place for a high-principled idealist. All we could do at the time was grin and bear it all. We had no alternative. We were too far away from any Catholic school. That was the reality. My idealism would have to wait.

The main game around Donacloney when we were growing up was cricket. Here discrimination raised its ugly head again. The other children would not allow us to bowl or bat as they were the two main features of cricket. We were allowed, however, to act as fielders as this involved a lot of running and hard work. My brother Dan and I were also good fielders and we certainly got plenty of practice at this particular skill. One could say that this was our first introduction to one of the main skills of Gaelic football. I have no doubt that this constant daily practice in a primary school playground helped us immensely throughout our football careers.

When I was growing up life was lived at a much more leisurely pace. Though times were much more difficult in terms of hard physical work with no regular financial income, we were happy. On the farming scene, money only came when we sold cattle, potatoes or other agricultural produce. We were luckier than most as we had a bar and my father also worked in the family quarry. This provided much needed revenue to keep a family of seven.

Government security measures also imposed restrictions on freedom during the war years. We had to have dark blinds on the windows of our houses. The people lucky enough to have cars had to place special protective covering on car headlights. Thus the cars could only travel slowly as the lights were so dim. As a result, life was made more difficult for potential German warplanes and made air attacks much more difficult to carry out. Coupled with these physical restrictions was the supply of rationing books by the Northern Ireland government. This meant that groceries and petrol could only be purchased through the use of coupons. The advantage of those imposed conditions was, however, that people depended much more on each other. Necessity dictated that people had to verbally communicate and help each other if there was a scarcity of any goods. Farmers grew a variety of potatoes and vegetables. Women made bread and jam and thus everyone was less dependent on the open market place. So in terms of communication and good neighbourliness the war had its benefits.

As far as I was concerned a technical and mechanical revolution occurred in our house in the mid-forties. It was the day that my father brought home a new Ford/Ferguson tractor. Fuelled by a mixture known as TVO (tractor vapourising oil), it made farming life much easier. It held pride of place until my dad bought the family's first car, a black Austin 10, in 1950. The horse and the bicycle with its famous carabide lamp were redundant.

My father was a sports lover. He did not confine himself to Gaelic football although it was his first love. When he stopped work each day he used to play soccer with Dan and myself in the yard. At that stage the GAA did not feature in my life, except for listening to the golden voice of Michael O'Hehir on the radio. As a young child I recall his commentary on the great Roscommon team, led by their captain Jimmy Murray, when they won two All-Irelands in 1943 and 1944. The famous All-Ireland final between Cavan and Kerry in New York in 1947 had us glued to the Bush radio in the corner of our kitchen, as did Meath's victory in the 1949 All-Ireland. For me these matches were only days of entertainment, far removed from the reality of our world. When the O'Neills came on holidays it was again soccer that predominated. Listening to Michael O'Hehir I never dreamed that the names of the O'Neills or Dan and myself would ever be uttered from the lips of the greatest ambassador the GAA has ever had.

As there was no Catholic secondary school in my immediate area, my parents had to make an important decision as to what I should do when my primary school days came to an end in 1950. In those times formal education ended for most children when they finished primary school. My parents strongly believed in the importance of secondary education. Despite the financial and personal sacrifices required, my two eldest sisters had already gone to the Assumption Convent in Ballynahinch. Now it was my turn. I was sent, as a boarder, to the Diocesan Secondary School in St Colman's College in Newry. If one wanted to go to university, or indeed become a diocesan priest, that was the route one had to take. Little did I realise then that this decision would have such a profound influence on my life.

I was not destined to become a great academic but I was about to discover a fantastic outlet for my physical energies and growing passion for sport. A new and wonderful world of Gaelic football awaited me when I entered that famed nursery of Gaelic games in September 1950.

3

St Colman's College – Where It All Began

The GAA has always maintained that the parish GAA club is the secret of its national success. This is because it is essentially locally based in geographical terms and therefore most people can readily identify with it. While I agree with this I would also strongly hold the view that the introduction of colleges' GAA competitions at both provincial and national levels has also contributed immensely to the development and popularisation of Gaelic games throughout the whole of Ireland. My alma mater, St Colman's College, Newry, was and is a leading exponent of this concept.

St Colman's initially competed in the Ulster colleges' football championship in 1926 and reached their first final in 1945 only to be beaten by St Patrick's of Armagh. At this time Fr John Treanor, Fr Hugh Connolly and Fr Bertie McGovern took charge of the college sides and left no stone unturned in their quest for success. Their endeavours were finally rewarded when Sean Blaney (father of Greg of 1990s fame) captained the college to their first provincial title in 1949. They repeated their initial MacRory Cup success when they edged out St Patrick's of Armagh in the 1950 final. Again Sean Blaney captained them. Among the players in those squads were my future colleagues Kevin Mussen and P.J. McElroy. Liam McCorry, who was on Armagh's All-Ireland-winning minor team in 1949, was also a member of St Colman's in that period of triumph.

Anyone who has ever gone to a secondary school with a good football tradition will realise the importance that is placed on past achievements. When I entered St Colman's in 1950 we were indoctrinated into this mindset. Great games of the past were always being recalled. Outstanding individual players were continually and fondly remembered. As a consequence there was only one thing I had to do. I wanted to play Gaelic football for the college and win as many trophies as I could.

On arrival, I found life very difficult, especially during the first few months. It was my first time away from home. Loneliness and hunger dominated my thinking. I would often lie in bed at night in the dormitory and wonder what was happening at home. The silence of that room at night was eerie compared to the hustle and bustle of the bar in Donacloney. The excitement of the calving of cows and the buzz of general farming activity were far removed from the rules and regulations of a boarding school. Slowly, however, as I got to know my newfound classmates a reluctant acceptance of my student life came to the fore.

Discovering the joys of Gaelic football, however, compensated for everything else. I took to the game right away. There were three separate college competitions at that time. The Corn na n-Óg Cup was basically for under 15 year olds, the Rannafast Cup was approximately for under 17 year olds and the MacRory Cup was for under 19s. Football wise my progress was good and I was selected for the Corn na n-Óg team at corner forward. We played well and won the cup in 1951. I was delighted and was immediately looking forward to many more successes with the college.

But that victory was as good as it got. During the rest of my college days no further honours came my way. On a personal level my football skills developed satisfactorily and I was selected in both Rannafast and MacRory teams during my stay. The only time we nearly won another competition was when we reached a Rannafast Cup final, only to be beaten by St Eunan's of Letterkenny in Omagh.

Malachy McGuinness from south Armagh, Harry Hoy from Lurgan and P.T. Treacy from Fermanagh were some of the footballers from outside Down who impressed during my years at the college. Future county colleagues such as Joe Lennon, Kevin Mussen and P.J. McElroy were ahead of me and Patsy O'Hagan came after me. The best footballer I saw during college matches was Patsy Kierans from St Patrick's College in Armagh.

In the mornings we got up at seven o'clock, washed and made our beds. Then we went to mass at eight and had our breakfast. This consisted of a bowl of porridge and tea with bread and jam. Class started at nine. Dinners at all boarding schools were more or less the same – barely edible. For supper we had bread and jam again before our second period of study. After this we retired to bed and lights were all out at ten o'clock.

All week we looked forward to a visit from our parents. They visited on Sunday and brought us extra food which we could use during the week. This more tasty food was not allowed. So after the parental visits we used to sneak our contraband into our lockers. Occasionally the dean raided the lockers and if he found illegal food we were punished. We did not like physical punishment but we always adopted the "tough guys don't cry" approach when this was dished out.

I was rather lucky because I had a regular source of supplementary food. The student who sat beside me in class was Henry Smith, now a dentist in Warrenpoint. Nearly every day Henry, who was a dayboy, brought in extra food along with his own lunch. I will always be grateful to him for providing me with such tasty sandwiches.

I was also a bit of a prankster during my student days. We put a rota system in place whereby, in turn, we pinched butter and homemade jam from the priests' cupboard. This was always done in the middle of the night. One student kept watch while another brought the butter and jam to the dormitory where it was hidden overnight. The next day we labelled the pots of jam. The new labels bore the names of Mrs McCartan or Mrs McElroy or whatever name we felt was appropriate. Each label was dated (e.g. 4/1/52) and placed in our own lockers.

Students also often pinched food from each other. This was accepted by most as a good-humoured exercise. Monday was a popular day for stealing food especially if you had a visit from your parents the previous day. Chocolates or sweets would be expected to be in your possession. Even though he was several years older than me, my future club and county colleague P.J. McElroy had a great passion for Mrs McCartan's food! While I would be trying to learn Latin or Shakespeare, a rubber would suddenly hit my head at a phenomenal speed. With the aid of an elastic band the rubber would do its job and I would have to reluctantly hand over some of Mrs McCartan's precious goodies. P.J. displayed the same accuracy and power then that would one-day torture defenders up and down the country!

Corporal punishment was a regular occurrence for the smallest of offences. In those days it was not the accepted procedure to complain about the excesses of corporal punishment or, indeed, what would be known today as verbal abuse. I never then or even now would blame the individual priests who inflicted such pain. They just happened to be the people in charge of a school at a particular time in their lives. The system in all aspects of life at that time was authoritarian. I also believe that many of the priests teaching us back then were in a job that they did not like or had not a flair for. They were there because the bishop of the day decided that there had to be a certain number of priests on the college staff. Despite these shortcomings I must point out the positive contribution these priests made at St Colman's. First of all there never was the remotest hint of sexual harassment or impropriety of any kind. Secondly, and most importantly, we owe a lot to them for their time and effort in providing us with a very good education. We were prepared well for the world outside.

I would never count myself as a model student even though I worked reasonably hard at my studies. I had the habit of sometimes taking the law into my own hands. Understandably this infuriated the authorities. Every Thursday morning in St Colman's each student was supposed to take the clothes off his bed and then turn the mattress upside down. This was known in student language as 'wrecking the bed'. The purpose of this procedure was to air the mattress. After football training each Thursday evening everyone was expected to remake their bed. One day, in order to have more time practising my football skills, I decided to remake the bed before training began. I was caught doing so and severely punished for breaking the rule.

On three other occasions I feared that I might be suspended for transgressing the rules. One serious incident I will never forget. A senior student hit my brother Dan, who was several years his junior, with the butt of an old butter knife. He did this because Dan took food from the communal dinner platter first, instead of allowing the older student to do so. In the eyes of students seniority always took precedence. When I saw this I immediately went over to the guy and hit him a good blow with my fist. The dean caught me and, as was the normal custom, I was sent to the president. As I nervously made my way to his office I was trembling with fear. I knew that suspension was probable and that even expulsion was a distinct possibility. It would not be nice to meet my parents if this should happen. However, the president, Fr Pettit, accepted my explanation and apology. He understood my impulsive reaction and I breathed a sigh of relief when I left his office with a word of warning as to my future conduct.

There was one priest in the college that especially impressed me. He was Fr James Haughey who was in charge of the college farm. A family decision, taken at Christmas during my last year, was to have a major impact on my future. My father was experiencing severe difficulty in getting suitable staff to run the bar and the farm. He himself was spending all his time at the family quarry business. He felt it was too much of a burden to expect my mother to look after it all, especially during the daytime. He asked me to take over the home place when I completed my senior certificate examinations the following June. Fr. Haughey knew this so he kindly gave me an opportunity to help out on the college farm when any of the farm helpers were either sick or unavailable. When this occurred he would wake me at 6.30 a.m. and ask me to help out with the milking and get the creamery cans ready for collection. My reward after this was to get a fry for my breakfast, before returning for class at 9 a.m. When June came I did my exams and was successful in them as I had been two years earlier when I sat my junior exams. Indeed, I got sufficiently high marks in my senior exams to enable me to qualify for a veterinary surgeon degree course in university. However, because of the family decision for me to return home, that was not to be. My days of full-time academic study were over. My dreams of being a veterinary surgeon were ended. My life of reading textbooks was exchanged for bar work and farm work. Donacloney was calling me and I was proud to answer the challenge.

Although I had left St Colman's I still continued to actively support the students in blue and white. During the 1960s St Colman's, under the tutelage of Fr Treanor, adopted a meticulous and professional approach to the training of college teams. County doctor Martin Walsh and county physio Jimmy Hocks were added to the management team. This thorough preparation finally paid dividends when St Colman's defeated St Jarlaths of Tuam 1-8 to 1-7 in the 1967 All-Ireland Colleges' final (Hogan Cup). Fr Treanor was assisted by former Derry player and teaching colleague Gerry O'Neill (a brother of well known soccer manager, Martin).

In 1970 former Down county player Raymond Morgan joined the college's teaching staff. In 1972 he started to train the MacRory and Rannafast teams and in 1975 St Colman's won both the MacRory and Hogan cups.

Throughout the whole campaign they surprised everyone with their fighting qualities and determination. The Hogan final against Carmelite College from Moate was an epic tussle. Captained by Declan Rogers of Ballymartin St Colman's came from four points behind in the closing minutes to win with a Michael McDonald point. This was an especially happy personal occasion for me as two cousins, John and Jim McCartan (sons of my first cousin Seamus), were members of the winning team.

Fifty years after entering colleges' competitions, St Colman's celebrated their golden jubilee by winning all the Ulster colleges' competitions in the one year – 1976. The sight of all four cups together, along with the Hogan Cup (won the previous year), in the trophy cabinet was a marvellous sight and one of which the students, staff and supporters were justifiably proud. After guiding Colman's to three successive Corn na n-Ógs, college teacher Dan McCartan stepped down as coach. He, too, had contributed immensely to St Colman's successes. In 1978 St Colman's again reached the Hogan final only to be well beaten by a powerful St Jarlath's side. In the same year, John McCartan and team captain and goalkeeper Patrick Donnan collected their third MacRory medal.

The King of Down Football

The MacRory Cup returned to St Colman's in 1979 and 1981. Three players of outstanding ability played on that '81 side. They were captain Greg Blaney, Paul Skelton and Martin Rogers. If Martin had not emigrated to America he would have been a regular on the Down senior team for years.

Due to the restructuring of the age level, the Rannafast Cup winners represented Ulster in the Hogan Cup in 1986. Colman's faced Dublin side St David's of Artane in the decider. Playing superb football they emerged victorious on a 3-19 to 0-7 scoreline. On that wonderful team were many future intercounty stars such as Brendan Tierney, Ollie Reel and Mark McNeill, all of whom came from Armagh, as well as two Down men, Cathal Murray (nephew of the 1960s star, the great Patsy O'Hagan) and Larry Duggan. From my own perspective I was exceptionally happy. Our two eldest sons, Brian and James, played at midfield and corner forward respectively on that team. Neutrals who watched the semi-final against St Mary's of Galway maintain that James' match-winning goal was one of the best ever by a colleges' player. One should also pay tribute to other St Colman's coaches at this stage. Fr Hackett, Fr Stevenson and Fr McCrory coached St Colman's teams to success in many subsidiary competitions during these years.

Down won their second minor All-Ireland in 1987 with Peter McGrath as manager and no fewer than eight college players, including our sons Brian and James, were on the panel.

In 1988 it took three games with St Patrick's, Maghera, to decide the destiny of the MacRory Cup. Eventually St Colman's, captained by Ollie Reel, emerged victorious thanks to a three-goal blitz from Tom Fegan in the deciding game. Again they reached the All-Ireland final, this time against St Mel's of Longford. Though St Mel's rallied strongly in the second period St Colman's held on to win deservedly by four points.

The next time the MacRory Cup was to return to St Colman's was in 1993. Again it was their great rivals St Patrick's, Maghera, that they faced in the final. Two stunning points from Aidan McGivern in the last two minutes saw Colman's take the title for the 16th time. I was particularly happy for our third son Charlie Pat who was a prominent member of that successful side. Going into the Hogan Cup semi-final, against St Patrick's of Navan, the team had to be reorganised as four of their main players were ineligible to play because of a three month age differential at All-Ireland level. It was unfortunate that Declan Toner, Michael McVerry, Tony Fearon and Charlie Pat lost out to this rule.

Despite this setback Colman's played terrific football to defeat the Meath team by ten points. This victory led to two of the aristocrats of colleges' football, St Jarlath's of Tuam and St Colman's, battling it out for the Hogan Cup in Pearse Park, Longford. It took a goal of spellbinding quality to decide this encounter. Jarlath's had just established a four point lead and for the first time in the game seemed poised for victory. Then Diarmaid Marsden shattered their confidence with a magical goal. A further five points were added without response. St Colman's had collected their fifth Hogan Cup by 2-10 to 1-9.

Two of that St Jarlath's side were to become household names a few years later, Michael Donnellan and Padraic Joyce. Likewise Diarmaid Marsden has made a huge impact for Armagh. Aidan McGivern, Finbar Caulfield and Charlie Pat McCartan played for Down seniors, as did the captain of the team Ronan Hamill for Antrim seniors.

Old adversaries St Patrick's were again the opposition in the 1998 MacRory final. The St Colman's boys put on one of their best-ever performances in the decider and won by 2-14 to 2-7.

When Roscommon CBS demolished St Jarlath's in the Connacht final everyone knew that Colman's were in for a testing time in the Hogan Cup semi-final against the westerners. However, Colman's reached their sixth Hogan final since Ray Morgan arrived. A game of tremendous tension, flowing football and resolute defence ensured Colman's beat Roscommon CBS by 2-15 to 1-15 after extra time. Leinster champions Coláiste Eoin from Dublin were their final opponents. After a rather nervous start the boys from Newry emerged convincing winners by 2-14 to 1-7. Declan Morgan (Ray's son) was the latest in a line of St Colman's players to march up the steps of the Hogan Stand to take the famous trophy. It must have been a particularly proud moment for Ray Morgan, his wife and daughters to watch their son and brother deservedly hold the Hogan Cup aloft. This was to be the last occasion that Ray would be in charge of a major final triumph. He had coached St Colman's to eight MacRory Cup and five Hogan Cup successes.

33 years had passed since Ray Morgan and his famous uncle Brian had shared a substitute bench for Down in the 1965 All-Ireland senior football semi-final. Like his wonderful predecessor, Ray's own football career had been badly curtailed by injury. Like Fr Treanor he turned to helping others. In the process he proved himself to be a coach par excellence with a keen tactical brain. How fitting that his last appearance on a national stage should provide such an exhilarating display of Gaelic football at its best.

Between 1998 and 2010 St Colman's experienced a barren spell regarding success at MacRory and Hogan Cup levels. However, that was rectified in 2010 when they stormed to a comprehensive MacRory Cup final victory over Omagh CBS before easily overcoming St Gerald's of Castlebar in the All-Ireland semi-final. They gave a commanding performance when comfortably defeating Munster kingpins St Brendan's of Killarney in the Hogan final. In a fabulous display of fast, open, combination football they cruised to an even more emphatic victory than the final scoreline of 1-18 to 3-5 would suggest. Incidentally Shay McCartan, who came on as a substitute in the second half and scored a terrific goal, is a son of 1977 Down All-Ireland minor-winning captain John McCartan and grandson of my first cousin Seamus who brought me to Glenn GFC many years ago. By the way, John and Shay belong to a very exclusive group of fathers and sons who have won Hogan Cup medals. One must also credit the capable management team of Declan Mussen (son of Liam and nephew of former colleague Kevin and ex-county board PRO Fintan), Barry Kelly, Eamon McEvoy and dedicated manager Cathal Murray on their contribution to St Colman's seventh Hogan cup success.

Of course it is the players who play the central role in any team's success. The dedication of all the players and the sacrifices that they made for the common good should never be forgotten. I will always be eternally grateful for the football education that I received from my time in St Colman's. Our five sons will say the same. Whatever I have achieved in football was initiated there. It provided me with a lifelong interest in the game itself and opened doors of friendship and camaraderie over the last 50 years. Most of all, this would not have been possible but for the voluntary commitment and dedication of all the mentors who made this happen. I am sure the rest will forgive me if I single out Fr John Treanor and Ray Morgan as being the two outstanding coaches in the history of St Colman's football.

In the centenary year of the GAA a plaque was erected in the foyer of the college. It read: "To commemorate the service of Michael Cusack on the staff of the College." Michael Cusack, a teacher of English and Mathematics at St Colman's in the 1870s, was the principal thinker behind the ideals and aims of the GAA when he helped to found it in 1884. Over a hundred years later two visionary teachers from the same college have implemented those aims to the utmost of their considerable abilities. Fr John Treanor and Ray Morgan deserve their special place of honour wherever and whenever Gaelic games and St Colman's College are mentioned.

4

Early Career

On leaving St Colman's College I enrolled for a one year dairying course at Greenmount Agricultural College. This helped me immensely as at that time we had a dairy herd and I was able to adopt a more structured approach to everything associated with milking cows and how to maximise milk yields. The importance of proper feed as well as maintaining strict hygiene procedures regarding milking utensils and a proper cooling system were continually emphasised. In addition I enjoyed the friendship of my fellow students, and my introduction to rugby was a definite bonus.

Initially I was disappointed about not going to university. This was not because I regretted the decision to return home. It was simply for a more selfish social reason. Every weekend my former student colleagues who had gone to university came home to enjoy the fruits of a fantastic social life. Dancing was their favourite pursuit. Saturday night was then the biggest night on the local dancing calendar. There were many different dancing venues within the county and beyond. However the "in" spot of the time was Ballymascanlon Hotel near Dundalk. Every Sunday after mass my friends regaled me with their stories of the latest big band that they had seen.

Unfortunately, for me, this was all forbidden territory. Friday and Saturday nights were by far the busiest times in the bar at Donacloney. Yours truly had to be there pulling pints, washing glasses and ensuring that all our many local customers were happy. I definitely enjoyed the work and the banter about the latest farming news from the area. Lurking in my mind, however, was the curiosity of what life must be like in "Ballymac"! There were other dancing places where I could go. They were usually held on a Friday or Sunday night. On Friday nights I was normally working too and somehow the Sunday night dances did not appear to have the same magical appeal of "Ballymac". However, with the advent of the growing showband scene some years later, the whole dancing scene was to change and I was no longer to be deprived of life's normal pleasantries.

Working in a bar did teach me one of society's most important values. I remember one Friday morning there were about 12 old age pensioners having a quiet drink when the Guinness rep suddenly appeared. As was his custom, he tasted the Guinness I was serving. He quickly spat it out and said, "That is rotten."

When he left I followed him outside and told him never to reprimand me in front of my customers again.

"I could not drink that Guinness," he insisted.

"I could not care less what you think of it. My customers love it that way and they are the only ones that matter," I replied. That evening the rep returned and apologised profusely. We had a great working relationship after that and I learned a lesson that you must always stand up for yourself when you see a wrong being perpetrated. That has always been my motto, in all aspects of my life.

Football wise there was very little underage activity during my teenage years. The first age group, which had any structured competitive football, was at U-16 level. However, there was no league in this group so U-16s were confined to championship football. As we had a small selection to pick from this usually meant that our team, who were known as Laurencetown St Patrick's, were weaker than most other clubs in our part of Down. Inevitably we were beaten in the first round of the championship. Minor football with Laurencetown was really the first serious football that I played at club level. Again, however, our shortage of numbers curtailed any hope of advancement. Despite these team limitations, through no fault of anyone, I was happy on a personal level with the progress of my own game. Things went so well for me that I was selected on the Down minor side at the age of 16 in 1954. I was picked at right corner forward and enjoyed the experience as we won both our first round and semi-final matches in the Ulster minor championship. Nevertheless, defeat to Armagh was our lot in the Ulster final on a scoreline of 2-8 to 0-9.

As a result of my good performances at underage level I was chosen to play for the Laurencetown senior team at Greencastle. This was the first occasion that I experienced annoyance and disappointment at club level. On the way home from the game I was left off at a place called the Devil's Elbow. It was about two miles from my home in Donacloney. Even though I was only 16 I had to walk home by myself. Both my mother and father were exceptionally angry. They would not allow me to play for Laurencetown again. I was now in an awkward position. I loved playing football but circumstances dictated that I was not able to follow my dreams. My cousin Seamus, who was a foreman in the family quarry business, provided me with a lifeline. He was very much involved as a player and indeed was captain of another club called Glenn, which was 15 miles away. It was agreed that I would join Glenn. He collected me for each match and left me home again. So began a long career that was to provide me with much enjoyment and success for the next 14 years.

In 1956 Ulster won the Railway Cup when they defeated Munster in the final on St Patrick's Day. There were four Down men on that successful panel. Kevin Mussen was right half back and Kieran Denvir was right half forward. George Lavery and Paddy Doherty were substitutes. At the same time a process of team building towards eventual county senior football success was underway in Down. A series of challenge games were played. The first of these was in April at Carlow. The team that achieved a 3-5 to 2-7 victory contained no fewer than nine players that the whole country would become familiar with in later years. They were George Lavery, Pat Rice, Kevin Mussen, P.J. McElroy, Jarlath Carey, Kieran Denvir, Tony Hadden, Brian Morgan and Paddy Doherty. An interesting footnote to this game was that Maurice Hayes persuaded Derry star midfielder Jim McKeever to play against Carlow. Jim was teaching in Downpatrick and Hayes reckoned that McKeever would be a huge addition to Down. However, the Derry man refused the invitation to join the Mourne men on a permanent basis and decided to remain loyal to the Oakleaf County.

Some footballing historians maintain that this was the day that our wonderful team was conceived. All nine men were retained for the team which beat Antrim 2-14 to 0-4 in the McKenna Cup a few weeks later. This was a fantastic day for me. I made my senior debut at right full back at just 18 years of age. Hopefully, I surmised, there would be many more days of sheer enjoyment to come. This was also the day that another promising footballer, Joe Lennon from Aghaderg, made his debut. My exhilaration at becoming a member of the senior team was completed when I was selected to play at full forward against Armagh in the first round of the Ulster senior football championship. On that day I marked the great Armagh full back, Jack Bratten. Jack was then at the peak of his career and had played in the same position for the Orchard County in the 1953 All-Ireland final against Kerry. Though well beaten on a scoreline of 2-5 to 0-6 I was happy and anticipating better and more successful days in the Down colours. But waiting around the corner was disappointment and a clash with one of the GAA's negative rules.

I was looking forward to making my second championship appearance with Down in the 1957 Ulster senior football championship. We were drawn to play Donegal in a first round game at Ballyshannon. As I waited for my lift to the game my heart was beating with excitement and anticipation. This was the big time for me. This was what I wanted to do since I first wore a pair of hard brown boots in my first practice session at St Colman's in the "Prep" meadow. Then a car which was to pick me up inexplicably drove past me. As I frantically waved the car rumbled on. Perhaps there was a mistake and that speeding car was not my intended mode of transport. I waited for what seemed ages for another lift to emerge. It did not. Despondently I returned home, put on the togs and boots and played soccer with Donacloney in a district league game.

However, a GAA player playing soccer led to another problem. Rugby, soccer, hockey and cricket were then deemed to be "foreign" games by the GAA. The GAA's *Official Guide* stated that any player who contravened this rule would be suspended for six months from the Association in the case of a first offence. If one violated this rule again the suspension would last for two years. In addition one could only be reinstated between the first of January and Easter Sunday in each year. As a result of my transgression an official of the South Down Board of the GAA reported me to the county board for playing soccer. To show how much I was discriminated against, he did not report a player from his own club who was also playing in the same soccer match. Just before the first game in the Lagan Cup, which was the name that the northern section of the National League was then known as, the chairman of the county board asked me did I play in a soccer game. If I had said no that probably would have been the end of the matter. However, I said I did and I was duly suspended for six months. This effectively meant that I could not play Gaelic football again at either club or county level until sometime in 1958. I was fuming at such a rule and my consequent suspension. How could playing soccer make me a less committed Gaelic footballer?

When 1958 came around there was only one thing on my mind. My suspension would soon be up and I could not wait to start playing again. In the 1958 McKenna Cup, Down easily overcame Fermanagh before being knocked out in the next round by our old adversaries, Armagh. After playing a series of challenge games the mentors were able to decide on their final 15 for the championship. As well as that, we were getting used to playing with each other. Each game we played our teamwork and general play improved considerably. I returned in the midst of these matches and saw immediately how the team had developed. The 1958 championship was considered to be up for grabs. Tyrone were aiming for their third consecutive title. Derry, Cavan and Armagh were very much in the frame. Our supporters and ourselves, however, reckoned that we could make our long-awaited provincial breakthrough.

Side by side with our senior title hopes was the progress of the Down junior team. As I had not played in the previous year's Ulster senior championship I was now eligible to play for the junior championship team. Paddy Doherty had been suspended in 1957 so he too was eligible to play junior football. As a result, we had a formidable junior team. Included were full back Leo Murphy, corner back Kevin O'Neill, right half back Patsy O'Hagan as well as midfielders Eamon Lundy and Tony Hadden (also back after a soccer suspension). None of these had played senior county championship football in the previous year. We had a very successful season, beating Monaghan in the first round, Fermanagh in the semi-final and Antrim in the Ulster decider. It was Down's first provincial junior success since 1949.

In the Ulster senior championship we played Donegal in the first round at Newry. We played particularly well in the first half and appeared to be coasting to an easy success at half-time. With just one minute gone in the second half Paddy Doherty scored a fabulous goal to leave the score Down 2-6, Donegal 1-2. It appeared the game was over but for some unknown reason we appeared to lose our momentum and Donegal scored 2-3 in next seven minutes. Then, just as quickly, every one of us seemed to realise the seriousness of the situation and we responded accordingly. To be fair, our supporters played their part in our comeback. Their support and cheering was deafening. Paddy Doherty was superb for the remainder of the game, scoring three excellent points. Corner forward Jim Fitzpatrick notched an opportunist goal before the superb Doherty added two further points. The final score of Down 3-11, Donegal 3-5 was a reflection of our eventual superiority.

After our indifferent display many of us thought that there would be several changes for the next match against Tyrone in the semi-final. However, the selectors kept faith with the starting 15 against the reigning Ulster champions. Incidentally there were 15 different clubs represented on those teams. Down performed brilliantly on this occasion. Playing fast expansive football we scored six points in the first half. Unbelievably Tyrone did not score at all in the first period. Shortly after half time Paddy Doherty scored a penalty and then added a point. Then Kieran Denvir scored a lovely point. There was only ten minutes left before Tyrone raised their first point. In the end we won by 1-9 to 0-2. I was satisfied with my own performance at centre half back. To cap a great day for Down's footballers the minors also reached the Ulster final. For the first time in 16 years a Down senior football team was in an Ulster final.

Going into the Ulster final we were confident of success. We knew that our display against Tyrone was not a fluke. It had been planned and worked on by both players and mentors alike. That visionary plan had been implemented after the county convention. We were professionally organised and prepared accordingly. We were working to a four or five year plan which would hopefully result in Down winning a senior All-Ireland football title. A series of trials had resulted in the establishment of a settled panel of committed, skilful players. Finally, management and players had come together to plot future strategy. The players for their part agreed to commit themselves to a rigorous training schedule. County secretary and team selector Maurice Hayes had promised us if we trained diligently and worked hard he would ensure that all issues concerning players' welfare would be properly and promptly addressed. Management would ensure that all medical problems, work problems, or any personal issues would be catered for. We all agreed with Maurice. As part of the structured part, a challenge match was arranged after the Ulster semi-final victory. We played the then reigning All-Ireland champions, Louth, in Knockbridge just before the Ulster final and beat them. Everything was in order, or so it seemed.

That 1958 Ulster final was against Derry. They, like us, had never won an Ulster title. So whatever the result a new name was guaranteed to be on the Anglo-Celt Cup. They had an excellent defence with goalkeeper Patsy Gormley and full back Hugh Francis Gribbin being real stalwarts. The half back line of Patsy Breen, Colm Mulholland and Peter Smith was one of the best in the country. The skilful, stylish and accurate Sean O'Connell was a brilliant forward. Most of all they had, in Jim McKeever, arguably, one of the best midfielders of all time. Nevertheless, as we arrived in Clones on Ulster final day I genuinely thought that we had more than a 50/50 chance of upsetting the favourites.

The curtain raiser was the minor final between Down and Cavan. Like ourselves, the minors were seeking their first Ulster title. In a terrific game they outclassed Cavan on a 3-9 to 3-1 scoreline. In a good all-round team performance one could not but admire the fantastic display of Sean O'Neill that day. The omens looked good for us. However, before our game began we had an unexpected and serious problem. Experienced and reliable corner back George Lavery had not appeared. In a repeat of what happened to me the previous year, he had not been collected for the game by the appointed taxi man. Despite all of our careful preparations, a basic misunderstanding had deprived us of one of our best players. One of course must remember that there were very few telephones, never mind mobile phones, at that time.

As a result of the mix-up, Kevin O'Neill was moved to corner back and Patsy O'Hagan was drafted in at right half back. For whatever reason we never really played well in the game. We were laboured in our movement and inaccurate in our passing. In short, as a team we didn't play anywhere near our full potential. It was a very wet day which did not suit our fast-running style. Still, it would be unfair to Derry to totally blame this for our inept performance. They were dominant in the first half with the magnificent McKeever lording it at centre field. His judicious passing of the ball to the forward line enabled the Oak Leaf men to lead at half time, 0-7 to 0-3. Shortly after half-time they scored again before I managed to send the ball to the net. Even though the goal gave a ray of hope, McKeever continued to dominate and landed a point. Then they were awarded a penalty which Charlie "Chuck" Higgins scored. Immediately afterwards Leo O'Neill (brother of Gerry and Martin) added a point. 15 minutes from the end Down, with young Leo Murphy outstanding at full back, upped the tempo. Our renewed efforts were rewarded when we were awarded a penalty. Paddy Doherty clinically dispatched the ball to the net to leave us only three points adrift. Perhaps, I thought, we could pull the game out of the fire. However, it was not to be as Derry scored two more points. It was at this juncture that Derry's goalkeeper Patsy Gormley produced three outstanding saves to prevent us from equalising or making it a more competitive encounter. Before the final whistle Kieran Denvir pointed in what was really only a consolation score.

The final whistle sounded to leave Derry Ulster champions for the first time on a score of 1-11 to 2-4. Leo Murphy, Kieran Denvir and corner forward Ronnie Moore were our best performers. Even though I scored a goal I did not do the primary job of a centre-half back. With my habit of racing forward too often I left too much space for the Derry centre half forward Brendan Murray to take advantage of. Nevertheless, we told ourselves that, despite not playing well, we were only beaten by four points.

Now a major dilemma faced the junior team selectors. Our successful Ulster-winning team was scheduled to play the All-Ireland semi-final against Meath at Newry the following Sunday. The GAA rules stated clearly that the only players who were not eligible to line out in junior championship football in the current season were those who had competed in the previous senior championship campaign. However, seven of us had played in the 1958 senior championship. Were we eligible or not? No one seemed able to give a definitive answer.

The selectors decided not to play any of us. So a new look Down junior team took the field at Newry. After his tour de force performance in the minor final, Sean O'Neill was selected on the junior side and he did not disappoint. Meath eventually ran out rather flattering winners by seven points. Likewise, luck was not with the minors when they succumbed to a 3-5 to 0-9 defeat to Dublin in the

All-Ireland semi-final. Despite our natural disappointment all of us instinctively knew that a new Down star had been born. Sean O'Neill's all-round performances in both games confirmed what a wonderful exponent of Gaelic football he was. My young first cousin who had helped us with the hay and kicked ball against a farmyard wall in Donacloney many years before was a definite star in the making.

There was renewed optimism within all of us when we returned to training for the Dr Lagan Cup competition which began in October. In the first game at Newcastle the ground was full as we met Antrim. The Glensmen started brightly and after ten minutes they led by four points to one. After that nervous opening we suddenly came to life. By half-time the game was really over as we then led by 14 points. The final score of Down 7-14, Antrim 2-3 told its own story. For the match I was switched to full forward and really relished the role. This was one day when everything seemed to go right for me. I managed to score four or five goals and four points. Those pundits who are into statistics maintain that it was one of the biggest scores ever recorded by any individual in the National Football League.

To the best of my knowledge the all-time record score ever achieved in the league was by Frankie Donnelly of Tyrone. Frankie scored 5-8 against Fermanagh when the O'Neill County faced the Ernesiders in 1956. However, I have always said that it is easy to score when the outfield players win so much possession and then pass the ball accurately into the forward line. Very often we give too much credit to the players who actually score and not enough praise to the men who win the ball.

In the next round of the cup we played Armagh and cruised to an emphatic 4-9 to 1-4 victory at Killeavy. Everything was going to plan but the real acid test of our progress would be tested in the next game. This was against Derry.

After beating us in the Ulster final they had gone on to shock the GAA world when they defeated Kerry in the All-Ireland semi-final. In a terrific all-round team display, and with the majestic Jim McKeever and the classy Sean O'Connell at their imperious best, they beat the Kingdom by a point. In the All-Ireland final they had come up against a fantastic Dublin 15 who eventually overcame them by six points. Now we were to face the All-Ireland finalists in Ballinascreen where the home side had never been beaten.

Down, in that game, began well and went into an early lead. Then we suffered two body blows. Kevin Mussen was injured after 15 minutes and Tony Hadden had to retire at half time. Initially this seemed to upset our rhythm. It was a marvellous game of free flowing football. The huge crowd constantly applauded as the game ebbed and flowed. At the end of the third quarter it was still nip and tuck. In the last quarter Derry took over and won the game: Derry 2-10, Down 1-5.

The National League then took its normal winter break. Though defeated we were not really despondent. 1958 had been a positive learning curve. Mentors and players were all satisfied that we could only go onwards and upwards. For me it was a case of roll on 1959. I just could not wait for the action to begin again. Surely an Ulster title, if everything went well, was there to be won. Any other success would be a most welcome bonus.

5

Our Time Has Come

Well 1959 did roll on but, as I have stated earlier, not to our complete satisfaction. After the disappointment of losing that year's All-Ireland semi-final to Galway we had made a pact. To a man, we agreed that no stone would be left unturned to ensure further championship progress. The year began with a banquet in St Colman's Hall, Newry, to celebrate the winning of Down's first Ulster senior football championship as well as McKenna Cup and Wembley Tournament successes. While this was a natural source of satisfaction for everyone it was, for me, more a case of unfinished business. That could only take place by achieving national honours on the playing fields.

Our first competitive action was in the Dr Lagan Cup where we beat both Armagh and Derry. This enabled us to qualify to meet Kerry in the National League semi-final. I was delighted to be back in Croke Park after our previous disastrous display in the home of the GAA. It was an exceptionally wet and blustery day. By the 13th minute Kerry led by three points to none. After gradually being able to come to terms with the elements we played brilliantly for the remainder of the half. Sean O'Neill, in particular, was outstanding. First of all he placed Tony Hadden for our opening point. Then P.J. McElroy sent a long pass in front of Sean O'Neill who was pulled down by a Kerry defender. Showing his instinctive skill he hit the ball with his foot as he was falling to the ground. The ball flashed into the net for a great opportunist goal. I managed to catch the ball from the resulting kick out, soloed forward and punched the ball to the net. Then after a fine passing movement, initiated by our defence, I again won the ball and sent it over the bar. Kerry responded shortly afterwards with two points from frees, just before our goalkeeper Eddie McKay made a superb save. Incredibly he was penalised for supposedly picking the ball off the ground. None of us, including the press, agreed with this bizarre decision by the referee. There was a sense of poetic justice when Kerry's Dan McAuliffe sent the penalty over the bar. However, Kerry's persistent attacking efforts were rewarded just before half time when they notched an equalising goal.

Gary McMahon gave Kerry the lead shortly after the restart when he scored a point. Soon we assumed the ascendancy again and both Sean O'Neill and I landed points to give us a one-point lead. By the three quarter stage another Kerry point had brought them level. In the last quarter we played splendidly. Brian Morgan caught the ball magnificently, turned quickly and sent the ball straight and true over the bar for the lead point. Paddy Doherty then struck an impressive purple patch by scoring four points in rapid succession, two from frees and another two from play. We were five points clear as the game neared its end. Eddie McKay brilliantly saved two fantastic goalbound efforts by the Kerry forward line. In the final minute Paudie Sheehy scored a consolation goal. When the final whistle sounded we had won our way to our first National Football League final.

This was a huge psychological boost for us as we had overcome, in the process, the acknowledged and traditional masters of Gaelic football. Eddie McKay, George Lavery, Pat Rice, Patsy O'Hagan, Sean O'Neill and Paddy Doherty had all played well. This feat was accurately commented on by Mick Dunne writing in the *Irish Press*: "From Croke Park comes the scoreline which marks the turning point in Down football – they are now ready to take their place amongst football's elite and survive in the most exalted company." From my own perspective, I had been relieved of my defensive duties and felt much more at home in the forward line, even though it was in my less favoured position of full forward.

That 1960 league final was unique in that it featured the first final between two Ulster sides. This novelty pairing of Down against Cavan (our Ulster final opponents of 1959) attracted a huge crowd of almost 50,000 people. Cavan began the decider the much stronger team and only terrific defensive displays by Eddie McKay, Leo Murphy, Pat Rice and the magnificent George Lavery prevented the Breffni side from totally overwhelming us. As it was, they held only a two-point advantage after six minutes. Sean O'Neill then pointed two frees before Paddy Doherty and O'Neill again scored to put us two points in front. Cavan's stylish forward Charlie Gallagher then scored a lovely point before P.J McElroy and Sean O'Neill added further points just before the interval. The half time score read: Down 0-6, Cavan 0-3.

In the third quarter, Cavan were much superior and scored four points without reply to leave us one point behind. At the beginning of the fourth quarter, the ever reliable Paddy Doherty scored two points, one from play and one from a free. Then Patsy O'Hagan got the ball and found Brian Morgan with a precise pass. He swivelled, turned and put the ball over the bar for a marvellous point. We were two points ahead. As the game entered its closing stages Cavan had responded with two points to make it all square again at 0-9 each. The brilliant O'Hagan then soloed through to give us the lead. Immediately after, Brian Morgan added another. On the stroke of full-time Sean O'Neill sent a lovely weighted pass to Brian Morgan and the Annaclone man gave us the insurance point. The full time whistle went and we had won our first senior national football title, by overcoming our fellow Ulstermen on a scoreline of 0-12 to 0-9.

The whole stadium erupted and Down supporters invaded the pitch in their thousands. Our outstanding captain Kevin Mussen had given a real inspirational display. John D. Hickey, writing in the following day's *Irish Independent*, confirmed this view: "He was a rallying force whose coolness, even in times of great peril, must have caused his team mates, or most of them, often to ask themselves why they were so agitated in less dangerous situations."

Life would be very monotonous if we all reacted in the same way to every type of incident. For example, on the way home after that league win Dad was stopped at a set of traffic lights outside Dublin when a Cavan supporter jumped out of his car which was in a parallel lane. He placed his blue and white Breffni cap on the insignia of Dad's vehicle. Immediately, my father and one of his passengers, my first cousin Seamus McCartan, dashed out of their car. In no uncertain terms they made the man remove the offending apparel and told him to have manners. Meanwhile, my mother calmly sat in the car and quietly observed, "I would not like to see their reaction if Down had lost!"

A week later came a match that, I feel, was to serve as an important wake-up call for the future. We played Kerry in a challenge game at Listowel. It was a most disappointing display. True, we started without Sean O'Neill and Jarlath Carey. True also that during the course of the game we lost Eddie McKay, P.J. McElroy and Pat Rice to injury. That, however, does not explain such a pathetic performance. Kerry dominated for the whole game and were not flattered by their comprehensive triumph. To be beaten by 6-6 to 0-9 was nothing short of a humiliation.

Kerry really rubbed it in that day because they did not like the fact that we had beaten them in the league semi-final. Their mentors kept telling the players during the course of the game to go for goals. When my father was leaving the ground he was continually being slagged about how useless Down were and how great Kerry were. He retorted, "It is only a friendly at the opening of a new pitch."

"We do not play friendlies," came the cynical reply.

Hopefully, we thought, all of this would serve as a timely reminder of what could happen if we did not maintain our high standards of meticulous preparation and personal discipline. We definitely needed to be on our guard when we faced old adversaries Derry in the McKenna Cup final on the following Sunday. We again flopped. Derry fully deserved their 1-11 to 1-7 success. Self-doubt was now beginning to raise its head amongst us but importantly our mentors kept cool. Before the Ulster championship began there would be another opportunity to restore our championship credibility. In the playoff for the annual Wembley tournament we had already overcome Cavan to qualify for another tilt at Galway in the famed English soccer arena.

Just like the previous year there was a huge crowd and another beautiful sunny day. Pace, power and skill were in abundance during this encounter. Paddy Doherty and Sean O'Neill scored some glorious points as we continually pressed the Galway defence. Brian Morgan was also on top of his game with his unselfish distribution of the ball to better placed colleagues. Good as they were I had no doubt that the real star of that wonderful Wembley win was Patsy O'Hagan. Just as in the previous year's tournament final he seemed to revel in the spaces of that Wembley pitch. He scored three fantastic goals in a real man-of-the-match performance. In an exhilarating game we beat Galway 4-11 to 3-7. Interestingly, one of the Galway goals was scored by George Glynn whom all of us in Down, and myself especially, would come to know in the years to come.

Now I looked forward with much more optimism as we prepared to meet Antrim in the first round of the Ulster senior football championship. Playing with a massive wind advantage we scored 0-11 in the first half without any reply from the Glensmen. In the third quarter Antrim played much better to score 1-2 without any reply from us. However, that really was the end of their challenge and we were triumphant in the end on a convincing score of 0-14 to 1-4.

The semi-final against Monaghan, in Dungannon, took place against the background of another day of heavy rain and gale force winds. Nevertheless, we played well and were much more content with our ball handling and general team play. Only five good points from the accurate boot of Longford-born Danny O'Brien kept Monaghan in the game. When the final whistle sounded we had scored a comfortable win – Down 2-11, Monaghan 0-7. Leo Murphy, Paddy Doherty and the consistent Brian Morgan were our stars. Things were also moving along nicely for me. I scored the two goals and my new home in the forward line was very comfortable.

Now, for the third year in a row, we were in the Ulster final. The press build up to the game was intense and the supporters of both counties eagerly looked forward to a rematch of the 1959 finalists.

Only 40 seconds had elapsed when the first decisive action occurred. Marvellous interplay between my brother Dan, who had taken over my old centre half back spot, Kevin Mussen and Sean O'Neill ended with the ball being passed to Paddy Doherty on the edge of the square. Unerringly he sent the ball to the net for a fabulous goal. Within a minute I got the ball about twenty yards out and hammered it to the net. Shortly afterwards Paddy Doherty added a point. Cavan then assumed control and Con Smyth scored a good goal. Sean O'Neill replied with a point from a close range free before the dangerous Smyth responded with a similar score for the Breffni men. Approaching half time, the hard-working James Brady scored for Cavan to leave the interval scoreline reading Down 2-2, Cavan 1-2. The reason for Cavan's resurgence in the second quarter was the great performance of their two midfielders. Both of them – the energetic Hugh Barney O'Donoghue and the sublime Jim McDonnell – were simply magnificent at this stage.

During the opening six minutes of the second half the very accurate Con Smyth pointed three successive frees. With the scores now level I was worried that Cavan were on a serious revenge mission to compensate for their failure of 1959. Then our selectors showed their astuteness when they made a game-changing tactical switch. Tony Hadden was moved from right corner forward to curb the midfield dominance of McDonnell and O'Donoghue. The move worked a treat as Hadden immediately and continuously won possession. In addition he ensured that we got quality ball. We were awarded two frees which Doherty and O'Neill duly pointed.

Cavan, however, were still a force to be reckoned with and that will o'wisp forward Charlie Gallagher was causing panic in our defence. Nevertheless, they held firm. Then came the match-winning moment. Gallagher broke through and appeared certain to score a goal. Eddie McKay saved magnificently and the ball was quickly transferred to Dan McCartan in the heart of our defence. He passed to Tony Hadden who flighted the ball across the field to the overlapping Kevin Mussen. Kevin sent a superb pass onto Paddy Doherty lurking on the 14-yard line. Paddy "Mo", as we affectionately called him, lashed an unstoppable shot to the back of the net for a stupendous goal.

Brian Morgan and Con Smith exchanged points before Tony Hadden and Jarlath Carey, who had now replaced P.J. McElroy at midfield, added two more to make us sure of victory. In the last five minutes the marvellous Jim McDonnell scored two points but the game was effectively over. When the final whistle went we had won our second Ulster senior football title. The scoreboard read Down 3-7, Cavan 1-8.

What was more significant about that 1960 Ulster campaign was that the selectors had finally decided what our best 15 was. The goalkeeping berth and full back line had already been well established. The introduction of Dan at centre half back had stabilised our defence. Unlike myself he had the natural capacity to play the anchor role very competently. This allowed both wing half backs, Kevin Mussen and Kevin O'Neill, to attack when necessary. Joe Lennon, P.J. McElroy and Jarlath Carey were three good midfield options. Kieran Denvir was also able to play there as well as in the forward line. If any of these were in difficulty, in any given game, we also could draft corner forward Tony Hadden into the midfield sector. Sean O'Neill, Paddy Doherty, Patsy O'Hagan, Brian Morgan, Tony and myself were settling into a regular pattern of play in the forward line.

Even more significant was that all the forwards and midfielders were capable of scoring. Centre half forward now seemed to be my most natural position. This allowed the whole forward line to knit as a unit. The fact that I had two of the most outstanding forwards in the game on either side of me made my task all the easier. Every time either Sean O'Neill or Paddy Doherty were on the ball the opposing defence threatened to panic. It was a no-win situation for the defenders. If any of us were fouled O'Neill or Doherty, depending on which side of the field the offence was committed, would point the resulting free. If they did not foul them, Paddy or Sean were likely to score from play. They were also very adept at creating scoring opportunities for the rest of us. Kieran Denvir, who missed the Ulster final because he was on his honeymoon in Rome, was also a very talented player. He could play in the wing or corner forward positions as well as midfield. Patsy O'Hagan was a very good target man in the full forward position and, as he showed in the Wembley tournament final, he was also a marvellous goal scorer. Brian Morgan was a hugely creative and inspiring left corner forward who certainly knew where the goal posts were.

In the All-Ireland semi-final Down faced Offaly who had just won the Leinster senior football final for the first time. Playing with a strong wind Offaly began the game impressively. They hit us hard but fair. They did not indulge in any fancy combination play. For them it was very much a matter of catching the ball and kicking it as far as possible into our defence. After about ten minutes they had scored three points without any response from us. Their midfielders were totally on top but we had managed to claw our way back into the game thanks to good individual scores from Patsy O'Hagan and Paddy Doherty. By the 20th minute the score was 0-4 to 0-3 in their favour. For the remainder of the half Offaly assumed almost total control. They then scored a goal. Just when we were trying to recover from that body blow disaster struck again. Offaly defender cum midfielder Sean Ryan sent a long ball into our goalmouth. There was a complete lack of understanding between our full back line and goalkeeper as Offaly forward Sean Brereton sent both goalkeeper and ball over the line to leave Offaly leading 2-4 to 0-3. That was a worrying score for us when the referee signalled the end of the first half.

With wind advantage we pressed continuously at the beginning of the second half. Paddy Doherty was especially prominent at this stage. After a minute he landed a spectacular point before Patsy O'Hagan added another. Then Doherty pointed a free before splitting the posts with another magnificent point from play. There were only five minutes gone and we had reduced the deficit to three points. It was now Offaly's turn to regain the upper hand. Har Donnelly scored a free and Tommy Greene notched one from play.

With our midfield of P.J. McElroy and Joe Lennon failing to gain parity our selectors then moved Tony Hadden out to the troublesome sector. Immediately the pattern of play changed. Hadden caught ball after ball and initiated many attacks. As a result Doherty scored a great point. Then in a fantastic move Kevin Mussen gained possession and passed to the overlapping Joe Lennon. He quickly distributed an excellent pass to Paddy Doherty who split the uprights again with an exquisite point.

We were now only three points behind on a score of 2-6 to 0-9. We kept attacking. Offaly right full back Paddy McCormack took the ball off the line as I attempted to score a goal. Their goalkeeper Willie Nolan produced three marvellous saves in quick succession. First he saved a thundering goalbound effort from Tony Hadden before producing two other wonderful saves, this time from the boot of Brian Morgan. I was beginning to wonder was this not going to be our day.

Then something which has since become immortalised in GAA folklore happened. I was at the centre of this controversy. There were only eight minutes left and the pendulum had definitely swung our way everywhere, except on the scoreboard. I had been switched to full forward to attempt to penetrate the

Offaly rearguard. I was standing on the edge of the square when I got the ball. I took one step forward and several Offaly defenders pulled me around. I was now facing outfield when the referee Tom Cunningham of Waterford blew the whistle. Much to the annoyance of Offaly players and supporters he awarded us a penalty. The photographs of the incident prove the referee to be correct. Offaly people said I was charging goalwards and insisted that it should have been a free out. Some media commentators agreed with this opinion. I have no doubt about the validity of the referee's opinion. If I had been charging goalwards, as my detractors alleged, I would have been facing the net. This was not the case. Therefore it was a definite penalty. The tension in the ground at this stage was unbearable as the Offaly supporters loudly voiced their disapproval. Unperturbed, however, the ice-cool Paddy Doherty hammered the ball to the back of the net. The sides were level and the whole stadium immediately erupted into a cauldron of noise and excitement.

All of us were extremely nervous for the remaining minutes of the game. Tony Hadden put us in front, for the first time, with an excellent point. But the delight of our supporters turned into despair when the referee awarded a close-in free to Offaly for an alleged pick-up off the ground by Pat Rice. The accurate Har Donnelly pointed the free to level the scores again. In the last minute a determined Offaly side launched another attack. Suddenly, the ever-dangerous Sean Brereton was racing towards the goals. My heart was in my mouth as I believed all our brave efforts were to be in vain. Another disappointing, though closer, championship exit at the penultimate stage now appeared to be our fate. But, incredibly, out of nowhere the vigilant and extremely disciplined Leo Murphy came to literally snatch the ball off Brereton's boot. His long relieving clearance went straight to Paddy Doherty. Though surrounded by a group of Offaly backs he managed to send a high shot towards the Offaly goalmouth. It appeared to be going over the bar but tailed off at the last minute to strike the outside of an upright and go wide.

The final whistle went. It was a draw: Down 1-10, Offaly 2-7. We were lucky to escape. Only Paddy Doherty's magnificent tally of 1-7 had kept us in the game.

After our close call with defeat our management decided to enlist outside help. They went to Navan to meet Peter McDermott who was very familiar with Down football. He had been joint trainer with the Down team that had won the All-Ireland junior football title in 1946. He had also trained the Newry Shamrocks club in the Down senior club championship. Furthermore, he was generally acknowledged as a very astute reader of the game. He, himself, was a double All-

Ireland senior medal winner with Meath in 1949 and 1954 when he was the team captain. The "man in the cap" as he was popularly known had also refereed the 1953 All-Ireland final between Kerry and Armagh. After the drawn encounter he had written to a friend, Alfie Matthews of Newry, pointing out flaws which he had observed in Down's performance. In a formal coaching session Peter addressed us and the selectors in St Malachy's school in Castlewellan. He talked about our strengths as well as our weaknesses. In short, as a result of his help we were instilled with a greater confidence and a greater will to win.

Thus we were very happy when we met Offaly again in September, with Michael McArdle of Louth as referee. The only change for the replay was Kieran Denvir at midfield instead of P.J. McElroy. 68,000 people filled Croke Park. This was a semi-final record crowd. Within the first five minutes both Patsy O'Hagan and Joe Lennon had scored points. Three minutes later, however, disaster struck. A Charlie Wrenn 45-yard sideline kick deceived our whole defence and landed in the back of the net. We constantly attacked but tended to overplay the ball. A hard-hitting Offaly defence repeatedly broke up our attacks. As a result, their more direct approach meant that the ball was quickly returned into the heart of our defence. Soon Tommy Cullen scored a point from play and Har Donnelly added another from a free. Then from the right wing Sean Brereton swung over another excellent score. Except for a goalbound effort by Patsy O'Hagan, which was well stopped by Willie Nolan, we were not at the races for the remainder of the half. The interval score was 1-3 to 0-2 in Offaly's favour. What was most annoying was the fact that we had not scored from the fifth minute of the first half.

In terms of possession we were much better at the beginning of the second half. Patsy O'Hagan was exceptionally unlucky when his effort hit the post and went wide. However, despite our initial territorial advantage it was Offaly who scored first when Har Donnelly converted a 21-yard free.

Still we continued to win a lot of outfield possession but our forward line tended to shoot too hastily and from too far out. As a result of this nervous play we shot four bad wides. Then Sean O'Neill gained control of the ball on the right flank of our attack and crossed it to me. I sent it over the bar. Within the next two minutes our forward line started to click into top gear. I scored another point from close range before Tony Hadden added one from far out. From a personal point of view I seemed to be getting into the game much more and was now more confident that we could take control in a more effective manner. Halfway through the second half Kevin O'Neill, who was having an excellent match, sent me a lovely pass. I duly dispatched the ball to his brother Sean who flicked it to Patsy O'Hagan. Again O'Hagan's well aimed shot was brilliantly stopped by Offaly net minder Willie Nolan but he failed to hold it. It broke loose to Brian Morgan and the Annaclone player punched it to the net. We were ahead by 1-5 to 1-4. Rain was now falling incessantly but that did not dampen our spirits as we surged forward in search of further scores. I won the ball on the 40-yard line, soloed through and slotted it over the bar. There were 11 minutes left and we were two points in front. A Paddy Doherty free a few minutes later gave us a three-point advantage. With just a minute to go Offaly's Tommy Greene went in search of an equalising goal but a brilliant tackle by Dan McCartan forced the Offaly man to be content with a point. At the very end Leo Murphy rose brilliantly to fetch the ball. When his typical long clearance landed in the centre of the field the full-time whistle was blown. We had won a tight, tense contest by 1-7 to 1-5. More importantly, however, we were in our first All-Ireland senior football final. The ghosts of the previous year's disappointing exit to Galway were now firmly laid to rest.

Our friend 'Linesman' summed up the feelings of all Down players, mentors and supporters very accurately in the next edition of the *Frontier Sentinel*: 'These are truly wonderful days for Down. We are living in the presence of football history.' And I could not help but think that we were sixty minutes away from landing the greatest prize of all.

In the final we were due to meet Kerry, the long acknowledged kingpins of Gaelic football. The interest in this pairing was unprecedented as 80,000 stand ticket applications were received in Croke Park for 20,000 seats. In the *Armagh Observer* a Tyrone GAA follower offered to sell three and a half acres of land for ten tickets. Our training sessions were attended by hundreds of supporters. The last team from Ulster to win the All-Ireland senior football championship was Cavan in 1952. No team of the six counties of Northern Ireland had ever annexed the Sam Maguire Cup.

One day, in the week before the decider, I was busy forking up bales of hay into our barn loft when I heard a familiar voice calling me. "You are an incredibly strong man the way you are able to put up those bales so quickly. What do you eat for breakfast?" the voice asked.

"A loaf of bread and a boiled egg!" I replied, good-humouredly. It was the one and only Michael O'Hehir. He had come to interview me. When I told him that we expected to beat Kerry he looked at me in disbelief.

"Both of us have fifteen players. The only difference between us is the colour of the jerseys." I told him. That was the contrast between Down and other good sides who played against Kerry at that time. Our management had instilled in us a total belief in our own ability. Other teams gave them too much respect because of their successful tradition. Our blend of youth, skill, teamwork and our natural ability to interchange positions almost at will, had captured the imagination of the public throughout the country. Women and children so long starved of something to cheer about had adopted Down in their thousands.

The two games with Offaly had brought the team on in a manner that no amount of training sessions could ever have accomplished. There were 31 counties behind us as we meticulously prepared for the greatest day in our lives. Peter McDermott returned to help us in the two weeks between the Offaly replay and the final. Kerry had 19 All-Irelands to their credit. We had none. Peter McDermott's last words to us were reassuring and positive: "Every time you make a breakthrough you get more confidence for the next step. You are good enough to win, but if you don't the Mountains of Mourne won't fall into the sea."

One final significant decision was agreed by both management and players. We would not repeat the pre-match travel and accommodation mistakes of the previous year when we stayed overnight in Butlins. This time we slept in our own beds on the Saturday night. We got a proper breakfast after we went to mass in St Colman's College in Newry. We got a police escort to the border and a garda escort to Dublin. Before we went to Croke Park we had a proper light lunch in our hotel. The sleepless night of 1959 was but a bad, distant memory. The AA on both sides of the border reported a massive volume of traffic as the whole of Ulster seemed destined for Croke Park. Every Ulster GAA supporter, outside of Down, had become an honorary member of the red and black brigade for the day.

On Sunday, 25 September 1960, the gates of Croke Park opened at noon. When the gates were shut at 2.15 p.m. 88,000 spectators had crammed into the ground. Thousands of disappointed supporters were turned away. They had to be content listening to the commentary on the match from Michael O'Hehir. Every bar and café echoed to the master's voice on the many radios that blared among the streets of the capital. The man who commentated on the great Roscommon, Cavan and Meath teams in our kitchen back in the 1940s was now uttering the names of Lavery, Mussen, Murphy, O'Neill, Hadden and Doherty. My mother, I know, was particularly proud to listen to the names of her two only sons and two nephews.

We could not wait to leave the dressing room. When we looked out on the pitch at half time in the minor curtain raiser, the excitement was clearly palpable. The red and black colours of Down clearly dominated. Personally I was cautiously confident but also acutely aware of what we had to do. We, the players of the county of Down, were the only people who could bring to fruition what our supporters wanted. What an awesome challenge it was. Kerry were in their 29th final. We were in our first, just one year after winning our first provincial title. Before we left the dressing room there were no impassioned speeches. Our manager Barney Carr told us simply and effectively to go out and play our normal game. Then an anonymous voice from our midst roared the most meaningful mantra of all: "Remember Listowel!" And to a man, inwardly and outwardly, we did. We wished each other the best of luck as Kevin Mussen led us onto the sacred soil to a crescendo of thunderous noise and applause. Brian Morgan and Patsy O'Hagan were the last people to leave. Hundreds of our supporters, who were locked out, knocked on the rear door of the dressing room. Just before they joined the rest of us the two players generously unbolted the door. Immediately, the delighted spectators burst in, ran out onto the side of the pitch, and took their unexpected places just outside the perimeter fence. There they stayed until the final moments of this wonderful occasion. One could not imagine that scenario happening in the ultra security conscious world that we now live in.

The only change in our side was Jarlath Carey at midfield instead of the unlucky Kieran Denvir.

The game began at a phenomenal pace. Three times Kerry attacked and three times they were repulsed by the combined efforts of Dan McCartan, Leo Murphy and George Lavery. George showed terrific anticipation as he beat danger man Tadhgie Lyne to the ball before directing a long kicked pass to Tony Hadden who was acting like a third midfielder in the modern game. Tony opened the scoring with a beautiful long range point from over forty yards out. Then that wonderful Kerry midfielder Mick O'Connell equalised with a point.

A few minutes later O'Connell sent a dangerous ball into our goalmouth but our goalkeeper Eddie McKay hurled himself through the air to spectacularly field the Valentia man's effort. The next few minutes was hectic end-to-end play before a free allowed Tadhgie Lyne to give Kerry the lead. Suddenly our whole team began to move with both purpose and penetration. Kerry goalkeeper Johnny Culloty saved magnificently from both Brian Morgan and Patsy O'Hagan. Then Joe Lennon gained possession and from forty yards out scored a fantastic point to equalise.

That score of Joe's inspired the whole team even further. So dangerous was our forward line, with their blistering pace and continuous movement, that the Kerry defence had to resort to fouling. As a result both Paddy Doherty and Sean O'Neill pointed to put us two points clear. I grabbed the ball, shortly afterwards, on the 40-yard line and soloed goalwards. My shot for goal was deflected over the bar by the agile Culloty. A minute later, as a result of good outfield play, Tony Hadden pointed. We had scored five points in five minutes and were now four points to the good with 15 minutes gone. The scoreline read 0-6 to 0-2 and I was enjoying our teamwork and our ability to take decisive scores. Tadhgie Lyne then scored two frees to narrow the gap. Just before half time Paddy Doherty and Tadhgie Lyne exchanged pointed frees to leave the half time score Down 0-7, Kerry 0-5.

At half time there was no panic in the dressing room. Barney Carr just told us to keep playing the way we were. We all, instinctively, knew what we had to do to bring the Sam Maguire Cup over the border for the first time. And we had thirty minutes to achieve our dream. In the second half Kerry were playing with the wind and almost immediately Mick O'Connell pointed to reduce the deficit to one point. Then right half forward Seamus Murphy dashed up the field to land the equaliser for the Kingdom. I briefly wondered would this be the start of Kerry assuming control.

I did not have to worry for too long as another defining moment in the history of this Down team was about to occur. Luckily, I was in the middle of it. Kevin Mussen sent a perfect free kick to me about forty yards out from the Kerry goal. I lobbed the ball as hard as I could into the goalmouth. The Kerry defenders were clearly watching and tightly marking the rest of our forward line as the ball spun over their heads into the apparently safe hands of goalkeeper Johnny Culloty. Johnny went up to catch the ball with both hands but, inexplicably, let it slip from them into the net for a fortuitous goal. A minute later I gained possession on the 40-yard mark and passed to Sean O'Neill in the right corner forward position. Sean sent a clever pass across to the perfectly positioned Paddy Doherty who was hauled down in the square by Kerry's corner back Tim "Tiger" Lyons.

As referee John Dowling of Offaly awarded the inevitable penalty I knew that if it was scored we would, in all probability, win the game. That lucky goal of mine had seemed to revive the whole team and inspire them to be more creative in their movement and even more determined in their tackling. For the second time in a matter of weeks Paddy Doherty slammed an important penalty to the net. We were now six points up. As the ball nestled in the corner of the net, Down supporters threw hats, scarves and coats up in the air in spontaneous gestures of unbridled joy. Paddy raced back to take up his customary left half forward position and a worried Mick O'Connell interrupted him. "How much time is there left?" the Valentia maestro enquired.

"About three hundred and sixty four days!" came the instant and witty reply from the Ballykinlar man.

Mick O'Dwyer scored a fabulous point for Kerry shortly afterwards with still 14 minutes left. Nevertheless, as all of us on the field started to look around at our excited supporters, we were automatically spurred on to display the full repertoire of our defensive and attacking skills. The immaculate Paddy Doherty scored three times as we headed towards the end. His last point was a score that really matched the occasion. He caught the ball with his back to the goal and nonchalantly kicked it over his head for a tremendous score.

All of us, including our supporters, impatiently awaited the final whistle. A whistle for a fifty was mistaken for the full time whistle by Down supporters and there was an immediate mini pitch invasion. Luckily both officials and ourselves managed to get the supporters back to their seats. When the final whistle did go, minutes later, the whole pitch became a seething sea of red and black. The score was 2-10 to 0-8 and my first thought was that we were champions of all Ireland.

In the process of that wonderful performance we had inflicted upon Kerry their heaviest defeat, until then, in an All-Ireland final. Some of my lifelong friends, such as my first cousin Seamus McCartan and good friend Seamus Fitzpatrick, were the first to greet me. It was an unbelievable feeling of joy and fulfilment.

A Down supporter climbed a goal post at the Hill 16 end and placed a red and black flag on top of an upright. Not to be outdone, my first cousin Columba Hylands put his Down hat on top of the other upright. We were all carried shoulder high across the field towards the central presentation area in the centre of the Hogan Stand. When Kevin Mussen raised aloft the Sam Maguire Cup I could not believe what I was seeing. After all the years of difficulty and hard work Kevin had now in his hands what we all wanted. The noise when he lifted the trophy was deafening in its intensity and overwhelming in its excitement. After the presentation our ecstatic supporters stayed on the pitch, cheering, shouting, blowing horns and ringing bells. It was an unforgettable experience to observe so much joy on so many supporters' faces.

Eventually the whole team made their way to the dressing room. Meeting my brother Dan and our first cousins Kevin and Sean O'Neill in the winners' dressing room was an unforgettable shared experience of complete exhilaration.

We had come a long way since the four of us had spent so many happy summer days, in the forties and fifties, back in Donacloney.

Suddenly in the middle of all this celebration there was something more important that I had to do. I dressed quickly and rushed outside into the street. It was heaving with thousands of excited, exuberant Down supporters. I stood on the footpath of Jones' Road looking for someone special. Then I spotted him on the far side with his arms around a family friend from Hilltown for whom he had secured a match ticket. Between us there were hundreds of delighted people. Then we saw each other. As we raced to meet, the crowds seemed to magically disappear like the dividing of the Red Sea in biblical times. As my father and I hugged we seemed to be suspended in time, totally oblivious to all that was going on around us. I was thinking of the scene the previous year in our yard at home. My then prophetic words had surely now answered his understandable frustration. With a beaming smile and tears streaming down his cheeks he spoke just six words of total satisfaction: "Jimmy boy, you kept your promise."

Of all the wonderful things that have happened to me, with the exception of my own family's joyous moments, this was the most fulfilling feeling of all. Even now, barely a day passes when I don't fondly recall that lovely experience that my father and I shared on Jones' Road.

We then went back to our hotel, The Maples House Hotel on Iona Road in Glasnevin. Before the celebratory banquet began Dr Martin Walsh told us to lie down for an hour and we dutifully obeyed. Unbelievably, Joe Lennon missed the celebrations as he had to be back in college in Warrington in England. Immediately after the game he had to catch a flight and was actually back in England after seven o'clock! It would be hard to envisage that happening now.

At 1 a.m. many of us went for a stroll down O'Connell Street in order to savour the joy of our accomplishment. Buying the early edition of the next day's papers and reading about our historic exploits crystallised for all of us the uniqueness of what we had achieved.

On Monday morning we visited Áras an Uachtaráin at the special invitation of President de Valera. De Valera had a particular affection for County Down as he had been M.P. for the constituency of South Down over forty years earlier. There was one particular funny incident in the Áras that morning, they ran out of soft drinks! As most of the Down officials and players were pioneers, the President's staff had to send out for additional lemonade. After we left the Phoenix Park we had our lunch. We then had an amusing diversion. The Sam

Maguire Cup was fastened onto the top of a car belonging to a Down supporter called Hugh Murdock. Hugh, though living in Dublin, was an avid Down fan and had played for the county in the past. With the Sam Maguire in place, Hugh led an impromptu cavalcade of Down cars all bedecked with the county colours. Through the whole centre of Dublin right onto O'Connell Street he led us on a journey of joy and happiness.

Then began the magic trip home. There were official receptions in Drogheda and Dundalk. Bands played lively, joyous music and thousands of onlookers kept cheering, clapping and congratulating us as we slowly made our way northwards. We stopped for a meal at Ballymascanton Hotel where I had often yearned to visit in my late teenage years. At the border the Gaels of Armagh, our keenest rivals, held a mini pageant in our honour. A group of Irish dancers danced jigs and reels. The people of Killeavy parish and their local GAA club formed a guard of honour as we left to enter our native county.

Over 40,000 people thronged the streets of Newry when we arrived at the victory platform. Here there were many speeches. Our manager Barney Carr introduced each of us individually to the ecstatic crowd and each of us was loudly applauded when we took to the podium. As we left Newry the surrounding hillsides of counties Louth, Armagh and our beloved Down blazed brightly as huge bonfires lit up the evening sky. It was a wonderfully uplifting sight. On we travelled to Mayobridge, then to Clonduff, home of our captain Kevin Mussen and Patsy O'Hagan. It was then the turn of Kilcoo to honour us. As we moved onwards to Castlewellan a brilliant torchlight procession greeted us. When we reached Downpatrick torchlight celebrations were again highlighting what a football team's success can mean to so many people.

We reached journey's end at Newcastle at about half past three on Tuesday morning. The vast crowds already there were augmented by those thousands who had joined us along the way on our glorious lap of honour. Eventually, tired, weary but happy, we sat down for a meal in the Donard Hotel. Life could not have been better. God was in heaven and we had won the Sam Maguire Cup. Before I went to sleep I thought about all those brave Down GAA people who had soldiered for so many years without any real success.

The best nightcap of all, however, was those precious words that my father uttered to me on Jones' Road: "Jimmy boy, you kept your promise." I will always be grateful to all who helped me, both on and off the field of play, to fulfil that farmyard pledge.

6

A Good Team Becomes Great

As all the celebrations in the county were coming to an end we were making our way back to Croke Park, a fortnight later, to play New York in the St Brendan Cup. This was an annual competition between 1954 and 1960 which pitted the National League champions against New York. Only magnificent defending by their full back Denis Bernard, who had played for Cork in the 1956 All-Ireland against Galway, prevented us from overwhelming the American side. As it was, our overall superiority was reflected in the final scoreline of 2-8 to 0-6. Along with the impressive Jarlath Carey, Kevin O'Neill had one of his finest ever performances in a Down jersey. The crowd cheered long and loud as we left the field to complete a very successful year for Down football.

During the course of the next few weeks we travelled to clubs, céilís and parades throughout the county. Many civic receptions were held in our honour. These were all thoroughly enjoyable but we still had the task of successfully defending our Dr Lagan Cup and National Football League titles.

After the Saint Brendan Cup triumph we trounced Antrim 6-12 to 0-6 in the first match of the Lagan Cup. A week later we faced Tyrone in the next round. They started in whirlwind fashion and led 1-3 to no score before Tony Hadden was brought to midfield. Thanks to his clever promptings we had drawn level by half time. In the second half we dusted off our celebratory cobwebs and won rather easily in the end, 1-11 to 1-5. Another win over Monaghan completed our pre-Christmas National League fixtures.

Just prior to Christmas I was awarded the Caltex Gaelic Footballer of the Year award. Paddy Doherty was selected as the UTV Sportsman Of The Year. (Incidentally the Ballykinlar man has yet to receive his winner's trophy!) The sports editors of 11 newspapers selected the Caltex award winners in different Irish sporting disciplines. Among those picked were John Lawlor who had come within inches of winning a bronze medal in hammer throwing at the 1960 Olympics in Rome. Kilkenny born Nick O'Donnell who had won All-Ireland hurling medals with his adopted Wexford in 1955, 1956 and 1960 was also picked. John Caldwell who had won a bronze medal in the 1956 Olympics was selected as the leading boxer. It was a personal honour for me when one considers that I was following in the footsteps of Jim McKeever. He had won the initial award in 1958 and Kerry's wonderful right half back Sean Murphy won in 1959. I must emphasise, however, that whereas it was nice to get it, the award was really an acknowledgement for what Down had achieved as a team. It could have easily, and probably more fairly, gone to several other Down players from that All-Ireland winning team.

After Down's record breaking performances in 1960 it was not surprising that ten Down men were picked on the Ulster Railway Cup team for the provincial semi-final against Leinster in Casement Park. However, the Ulster selectors caused a huge sensation when I was not selected and, indeed to make the selection even stranger, they picked me as last substitute. Those sentiments that I have just written were not mine alone, more a summary of what many GAA correspondents of both the national and local press had stated. Ulster, who had won the Railway Cup the previous year, were beaten by a point.

Of all the games that I sat on a substitute bench this was easily the most frustrating. I kicked every ball that was kicked. The net result of this was that there was a huge hole in the sand in front of the subs' bench seat at the end of the match. During the course of the whole game a large majority of the crowd kept chanting: "Bring on McCartan, bring on McCartan." I felt that this only discouraged the selectors from making a decision to bring me on at all. My view on this is borne out by the fact that they brought me on just thirty seconds before the end when the game was effectively over. What made their decision even more galling was the fact that on the previous day I was selected to represent Ireland in the annual representative game with the Combined Universities. To add salt to my already injured ego, I was chosen as the Irish captain.

I have never really found a definite answer as to why I was so unfairly treated by the Ulster selectors. The only reference that I remember being made by any of them was when the late Alf Murray said something to the effect that they would not be influenced by a section of the Dublin media as to whom they would or would not choose. Coincidentally, in an unrelated dispute some years earlier, Alf had objected to me playing for Clann na nGael minor team in the Armagh minor football championship. Donacloney is situated relatively close to the Armagh border. Indeed my postal address was Donacloney, Lurgan, County Armagh. However, in that Armagh minor championship Clann Na nGael were drawn against Clann Eireann who were also a Lurgan-based side and thus keen rivals. When Clann Eireann heard about me playing they objected on the basis that I was from a different county and was therefore illegal. The man who led their objection was the same Alf Murray. In the final analysis I had to stop playing for Clann na nGael. That being said he was technically correct, as I did not fulfil the necessary qualifications for playing in County Armagh.

Incidentally, Alf had been an outstanding footballer with both Armagh and Ulster in the forties. Furthermore his GAA credentials as an outstanding administrator could not be called into question. This was further emphasised when he was elected to serve as President of the GAA between 1964 and 1967.

Returning to the fact that I was not picked for Ulster doesn't mean that my inclusion would necessarily have ensured an Ulster victory. All I wanted to do was to be given the chance to make a contribution, which I think I deserved on my form at the time. This was an opinion that was widely shared by most supporters and media people.

Writing in the *Sunday Press* on 12 February 1961, sports columnist "Fergus" stated: "How the selectors reached the decision that James McCartan is not worthy of his place mystifies me. I say that it is a rank injustice that he has been left out – and then being named, as last substitute is ridiculous. Better in the circumstances not to have his name on the list at all."

After Ulster's shock exit, "Linesman" wrote in the *Frontier Sentinel* on 25 February: "The ovation that McCartan received when he took his place on the subs' bench was unprecedented to say the least of it – he appeared to be something of a shuttlecock between the respective selecting bodies with disastrous results for Ulster."

Between 1950 and 1967 annual representative games in football and hurling took place between Ireland selections and the Combined Universities. In some years the Irish Army also fielded teams in those then prestigious competitions. The players selected on those teams were considered to be the best players in Ireland at the time. On 19 March I had the honour of captaining Ireland to a 3-13 to 2-8 victory over the Combined Universities. Also included in the side were my Down colleagues Leo Murphy, Paddy Doherty and Patsy O'Hagan. Offaly men Paddy McCormack and John Egan flanked Leo at full back and the midlanders' talented Sean Brereton was at right full forward. Aidan Brady of Roscommon was goalkeeper, Kerry's Mick O'Dwyer was left half back and Galway's Mattie McDonagh was at centrefield. My future brothers-in law Felix McKnight and George Glynn were included in the Combined Universities side along with Sean O'Neill. Like the Railway Cup competition, this tournament allowed players from the so-called weaker counties to play at top level. Such star performers as Mick Carley from Westmeath and Cathal Flynn from Leitrim got a chance to show their outstanding football prowess. On that March day in 1961 they really showed how good they were.

After a convincing win over Armagh in the semi-final of the Lagan Cup, Down qualified to meet Derry in the final. As I said before Derry always had good footballers and on this occasion we found it extremely tough to overcome them in a very exciting game. Playing superb football they held a 1-6 to 0-3 interval lead. The third quarter proved to be more evenly matched as both sides scored four points. Then Paddy Doherty scored an opportunist goal to narrow the gap to three points. However, for the remainder of the game Derry exerted their superiority when they scored another goal after a fantastic passing movement. The game was over. They emerged deserving winners on a 2-10 to 1-7 scoreline.

Like everyone else, I was not satisfied with our performance. Perhaps we were taking things for granted. We had now got into the annoying habit of overplaying the ball and attempting to score goals from impossible situations when points were there for the taking. This had played right into Derry's hands. They were much more direct and purposeful in their play.

Nevertheless, another opportunity soon presented itself to rectify the mistakes we had made in the Lagan Cup final. We were again scheduled to play the same opposition in the McKenna Cup semi-final in the middle of May. In a good, all-round display we triumphed by 0-11 to 0-8. If we had been more accurate in our shooting the margin could have been greater. On a very wet day at Dungannon, we played very well to register a comprehensive 2-10 to 1-6 success over Monaghan in the McKenna Cup final.

It was now with much more confidence that we headed for the third successive year to the Wembley tournament final at Whit weekend. This competition always seemed to act as a catalyst for better performances and so it did it again. This time we faced Kerry. In a fantastic team performance we overran them by 4-5 to 1-7. Eddie McKay was impressive in goal and the whole defence played competently throughout. Our midfield was outstanding. Jarlath Carey, who was now playing the best football of his career, dominated the often magnificent Mick O'Connell. Alongside him and despite playing with an injured right foot, Joe Lennon gave a very commendable display. Tony Hadden's roving tactics unsettled the Kerry defence. This allowed the rest of us to score. Paddy Doherty and Brian Morgan were particularly good in ensuring our success. So, as a result of the McKenna Cup and Wembley successes our confidence had again risen considerably. We looked forward with eager anticipation to defending our Ulster title against Fermanagh in the first round of the provincial championship at Newry.

From the start the Ernesiders tore into the game with rare abandon. They upped the physical stakes and initially we found this difficult to cope with. Still, Paddy Doherty scored three points in quick succession. Fermanagh fought back to level the scores but in the second quarter we took over and went in at half time 0-9 to 0-4 to the good. At the beginning of the second half, points were exchanged before I obtained possession just inside our own half. I soloed upfield and sent over what I reckoned was a good point. However, the referee disallowed the score and awarded us a free but Paddy Doherty missed the opportunity to put us further ahead. Fermanagh then reduced the deficit with two well-taken points. In the closing minutes we came back to score two really good points from the accurate boots of Patsy O'Hagan and Kevin O'Neill. Kevin O'Neill's point must have been from about 50 yards out. After a very dour, tough battle we won on a scoreline of Down 0-12, Fermanagh 0-7.

Just as the full time whistle went, everything, momentarily, seemed to go sour. A section of the Down supporters invaded the pitch to vent their anger at the roughhouse tactics of some of the Fermanagh players. They were especially annoyed at the Fermanagh player who had committed a terrible tackle on Kevin Mussen. This forced Kevin to retire from the game midway through the second half. I have always felt that this played a factor in Kevin's later performances during 1961. Thankfully, match officials and stewards brought the pitch invaders under control and normality was restored. I have often felt sorry for the vast majority of good sporting players whose reputations are sometimes tarnished by the actions of a few of their colleagues.

Now we were in our fourth successive Ulster semi-final and, for the third time within a few months, meeting Derry. With one win a piece this was the real acid test for both teams. The game itself turned out to be one of the best ever contests in the Ulster championship. Derry opened the scoring with a well-taken point. I then scored a goal before Denis McKeever did likewise for Derry. With Jarlath Carey and Joe Lennon dominating the midfield exchanges, our forward line got a plentiful supply of ball. Leo Murphy added another dimension to his developing game by pointing a 50. Sean O'Neill and Tony Hadden added further scores before Derry got one back. Then Paddy Doherty went on a scoring spree with a goal and two points to his credit. In the last ten minutes both sides scored two points to leave the interval scoreline reading Down 2-7, Derry 1-4.

Surprisingly, Derry had started the game with their ace midfielder Jim McKeever playing at centre half forward. This had suited us as Lennon and Carey were able to dominate Derry's selected midfield pairing. After both sides each added a further two points in the second half, Derry drafted McKeever to midfield. Immediately, the whole trend of the game changed. Thanks to McKeever, the Derry team came at us in waves continuously for about ten minutes. Our lead narrowed down to a three-point advantage. There were five minutes left in the game as the speedy Leo O'Neill dashed through our defence. A goal was definitely there for the taking. Unluckily for Derry and fortunately for us O'Neill shot inches wide from the edge of the square. Moments earlier Phil Stuart seemed destined to score a Derry goal only for Eddie McKay to make the most spectacular save of his career. Derry folded and we added two further points. When the whistle went we had recorded a 2-12 to 1-10 victory. This was one of the best games of football that I ever played in.

John D. Hickey, writing in the next day's *Irish Independent*, agreed: "The game was contested with an intense fury, frequently with superb individual efforts and more importantly some magnificent combined movement. Derry's heroic fightback and the titanic finish of Down will long live in the memory."

In the Ulster final we were pitted against our near neighbours Armagh. A record crowd turned up at Casement Park for another thrilling encounter. However, for me this was not a particularly happy occasion. I had hurt my shoulder in the Derry game and was not able to start the final. I was shattered as it was my first game, of real substance, to miss for four years.

Armagh started the game at a tremendous pace and their midfield pairing of Gene Larkin and John McGeary controlled the sector for most of the first half. This enabled their talented forwards to really test our defence. Pat Campbell, Kevin Halpenny and that tearaway forward Jimmy Whan were particularly conspicuous in the first half. At half time the Orchard County led by 1-7 to 1-2. I had never seen such determination and fighting spirit from an Armagh side as I did during the first half. We all knew we had a real game on our hands if we were going to turn things around after the interval.

During half time our management decided that I should enter the fray at full forward and Patsy O'Hagan was switched to right half back. For one of the first times in his long career Kevin Mussen, who was not having a good game by his high standards, was replaced. In the first seven minutes of the second half Paddy Doherty scored three points to reduce the deficit to two. As I was not fully fit I decided to compensate by throwing myself more wholeheartedly into the game.

This seemed to spur on the crowd and our supporters really got behind us. Then luck came my way. A long ball came in from Paddy Doherty and hit an upright. It rebounded towards me on the edge of the square. I collected it and slammed it to the net. We were in the lead by a point, 2-5 to 1-7.

Suddenly the whole team seemed rejuvenated. We scored three further points as the team played brilliant combination football. Armagh pulled a point back before sharpshooter supreme Paddy Doherty put us into a three point lead again. With time almost up, Armagh landed one final attack. John McGeary lobbed a magnificent long 50-yard kick into our goalmouth. Unexpectedly out of the crowded parallelogram came our goalkeeper Eddie McKay with the ball clutched firmly to his chest. The Down fans roared loudly. A free out was awarded and the full time whistle went. Down had won their third consecutive provincial title on a scoreline of 2-10 to 1-10.

After the game some of the Armagh supporters and indeed some of their officials claimed that the ball had crossed the line in that last minute goalmouth scramble. However, the umpires who were closest to the scene were adamant that this was not the case. The Armagh players, nevertheless, were very gracious in defeat and accepted the referee's decision. They then all wished us well for the next stage of our 1961 championship campaign. One player, John McKnight, who was over 150 yards away in the Armagh full back line at the time, maintained that the ball was definitely over the line. He repeated this assertion in a Sunday newspaper the following week.

Shortly afterwards my sister Delia got engaged to John's brother Felix. Many members of both families attended an engagement party for the happy couple. During the course of the festivities John McKnight innocently said to my father, in answer to some unimportant question, "I did not see that."

Quick as a flash my father retorted, "That's surprising coming from a man who has such fantastic long range vision!" Wisely, John did not blink an eye and ignored the teasing comment. An interesting fact from this game was that Armagh's free taker Mick McQuaid was not really Mick McQuaid! The Catholic Church had a rule that no clerical student or Catholic priest could play intercounty football at that time. As Father 'X' came into this category, he adopted the name of Mick McQuaid, of tobacco advertising fame.

The All-Ireland football semi-final was a real mouthwatering clash, especially for neutrals. It was a renewal of acquaintances for Kerry and us. Kerry were the reigning National Football League champions who had completely overwhelmed our conquerors Derry in the league final. After we had beaten Kerry in the 1960 All-Ireland final there were three reasons offered for Kerry's defeat. Most of these reasons, or excuses as I preferred to call them, came from within Kerry. Several leading pundits from outside the Kingdom agreed with these.

One of them was that there had been a lot of internal dissent within the Kerry camp the previous year. This had led to the premature retirement of their legendary long-time trainer Dr Eamon O'Sullivan. Secondly, their experienced and powerful midfielder John Dowling was badly hampered by injury during the final. Several other players were allegedly not fully fit when they togged out for the final. Whatever about the third reason, the first two were substantially true. Another hurtful criticism mentioned by some critics was that Kerry were outmanoeuvred in the All-Ireland final by a bogus team. By this they meant that Kerry's traditional catch-and-kick style was overcome by a team which did not really play Gaelic football. This was a reference to our combination style of play.

Now Dr Eamon O'Sullivan was back with Kerry and the whole team was pronounced fully fit as they prepared to meet us. This time there would be no need for excuses.

When the Down team was announced there was a surprise development. Our captain Kevin Mussen was not included. Kevin had not been playing particularly well throughout the Ulster championship but we never expected him to lose his place. It is always hard to gauge why any player can lose form. The serious injury to him in the Fermanagh game certainly took its toll. In addition, Kevin had been playing for Down at a consistently high level since his college days in St Colman's. Patsy O' Hagan was selected in Kevin's right half back position and P.J. McElroy was now the team's full forward.

Also missing from the team that played Kerry in the previous year's final was left half back Kevin O'Neill. I felt that Kevin was decidedly unlucky to have lost his place. His replacement, John Smith, from Ballykinlar, was definitely a very good footballer but Kevin had been one of our most consistent performers and had done nothing wrong. Still, it is the prerogative of a management team to select a team and so far they had always proven themselves correct in this regard.

Another bone of contention raised its head before the All-Ireland semi-final. As George Lavery was our vice captain I automatically assumed that he would be selected as captain against Kerry. The management decided to select Paddy Doherty instead. I never had any problem with Paddy's ability to lead us, I just thought that George's years of loyal service should have been rewarded. No man that I knew of had played as many high quality games for Down since he first donned the county jersey nine years earlier in 1952. When you speak of individual outstanding performances I think George's display in the 1960 All-Ireland final must be accepted as his best ever exhibition.

We knew the only way to overcome our detractors was to prove ourselves on the field of play. Only 45 seconds into the game Dan McCartan expertly intercepted a Kerry attack. Dan sent a long ball to Paddy Doherty about 50 yards out and on the left hand side of the field. Paddy spotted Sean O'Neill in front of the goalmouth and quickly transferred the ball across to the Newry Mitchel's man. Without hesitation Sean accurately planted the ball in the back of the net. Timmy O'Sullivan immediately replied with a point for Kerry.

Then I got the ball about 40 yards out. When I kicked the ball it bounced on the ground outside the parallelogram but then went over the bar. Kerry's Timmy O'Sullivan pointed twice to leave us ahead by the minimum of margins. However, we were starting to play really well. Our defenders and midfielders were winning the ball first time and our attack was moving smartly as a unit. In four minutes we scored four excellent points. First Paddy Doherty raised a white flag before a spectacular clearance from new man John Smith found Tony Hadden and the Newry Shamrock's man punched over a great point. Doherty then added another before P.J. McElroy put his name on the score sheet. At the end of the first quarter we were leading 1-5 to 0-3 and apparently coasting to an easy victory.

Things, nevertheless, are never as simple that. For the remainder of the first half Kerry were much the better side. Teddy O'Dowd started their comeback in the 17th minute with an excellent point. Moments later he was on his way through for a possible goal when he was fouled by one of our backs. Inexplicably, the normally accurate Dan McAuliffe sent the ball wide. A 50 by Mick O'Connell was finished over the bar by substitute Tom Burke. Our defence, which had coped admirably with this intense pressure, was forced to concede frees, two of which the accurate Mick O'Dwyer put over the bar. Just before the short whistle, Dan McAuliffe pointed to leave the half time score Down 1-5, Kerry 0-8. We were level and exceptionally lucky that we were not trailing the Munster men.

After the interval Down again started to play really well. Within a minute Paddy Doherty scored a point to give us the lead. It was during this third quarter that we really came into our own. Personally, on the field of play I have always loved trying to anticipate where the ball is going to land. Sometimes this works. Sometimes it does not. On this particular day I was really lucky, as my actions seemed, repeatedly, to be in tandem with my intuition. If I went to the half back line the ball appeared to be waiting on me, likewise in midfield and in attack. As a consequence I had a lot of possession. To complete my feelgood factor was the fantastic support play of Sean O'Neill and Paddy Doherty, playing on either side of me. They were simply magnificent in everything that they did. To make matters worse for the Kerry defence, both Tony Hadden and Brian Morgan tracked back to support the player in possession. This is a common tactic nowadays but back in 1961 it was a natural instinctive ploy by such gifted players as Tony and Brian. Brian Morgan was the next to land a fabulous point. Then Tony raced through the whole defence and was brought down inside the square. Both supporters and players were certain that Paddy Doherty would score the spot kick. Unbelievably, Paddy miskicked the ball and it literally rolled into the happy hands of goalkeeper Johnny Culloty.

Kevin Mussen was now introduced for Patsy O'Hagan and he immediately resumed his normal classy type of play. Both our midfielders Joe Lennon and Jarlath Carey were having superb games and the immaculate Tony Hadden added another point to put us three points clear. For the next ten minutes Kerry regained their superiority and constantly pounded the Down rearguard. Five Kerry 50s landed in the goalmouth in quick succession. Five times our defence cleared the danger. Individually and collectively our goalkeeper and the full back line was outstanding throughout the game but particularly at this juncture. Kevin Mussen had brought a sense of calmness and reassurance to the half back line. Dan McCartan's anticipation and general positional sense were top class and John Smith, making his Croke Park championship debut, was simply outstanding.

For all this continuous Kerry pressure they only managed a solitary point from Tom Burke in the 17th minute. This proved to be their first and only score of the second half. By the 22nd minute of the half Down had taken over completely. Again Paddy Doherty seemed to be at the heart of every attack and he initiated our scoring comeback with a brilliant point. Then Joe Lennon was injured and had to retire. Kevin O'Neill replaced him. It was good to see both players who had been unlucky to be dropped now back on the field of play. Shortly after Paddy's point I soloed through before parting to the Ballykinlar flyer who scored our side's tenth point. Before the end Paddy and I added further points. When referee Jimmy Martin of Roscommon blew the full time whistle we had won convincingly on a scoreline of 1-12 to 0-9.

This game has been acknowledged as having been a tremendous advertisement for all that is good in Gaelic football. I also felt that no one could now dispute the overall quality of our team and nobody could offer any realistic excuses for Kerry's defeat in the 1960 All-Ireland final. In the next morning's *Irish Independent* GAA writer John D. Hickey was lavish in his praise for the quality of the match in general and my own display in particular:

> *The splendid endeavours of Joe Lennon, the excellent save of Eddie McKay, the whole full back line but especially the reliability throughout the hour of George Lavery were commendable features. Most of all I would like to record the strength, accuracy and football splendour of James McCartan, a deep lying centre half forward who wrought havoc, in Kerry eyes, in the general midfield area all through but especially in the second half.*

We were now through to our second successive All-Ireland senior football final. What made the game more intriguing was the fact that Offaly were to be our opponents. Both of us had made fantastic progress as neither of us, up to two years previously, had ever even won a provincial senior title. From an Offaly viewpoint this occasion would prove to be an ideal opportunity for them to seek revenge for their failure at the penultimate stage in 1960. For us it was the perfect chance to prove that we really were a better side than the midlanders. While our supporters looked upon us as hot favourites to repeat the previous year's success, the team and the mentors were much more guarded. As part of our preparations we played both Dublin and Meath in challenge games and emerged easily victorious on both occasions. In those matches the management gave players such as Kevin Mussen and Kevin O'Neill further opportunities to stake their claims for starting positions on All-Ireland final day. Even though both performed well, the selectors decided to stick with the side that had started against Kerry. To curb the effectiveness of the very strong Offaly full back line of Paddy McCormack, Greg Hughes and John Egan it was felt that P.J. McElroy would provide us with our best option at full forward.

Initially it was thought that my brother Dan would not be able to play as he had suffered a bad finger injury during the challenge game against Meath. Thankfully, he recovered sufficiently to be passed fit.

As Offaly were in their first senior All-Ireland final the spectator interest was even greater than it was in 1960 when a record crowd turned up. This was surpassed in 1961 when 90,556 viewers passed through the turnstiles. That figure still remains the biggest crowd to attend any final.

A Good Team Becomes Great

In the week prior to the game a major controversy arose about the appointment of Mick McArdle of Louth as referee by the GAA's Central Council. Offaly objected to him and Jimmy Martin of Roscommon was then offered the position. Again Offaly objected. This was presumably because Martin had been widely praised for his performance in refereeing our semi-final against Kerry. On the Thursday we learned that Offaly had agreed to Liam Maguire of Cavan to take up the whistle. We did not dwell unnecessarily on those side issues and prepared for the final as best as we could. Again, I was quietly optimistic but also acutely aware that Offaly would be no pushovers. If we were to overcome them only a first rate team display would suffice.

Within 12 seconds of the start of this game Paddy Doherty steered the ball over the bar for a well-taken point. Offaly replied with a vengeance. A forward ball from Mick Casey deceived our whole defence and landed in the back of the net. Har Donnelly added a point three minutes later before we suffered another devastating body blow. Donnelly sent a dangerous ball into our goalmouth. Both Eddie McKay and Leo Murphy seemed to have it covered. Incredibly, the unmarked Peter Daly was allowed to nip in between them to score a rather easy goal. Within a space of just four minutes we had conceded two gift goals. The scoreline now read Offaly 2-1, Down 0-1. For the first time I felt we were in real trouble. I knew it was very early in the game but I feared that our capacity to give away soft goals would be our downfall.

Before the kick out after the second goal I walked over to Sean O'Neill and aired my misgiving. "Sean," I said, "we are in desperate trouble."

"Not really," said the cool Sean. "It will only make it a bit harder now."

Six points down and only six minutes gone. "Must try harder" appeared to be the new collective mantra of every Down player. For the next 15 minutes all of us performed to our very limits. Sean O'Neill was the first to score, a real beauty of a point. For the next 12 minutes we played superb football, winning a lot of possession and creating great opportunities to move within scoring distance. However, the Offaly defence was equal to the task, displaying great qualities of resilience and determination.

Eventually our barren scoring spell was broken when Paddy Doherty lobbed a high ball into the Offaly goalmouth. With my back to the goal I rose to catch and quickly turned in mid-air to send the ball left-footed into the back of the net. This seemed to lift the spirits of the whole team and our supporters roared us on to greater efforts. With Jarlath Carey giving an impeccable performance in the centre of the field we were soon on our way again. Paddy Doherty got the ball and speedily soloed down the left wing. He floated a dangerous, weighted ball across the goalmouth. Sean O'Neill rose magnificently to field it and then neatly sidestepped an Offaly opponent. With his left foot he unleashed a powerful shot that went through the net for a spectacular score.

Within two minutes we had transformed the game. The score now read 2-2 to 2-1 in our favour. Then Tom Cullen for Offaly and Tony Hadden exchanged points before Har Donnelly brought the game level. The whole team was now on song but Offaly did not give up easily. They mounted a serious attack. I raced back to help out our beleaguered defence, intercepted the ball and soloed upfield. Several Offaly players hit me hard but fair. I managed to escape their clutches and kept going before passing the ball forward to Paddy Doherty. Instinctively he lobbed the ball into the square. Offaly full back Greg Hughes and P.J. McElroy rose high together. In a moment of inspiration the astute McElroy palmed the ball down to the onrushing Brian Morgan. The outcome was another powerful left footed shot, another goal for Down.

The half time whistle went. The scoreboard had a surreal look about it. It read Down 3-3, Offaly 2-3. At the interval we were acutely aware of both the deficiencies and strengths in our first half display. We felt that if we could tighten up in defence our forwards had the ability to penetrate the Offaly rearguard.

The second half was a dull, dour encounter with both defences on top. Nevertheless, our midfield pairing of Joe Lennon and Jarlath Carey reigned supreme despite facing several, different Offaly players. Shortly after the restart I pointed from 20 yards out only to see Har Donnelly scoring for Offaly soon afterwards. Six minutes into the second half Offaly appealed for a penalty because they felt that left half forward Tommy Greene had been fouled in the square. However no free was given.

Both sets of supporters raised the noise level to deafening proportions and the tension became unbearable. First Paddy Doherty scored. Then Har Donnelly replied. Jarlath Carey was the next to split the posts with a wonderful effort from play. Not to be outdone, Har Donnelly responded with a point from a free. For the next eight minutes the game ebbed and flowed with neither side able to score. When Sean Brereton landed a free in the 29th minute there was only two points between the teams. This was and is the most dangerous lead of all, especially when the time is nearly up. The whole occasion was nervewracking.

A Good Team Becomes Great

With our supporters whistling for full time, Offaly got another close-in free. Har Donnelly sent it over the bar. Just a one-point game now. Thankfully, immediately after the kick out, the full time whistle sounded. By the narrowest of margins we had won our second All-Ireland senior football title.

Despite a terrible start our defence had settled down and displayed their usual composure under pressure. Pat Rice who had to leave the field of play in agony, owing to a split thumb, insisted on returning to the action. He proceeded to play a real heroic part in our victory. George Lavery appeared set to have another great final but he was cruelly taken out of the game by a blatant foul and had to retire. The whole half back line was solid throughout and consistently provided an excellent platform for the rest of us. Sean O'Neill was outstanding in the forward line. His brother Kevin, who originally replaced Pat Rice, had a terrific game, as did Pat when he came on for George Lavery. In essence it was a great team victory.

Our dressing room after the game resembled a hospital unit. As well as George Lavery and Pat Rice, Brian Morgan had also played through the pain barrier. His expertly taken goal just before half time was the catalyst for the rest of us to play with our natural confidence. Tony Hadden who received a knock on the head early in the game played the rest of the contest in a dazed state. Indeed it was not for several hours after the game that he fully realised where he was. Halfway through the second half I received a similar blow to the head and I have no recollection of what really happened in the last quarter.

"Linesman" in his weekly column after the game accurately summed up the true worth of our victory, particularly considering our disastrous start:

> *It was then that Down appeared for what they are, a set of men apart from any other that ever graced Croke Park. With such strokes of adversity most other teams would have died, but they only served to bring out the best in the champions. No final ever produced goals of such vintage, for each of them was a masterpiece of its own. As long as Down men talk of the 1961 final they will talk of those three left-footed thunderbolts … When the All-Ireland medals are presented to those Down men they should be inscribed also with the words "for valour", for no sporting decorations have been so hard earned.*

I was absolutely delighted to have won my second All-Ireland medal. What made the victory all the sweeter was the fact that we had overcome our two leading rivals in the process. It proved without any shadow of doubt that we were really worthy All-Ireland champions, not only for 1961 but for 1960 as well.

We had a wonderful night of celebration in our hotel on the Sunday night. On Monday we went on a sightseeing tour of Dublin. It ended with a visit to the historic setting that is Kilmainham Gaol. Then we made our triumphant journey home. The people of Louth and Armagh came out in their thousands to greet us. Yet again, we experienced the hospitality of the staff of Ballymascanlon Hotel. For the first time BBC television had televised a final and special arrangements had been made in "Ballymac" to ensure that we saw a recording of the game. Seeing ourselves on the television screen made the occasion all the more memorable. The reality that we were really All-Ireland football champions had now sunk in. An added bonus was that the commentator was Derry footballer, Jim McKeever. Two months prior to this, with his soaring midfield performance, he nearly prevented us from having our second glorious triumph. Now he was singing our praises as we headed homewards.

When we arrived in Newry the massive size of the ecstatic crowd and their spontaneous joyous reaction told us all we wanted to know. We were a great team who had brought glory to our native county. This time across the whole country there were no doubters, no begrudgers. When I saw my father for the first time after the 1961 final there was that great big beaming smile, mingled with uncontrollable tears of joy. It was great to come home once more, with our newfound friend Sam Maguire still by our sides.

My parents, Brian and Delia McCartan.

"Lagan View" – My Home and Licensed Premises for almost 60 years. Marie and I spent our married life there from 1967 to 2002.

My brother Dan (on left) and myself on the Massey Ferguson tractor (in 2010) which I had intended to use to tow away a bomb which had been left at our bar lounge door in 1973.

My father, Brian (on left), with a friend in Tullyraine Quarry in the early 1940s.

Marie and myself on our wedding day in 1967. From left to right, my brother Dan, mother Delia, myself, brother-in-law George Glynn, Marie, father Brian and sister Gay Glynn.

Family group at our daughter Maria's wedding.
Left to right – Eoin, Delia, myself, Maria and her husband Plunkett McConville, Marie, Charlie Pat and James. Kneeling in front – left to right – Daniel and Brian.

Family group at our daughter Delia's wedding.

Left to right – Charlie Pat, Eoin, Maria, myself, Michael McCarron (Delia's husband), Delia, Marie, Daniel, John Byrne, James and Brian.

Immediate and extended family group photograph taken on my 70th birthday in 2007.

1960 The History Makers. A new tradition is born – the first senior All-Ireland to come across the border.
Back, left to right: James McCartan, Joe Lennon, Jarlath Carey, Leo Murphy, Dan McCartan, Seán O'Neill, Kevin O'Neill, Pat Rice. Front, left to right: Eddie McKay, Patsy O'Hagan, Paddy Doherty, Kevin Mussen (captain), George Lavery, Tony Hadden, Brian Morgan.

Down – All-Ireland senior football championship winners 1991
Front, left to right: Ross Carr (Clonduff), James McCartan (Tullylish), Gary Mason (Loughlinisland), Brendan McKernan (Burren), Mickey Linden (Mayobridge), Paddy O'Rourke (captain, Burren), D.J. Kane (Newry Shamrocks), Peter Withnall (Drumaness), John Kelly (Carryduff).
Back, left to right: Eamonn Burns (Bryansford), Paul Higgins (Ballymartin), Conor Deegan (Downpatrick), Neil Collins (Carryduff), Barry Breen (Downpatrick), Greg Blaney (Ballycran).

Yours truly and a lifelong friend Seamus Fitzpatrick (R.I.P.) in Croke Park just after the final whistle sounded at the end of the 1960 final.

Punching the ball away from my brother-in-law Felix McKnight of Armagh in the 1961 Ulster final.

My brother Dan, Kevin O'Neill and myself attempt to "arrest" Maurice Hayes and put him in Boston Prison during our American trip in 1962!

Pictured along with bookmaker Des Fox (R.I.P.) on the extreme left, trainer Ando Moriarty (R.I.P.) and Bernadette Fox after my dog "Hymenstown Joe" had won an inter-track competition between Tralee and Dunmore in June 1986. This was the dog that was stolen by loyalists the previous October.

Marie and myself at the presentation of The Greyhound Hall of Fame Award in 2008. Sports Minister John O'Donoghue did the honours.

The Gresham Hotel, Dublin, was the venue for the presentation of the 1960 Caltex Sports Awards.

Back row (L to R) – Seamus O'Hanlon (cycling), James McCartan (Gaelic football), Tommy Caffrey (table tennis), Dr Pat O'Callaghan (Hall of Fame), Joe Carr (golf) and Fionan Fagan (soccer).

Front row (L to R) –Nick O'Donnell (hurling), Taoiseach Sean Lemass (who made the presentation), D.J. Langan (sponsor's representative), Jennifer Cassidy (swimming) and John Caldwell (boxing).

Pictured with from left to right – Eoin, Shay McCartan, Marie and Daniel. 16-year-old Shay, who won MacRory and Hogan Cup medals with St Colman's College in 2010, is a son of my cousin John McCartan and his wife Siobhan. He signed for Burnley FC in England in summer 2010.

One of my favourite GAA personalities was 1993 Derry All-Ireland winning manager, Eamon Coleman (R.I.P.). This snapshot of Eamon and myself was taken at Clones in 2006 when Eamon was Cavan manager.

7

America Here We Come

Three weeks after our second All-Ireland victory we beat Roscommon in the semi-final of the Grounds Tournament and qualified to meet Offaly in the final. That match began as a good sporting contest and we went into an early lead. However, Offaly fought back strongly to ensure that the half time score was 0-6 each. Within seconds of the restart it was abundantly clear that the midlanders were on a real revenge mission. The first five minutes involved some of the worst excesses ever performed by any side on a football field. It was obvious to me that there had been a collective decision taken at half time to considerably increase their physical approach.

Now, I had no problem with that attitude in itself. Nevertheless, what happened in the third quarter went far beyond the bounds of acceptability and four Down players were seriously injured as a result of this behaviour. Two of the players, Kevin O'Neill and Pat Rice, were so badly injured that they were carried off the field. Another player, Paddy Doherty, remained on the field but he was unable to make any worthwhile contribution. Patsy O'Hagan was the fourth man to suffer the ill effects of a shocking tackle. Luckily, after treatment, he was able to resume.

The worst attempted tackle was on Dan McCartan. Writing in *The Sentinel*, "Linesman" explained: "An Offaly player jumped over a fellow forward to land himself on all fours on Dan's chest. It was a mercy that Dan McCartan was not seriously injured. All of these incidents happened within five minutes of the resumption and surely indicates as vile a plan of campaign as any side ever put into action."

After such an unjustified attitude by some of the Offaly players it was, naturally, very difficult for us to assert any momentum or indeed any great interest in overexerting ourselves. True, we had alwa ys played with great endeavour but given the circumstances we were happy to see the end of the game. Even though Offaly finally won the contest by 0-11 to 0-8 we recognised we had won the games that really mattered against them. Our eventual win in the 1960 All-Ireland semi-final and our victory in the 1961 All-Ireland final were a testament to this line of thought.

In the Lagan Cup matches before Christmas we easily overcame Tyrone, Antrim and Monaghan to qualify yet again for the semi-final of the competition. Along with Liam Devaney of Tipperary, who received the hurling honour, I was selected as Caltex Gaelic Footballer of the Year again for 1961. In my acceptance speech I acknowledged the personal honour it was but stressed it really was a public affirmation of what the whole Down team had accomplished in winning successive All-Ireland senior titles.

When it came to the time for the announcement of the 1962 Railway Cup team there was much press speculation, at both local and national levels, whether or not I would be chosen. This time, however, I was picked at centre half forward for the provincial semi-final against Connacht. Personally everything went well on the day and I scored three goals and a point. More significantly, we won the game on a scoreline of 5-6 to 1-7. Nevertheless, we lost the St Patrick's Day final with Leinster by three points. On this occasion I was joined on the side by seven of my county colleagues: Leo Murphy, Pat Rice, Dan McCartan, Jarlath Carey, Sean O'Neill, Paddy Doherty and Brian Morgan. In addition Tony Hadden came on as a substitute in the final.

In the Lagan Cup semi-final we easily beat Armagh to once again qualify for the final against Derry. We had a player sent off in the decider and, especially after having been five points down, we recovered well to earn a draw. The replay was a terrific game of football played in very blustery conditions. Derry performed superbly all through and with seven minutes to go they held what appeared to be an unassailable lead of six points. Incredibly, when Brian Morgan and I scored two goals and Paddy Doherty added a brilliant point over the next three minutes, Down were ahead by a single point. For the remaining four minutes the huge crowd witnessed a contest of great intensity and no little skill as Derry desperately tried to regain the initiative. Thanks to our well disciplined defence we held out for a win that did not seem remotely possible such a short time before. One had to feel sorry for Derry, as they had been the best side for the vast majority of the game. However, in those days, in tight situations, we tended to hold the upper hand because we had six forwards who could score under pressure.

In the semi-final of the National League we met surprise packets Carlow. Like most Down supporters and players I have a soft spot for Carlow. In our years of team building, prior to our All-Ireland successes, Carlow were exceptionally good in facilitating us with challenge games. However, we had never played each other in a competitive match. In their league campaign of 1961/62 Carlow had surprised everyone by beating Cork, Kildare and Kerry at home in Tralee, on their way to qualifying for the semi-final. In the game itself Carlow began superbly and by the 20th minute they were seven points ahead. Subsequently, we notched two further points to leave us trailing at the interval on a score of Carlow 2-3, Down 0-4. After the resumption we gradually whittled down their lead and by the 15th minute we were a point ahead. Points were then exchanged before Down finally scrambled to a 0-13 to 2-5 triumph.

In the National League final we played Dublin. During the first period the Metropolitans were totally on top and they led at the interval by 1-3 to 0-2. At the start of the third quarter we improved considerably to draw level but then Dublin seized the initiative again. With four minutes to go they held a three point advantage. Then, just as we did against Derry and Carlow, we upped the tempo. First Paddy Doherty scored a fantastic point. Brilliant Dublin defending deprived certain goals from Sean O'Neill and Kevin Mussen who had now moved to right half forward. However, Lar Foley had stopped Kevin's goalbound effort by touching the ball on the ground. It was a penalty. Our alternative penalty taker Sean O'Neill drove his kick straight to the back of the net. We were leading by a point as the full time whistle was approaching. Dublin, not to be out done, mounted a series of attacks. In the first of these Dan McCartan's first time clearance sent the ball to safety. In the last attack a Dublin 50 landed in our goalmouth but, collectively, our defence managed to relieve the pressure. The full time whistle went. We had got out of jail for the third consecutive game. For the second time in three years we were National League champions. The scoreline at the end read Down 2-5, Dublin 1-7.

After our All-Ireland victories our management team, at the behest of Maurice Hayes, promised us the trip of a lifetime to the United States of America. Nowadays this may not seem as any big deal but in those times it certainly was the ultimate reward for our historic achievements. Back then, going to America was normally associated with emigration to seek better job opportunities. The trip was to be divided between sightseeing and a series of challenge games with American teams. Consequently the Central Council of the Association approved a tour invitation to the Down team which had been initiated by the North American GAA Board.

Two days after our latest National League success was the date set for the commencement of our historic trip. So, on Tuesday, 15 May 1962, we assembled at Newry where a huge crowd had gathered to give us a rousing send-off. Then, three hundred other supporters followed us down to Shannon airport in a cavalcade of cars. Car horns blared continuously, in salutation, as we wound our way through the midlands of Ireland.

When we reached Shannon another welcoming party of friends, who had come from Dublin and other counties to wish us bon voyage, serenaded us. The Mayor of Limerick praised us for all that we had done for the popularisation of Gaelic games. As we boarded the plane a band played "Come back to Erin" and "The Star of the County Down".

Six hours later we arrived in New York where we were once again serenaded. This time the County Down Men's Fife and Drum Band did the honours. A four-week tour and a 9000-mile coast-to-coast journey had begun. Those weeks were to become an unforgettable mixture of sightseeing, matches, receptions and friendships of the highest order. We were treated like royalty with motorcycle escorts and limousines guiding us from inland airport to inland airport. Those send-offs from the various city destinations made one proud to be a Down man, lucky to achieve what we had accomplished and to be so well rewarded for doing so. To see the tears of joy and happiness on so many faces as we travelled across America has left an indelible mark on my mind. The then President of the GAA, Hugh Byrne from Wicklow, journeyed with us in his official capacity. Michael Cavanagh, President of the North America GAA Board, warmly greeted him. After a midnight trip around the centre of New Yor, on the day that we arrived, we retired for the night, tired but happy and excited.

The following day we were taken on a guided tour of the city after we had attended mass in St Patrick's Cathedral. Times Square, the U.N. headquarters and the Empire State Building were among the more famous places that we visited. We were welcomed by the Irish Consul General, a Mr Shields, who regaled us with stories about his visit to the Mourne mountains before the beginning of World War II. That night, too, we had the first of many receptions by the Down Men's Association in America.

We also met hundreds of people with both family and Down connections. Thanks to the radio and Michael O'Hehir's commentaries most of the guests knew our names. They enjoyed recalling our individual and collective performances during our two All-Ireland victories. They were also very familiar with the writings of "Linesman". When they met our manager Barney Carr they found it incredible that Barney and "Linesman" were the one and same person. Relatives and friends had sent his weekly GAA reports to their American contacts over the previous five years.

On Thursday morning we arose at 7 a.m. and travelled by coach to Boston where a whole week of matches, tours and civic receptions had been arranged. Having two of Ireland's leading GAA journalists of the time, Mick Dunne and John D. Hickey, with us made the trip extra special. Further importance to our tour was added in Boston when Michael O'Hehir joined us. On a daily basis both John D. and Mick sent bulletins on what we were doing back to Ireland. This made me feel acutely aware of what Gaelic games must mean to every Irish person as well as the significant impact that we were making in the United States.

In Boston we met John Lawlor, the Irish Olympic hammer thrower who won a Caltex sportsman of the year award with me just 18 months earlier. We also met Cardinal Cushing and Mayor Collins. During our stay in Boston we were taken on a tour of Massachusett's State Senate where the President of the Assembly interrupted the business of the house to welcome "our visitors – the Irish soccer players"! That mistake made us all laugh and realise not everyone knew of the existence of Gaelic football. After this we were entertained at the residence of Irish Vice Consul, Con Howard.

Before we left Ireland we had experienced several tedious days waiting patiently as a tailor took measurements for our touring uniforms. We wore these at all official functions. Our visit to the Vice Consul was the first occasion that we had an opportunity to don our black blazers, cavalry twill trousers, white shirts and Down ties. Incidentally, Charlie Carr and my father sponsored the cost of the blazers. Like most of the touring party I did not particularly like the local American food which was on offer at many of these formal receptions. However, when we went to the house of the Columban Fathers religious order we had a special surprise. I really appreciated their lovely homemade brown bread and a cup of properly brewed tea in a decent sized cup. When someone pointed out that the tea came out of a fancy teapot with the immortal words "A Present From Warrenpoint" inscribed on it, there was laughter all round.

The following day we had our first game. It was played in a sweltering 93 degrees fahrenheit in the shade. The only player missing was Sean O'Neill who had stayed behind in Ireland to do important examinations. An American league side drawn from cities like Chicago, Boston, Montreal and Buffalo provided the opposition. On our American debut we triumphed by 4-10 to 2-5.

The next stop, a week later, was the windy city of Chicago. What a difference there was in the weather conditions! When we awoke on the Sunday morning torrential rain greeted us. Later that morning we attended the annual parade of St

Jude's Police Association. The heavy downpour continued until minutes before the match began at Hanson Park in the early afternoon. Such poor weather conditions naturally kept the attendance down to about 2000 hardy souls The game was played on a mud-churned quagmire of a pitch that was very small compared to normal GAA pitches. In a very disappointing display we won on a scoreline of 1-8 to 0-5. After the conclusion of his exams Sean O'Neill had now joined us. There were actually two Down natives on the opposing All-American League side: Frank Clements of Banbridge and Pat McAteer formerly of Newry Mitchels.

What made the Chicago stopover all the more enjoyable was the fact that a large party of Down people from everywhere took a week's holidays to be with us there. Some of them had made the trip from home but many of them were now living in different parts of America. They brought us on many excursions and generally left themselves at our disposal in terms of transport and hospitality. Every night that we spent in the Windy City there was a separate function held in our honour.

After leaving Chicago we went to Cleveland for a midweek game. A morning of bright sunshine soon gave way to a really miserable day. Despite the inclement weather almost 1000 people turned up to see us beating another All-American League side by 1-14 to 0-6. A Down native, Gerry Butterfield from Mayobridge, played on the American side. Gerry, who had captained Abbey CBS to MacRory Cup success in 1954, was one of the most talented footballers that I ever saw. I have no doubt, had he not emigrated, he would have been an outstanding member of our All-Ireland winning teams. A well-known figure on the American team was Father Peter Quinn who had won All-Ireland senior medals with his native Mayo in 1950 and 1951.

The morning after the Cleveland game we got up at 5.30 a.m. to undertake a ten-hour, 423-mile journey down the Ohio and Pennsylvania turnpikes. Travelling on a Greyhound bus we then proceeded through the Allegheny Mountains to Philadelphia. Here on 3 June we had our last game against a full American League selection. Thankfully the sun shone again and 5500 spectators turned up to watch the game. The attendance included several busloads of Down supporters from New York.

At a welcoming dinner for us in Philadelphia we got our first and only taste of nastiness. An American League player had expressed the belief that it must now be easy to win an All-Ireland senior football championship, especially since a team like Down had won it twice. This really annoyed us so we upped the tempo. As a result we gave a sparkling display of first class football and emerged convincing winners by 3-11 to 0-7. After that there were no more begrudgers amongst our All-American League opponents.

Prior to our game there was a curtain raiser between a Philadelphia selection and a Down junior team from New York. There were two sets of lovely trophies for both the winners and losers of the senior game. They were presented by the Philadelphia Clann na nGael society in memory of the late Joe McGarrity. He had been a native of Carrickmore in County Tyrone and had emigrated to Philadelphia in 1892 at the age of 16. Until his death in 1940 he had been closely associated with the movement for a united Ireland. Here again the North American Board President of the GAA, Michael Cavanagh, proved to be an excellent host and guide by showing us many places of historic interest in the greater Philadelphia area. For example, we were taken to the State House where the famous Liberty Bell was on display and we were also shown copies of the American Declaration of Independence.

Our final American destination was San Francisco on the western seaboard. Before we arrived there we experienced some airport frustration. First of all there was a delayed start to our scheduled flight from Philadelphia International Airport. Second, there was further anxiety at Chicago's O'Hare Field Airport. Our team's Convair 880 superjet had to circle the airport there for 60 minutes before we eventually got flight clearance. At last we reached San Francisco, more than four hours after our planned arrival.

At Bilbao Stadium on 10 June we faced a San Francisco selection that included a Greek-American goalkeeper called George Roussakis. He was certainly a formidable figure with his American football shoulder pads. At midfield there was a Polish-American by the name of Walt Pudlowski. To make us feel more at home two Down men, by the more familiar names of Charlie Downey and Sean Spiers, played in their forward line. Sean had also been a former county footballer. If he had not emigrated his natural ability would have earned the Clonduff star a definite place in our senior winning squad. This match was played in the best and biggest stadium we had encountered in America. We gave a magnificent display of Gaelic football as we trounced the home side in our last tour appearance. The final score of 7-13 to 1-8 was a fair reflection of our overall superiority.

Before we left San Francisco we met many people with Down family connections. I also had the good fortune to meet Fr James McKnight from Killeavy in County

Armagh. Fr James was a brother of Michael, John and Felix McKnight, all of whom gave outstanding service to Armagh football in the 1950s and early 1960s. Indeed, if Fr James had not become a priest it has often been said that he, too, would have become an outstanding defender for the Orchard County.

Before we boarded the plane to New York for the first leg of our homeward journey there was a huge emotional send-off to us from the people of San Francisco. When we reached New York there were still a few hours left before the commencement of the last leg of our flight back to Ireland. For those three hours the passenger lounge at New York's Idlewild Airport was treated to a concert of Irish music. "The Little Town in the Old County Down" and "The Star of the County Down" took centre stage before our farewell proceedings concluded with a rousing rendition of "The Soldier's Song".

Almost four weeks of fantastic hospitality were now at an end. However, the generosity of our hosts was not finished. On the homeward flight Patrick McAlinden from Cabra, outside Newry, handed over a gift-wrapped box to our county chairman George Tinnelly. Inside were presents, which had been entrusted to him, from the Gaels of Chicago. It contained Parker 51 writing sets for every member of the official travelling party as well as a substantial cheque for the Down football training fund. Each of us was also fully laden with mementoes and souvenirs of a wonderfully happy visit.

Accompanying the players on the trip were members of our management team as well as several county board officials. Men like George Tinnelly, T.P. Murphy, Maurice Hayes, Barney Carr and Danny Flynn had helped us in so many different ways to make all our dreams come true. It was only fitting that they should also participate fully in this trip of a lifetime. The Chairman of the Ulster Council, Paddy MacFlynn, was also in the travelling party. Among the many loyal Down supporters who toured with us were Mickey King and my father Briney. Mickey had the honour of captaining Down to their first senior success. In 1944 he led Down to their initial McKenna cup triumph. My father had played for and captained Down in the 1920s and 1930s. For both of them this trip was an experience of total satisfaction and sheer enjoyment.

All in all it was a very happy and contented group of Down GAA people who arrived back at Shannon. Again there was a huge welcome for us from a large crowd of relatives, friends and supporters who waited at the airport terminal. Once more they followed us in joyous triumph back to our home county.

Another enthusiastic crowd cheered us when we arrived in Marcus Square in Newry on 13 June 1962.

Our world of fantasy and merriment was over. The reality of what lay ahead now dawned. There was the little matter of defending both our Ulster and All-Ireland senior football titles to be attended to. And there were only two weeks left before we had to cross the first hurdle.

8

The Last Goodbye

Down travelled to St Molaise's Park in Irvinestown for the opening game of the 1962 Ulster senior football championship against Fermanagh. Despite speculation that travel weariness and jet lag might affect us we put on a powerful performance to comprehensively defeat the Erne men by 4-10 to 1-3. This was a game in which Sean O'Neill was truly outstanding, scoring a fabulous goal himself and creating a brilliant opening for Tony Hadden to add another. A fortnight later, in the provincial semi-final, with Hadden again on song we reached our fifth successive Ulster decider by recording a 1-12 to 1-6 victory over Tyrone.

That year's Ulster final against Cavan was one of our worst ever displays. Nothing went right. Shortly after the start we conceded a soft goal. Then Eddie McKay had to retire injured and was replaced by substitute goalkeeper Gerry McCashin. The bad luck continued when a long ball bounced off George Lavery's chest into the grateful hands of Cavan forward Jim Stafford who goaled from close range. At half time we were behind by 2-3 to 0-4. There was nothing particularly strange about that type of situation. Prior to this we always seemed to have the capacity to overcome such difficulties. As this game progressed, however, I had a very eerie feeling about our chances.

In the second half Cavan were much hungrier, much sharper. In addition our injury hoodoo continued. Two substitutes who came on, Kevin O'Neill and Kevin Mussen, both got injured just after coming into the game and were unable to make a worthwhile contribution. Ten minutes after the resumption came the greatest blow of all. The wily Stafford again spotted a gap in our defence and coolly slotted the ball to the net. We all tried as hard as we could but we just continued to be lethargic and lifeless. Traditionally when the chips were down we, collectively and individually, raised our game. That day our hearts were willing but our bodies just refused to respond. After Jim Stafford's second goal I knew that the great days of our team were over. People often overanalyse such developments as the careers of individuals and teams reach saturation point. When the referee blew the full time whistle Cavan had deservedly won the game by 3-6 to 0-5. We were beaten by ten points and had only scored one point in the second half.

The sad fact, however, was that Cavan were a mediocre side. Their subsequent loss to Roscommon in the All-Ireland semi-final was proof of that. Hindsight is a wonderful gift! It is my humble opinion that the American trip dulled our playing enthusiasm. More than anything else, I feel that this prevented us from winning not only another Ulster title but also our third All-Ireland. After all there was no other outstanding team in that season's championship. By their normal high standards, eventual winners Kerry were a very ordinary team.

When the new football season commenced in the autumn of 1962 with the Lagan Cup competition, we redeemed ourselves somewhat by accounting for Antrim, Tyrone and Monaghan. The cup was retained thanks to a last-minute thrilling victory over Donegal at Dungannon.

In the National League semi-final against Galway I was heavily stamped upon by one of their defenders. Such was the pain that I immediately got up and instinctively struck the offender with my fist. As so often happens the retaliation was spotted and the cause of the incident was not. Consequently I was sent off. Despite being a man down we led by 1-3 to 1-0 at half time. In the second half the team continued to play well and with only seven minutes to go Down were seven points in front. However, the Tribesmen made a fantastic comeback and with just 40 seconds left they scored a goal to equalise. As the referee looked at his watch, Paddy Doherty notched a tremendous winning point for us to leave the full time score having a very peculiar look to it. Very few games end with a scoreline of 2-8 to 4-1 but this one did.

I was suspended for the final against Kerry. We did not play well in the first half of that match and at the interval Kerry led by 0-9 to 1-0. Incredibly the Kingdom did not score at all in the second half but our tally of five points in that latter period was not enough to overtake them. So, as well as no longer being All-Ireland champions, we had also surrendered our league title. Watching the game gave me an insight into the inconsistency of refereeing standards, a problem that, unfortunately, is still very prevalent today. Compared to the offence for which I was sent off for in the semi-final, there were far more serious and unprovoked dangerous tackles in the final. Yet, in most cases, the referee did not even allow a free for the victims of those tackles.

In the McKenna Cup final replay we lost to Cavan and for the first time in five years we did not qualify for the Wembley Tournament final. However, we totally outclassed Monaghan in the opening round of the Ulster championship by 6-11 to 1-3 and then we defeated Armagh in the semi-final by 0-9 to 0-5. In the Ulster final we met a fine Donegal side that were making their debut appearance in an Ulster decider. However we gave a scintillating performance, with our new championship boys Patsy McAlinden and Brian Johnston acquitting themselves really well. When the long whistle sounded we had recorded a convincing 2-11 to 1-4 triumph. My favourite memory of that occasion was to see our captain George Lavery receiving the new Anglo-Celt cup. For his longevity of service and dedication to Down football no one deserved the honour more.

In the All-Ireland semi-finals Down featured in both the minor and senior games and my young cousin Val Kane had the distinction of playing in both contests. The minors lost the curtain raiser to Westmeath before we took the field against Dublin. In the first quarter, despite a wonderful display at centre field by Joe Lennon, we failed to take advantage of the many scoring opportunities that his dominance created. I had the misfortune to strike the crossbar when I was sure I was going to score a goal. Dublin gradually took complete control of the match and by half time they were leading by 1-5 to 0-2. Within ten minutes of the resumption Dublin had added another goal and two points. Only magnificent individual performances by Joe Lennon and Sean O'Neill kept the deficit down to a reasonable margin. Dublin eventually emerged deserving winners by 2-11 to 0-7. When I trooped off the field, I instinctively knew that the halcyon days of 1960 and 1961 would not be returning for many of that side.

Two months later we returned to Croke Park to play Galway in the Grounds Tournament semi-final and lost by two points. In retrospect this was an excellent performance, especially considering that Galway were on the threshold of securing three successive senior All-Ireland titles between 1964 and 1966.

In the spring of 1964 I won another Railway Cup medal when Ulster defeated Leinster 0-12 to 1-6 in the final. (The previous year I had won my first provincial medal when I came on as a substitute in Ulster's 2-8 to 1-9 success, also over Leinster.) We were also victorious in the Lagan Cup for the third successive year. This qualified us to play Cavan in the semi-final of the National League. Though we did not play well, we scraped our way to a home final against Dublin. Like our encounter in the championship we again started well. Only this time our scoring was much better. By the 28th minute of the first half we were ahead by 0-6 to 0-1. Then an inexplicable mix-up led to a Dublin goal, followed shortly afterwards by a point. Thus the Metropolitans were only a point behind when we retired for the interval. The omens were not good; particularly as we were due to face a gale force wind in the second half.

Shortly after the restart I scored a point that turned out to be our only score of the second period as Dublin coasted to a 2-9 to 0-7 victory. For whatever reasons, our injury count over this unsuccessful time seemed to mount considerably. In this game alone Dan badly hurt his arm and both Leo Murphy and Patsy O'Hagan had to retire through injury. However, these injuries only served to ignore the blatant fact that we were really a spent force in All-Ireland winning terms. The hunger, the heart, the exciting combination play were all but a distant memory.

Even though we won the McKenna Cup and again reached the Ulster final the "X-factor" that differentiates between a good side and a great one was missing. In the provincial decider we again started brightly and actually led at the interval on a 1-5 to 0-4 scoreline. But Cavan began the second half in terrific fashion and within a four minute spell the talented Peter Pritchard scored two goals for the Breffni men. Sandwiched between those green flags was an exquisite point by Charlie Gallagher. Cavan had dramatically transformed a four-point deficit into a three-point advantage. When Cavan scored their second goal George Lavery had gone off injured and had not been replaced. I know when one gets beaten one tends to dwell on such negativity as injuries and bad luck. Our new star corner back Tom O'Hare also spent much of the game in a confused state of mind as a result of an elbow to the face. But, in the final analysis, Cavan won because they were the better team on the day. When the full time whistle sounded we had lost by 2-10 to 1-10. No amount of debate could change that cold, hard fact.

At this stage of my career I was not really enjoying my football any longer. Even though I was only 26 years of age I had lost some of my natural enthusiasm. There were several reasons for this. My business and farming commitments were consuming a lot of my attention and I was finding it increasingly difficult to devote the necessary time to train properly at such a high level. When I had a personal disagreement with a member of the management team my voluntary decision to retire was made all the more easy. So, in the autumn of 1964, I informed the management team of my intentions to retire from county football. For the ensuing weeks representatives of the management team, the county board and my playing colleagues tried to get me to rescind my decision but I was determined that I would not change my mind. Many GAA columnists penned kind tributes to me.

John D. Hickey, in the *Irish Independent*, wrote: "He had scarcely reached man's estate when his name was a household word everywhere the game was played, and his football valour was respected as much as it was feared among all opposing sides."

The *Sentinel* also recorded some nice words: "No more will be seen the bustling becapped young Glenn giant blazing his way through the toughest of defences to turn the fast-ebbing tide in favour of his red and black colleagues."

During the next year I watched intently as my former colleagues suffered their first Lagan Cup match defeat since March 1961 when they were beaten by Derry. By now there was a new senior football management team in place. Brian Denvir was the manager and former Antrim star Paddy O'Hara was the trainer. The team's bad form continued when Donegal defeated them in both Lagan and McKenna Cup ties. The latter game at Ballybofey was to see the Down team receive a torrent of physical and verbal abuse from the home supporters. Sods of clay and items of fruit were thrown at the players. This was something that I could not understand, as there was no history of bitterness between the sides.

In the 1965 Ulster championship Down recorded a convincing first round victory over Tyrone. In the semi-final they played poorly and were lucky to eke out a narrow two-point win against Antrim. In their eighth successive Ulster final they met Cavan for the fifth time in that sequence. Playing extremely well the Mourne men were victorious on a 3-5 to 1-8 scoreline. Sean O'Neill, Paddy Doherty, Patsy O'Hagan and Joe Lennon were all brilliant. Coincidentally those four, along with Dan McCartan and Leo Murphy, were the only remaining All-Ireland medal winners who started that day. Of all the magnificent matches that Sean O'Neill has played I would rank his 1965 Ulster final exhibition as one of his best ever. Sean, in his first year as team captain, had the honour of lifting the Anglo-Celt Cup.

Meanwhile at home my father had kept trying to persuade me to return to play county football. Scarcely a week went by that he did not mention the subject. As I saw Down making progress my yearning to again don the red and black jersey intensified. However I knew, if I did so, it would be totally unfair on all the players who had done all the training.

For the time being my father's pleading and my desire to return would be put on hold. In the All-Ireland semi-final Down were meeting a fantastic Galway team that had won the previous year's All-Ireland final. Looking at Down's Ulster final performance I knew that we had a nice mixture of talented youth and seasoned campaigners. Tom O'Hare was an accomplished defender. George Glynn and Larry Powell were a strong midfield partnership. In attack the skilful Felix Quigley, Val Kane, Brian Johnston and Jackie Fitsimmons supplemented the experienced class of Sean O'Neill and Paddy Doherty. Defensively and in terms of winning possession Down did really well in the first half of the game. However the forward line failed to capitalise on this. Eventually Down succumbed to a three-point defeat. After that Galway side went on to win the All-Ireland against Kerry, I decided to bow to the inevitable.

I could not suppress or delay my feelings any longer. It was only when watching Down play that I realised how much the red and black jersey meant to me. It was not just when they were winning that I wanted to play. In fact it probably was when they were losing that my desire was greater. I came to the conclusion that representing Down would mean more to me than any work commitments or personal dispute with an individual. So when my father came calling again, in the autumn of 1965, there would only be one answer. After a year in the football wilderness I returned to county training.

That year the Ground Tournament semi-finals were hosted, as a double header, in Croke Park. Down played Kerry and Dublin were Galway's opponents. When I raced onto the field I got a fantastic reception from the supporters of all four teams. I highlight this experience not to emphasise any arrogance on my part but to reiterate the intimate common bond that unites all members of the GAA fraternity. In an entertaining game we beat Kerry by two points and in the decider against Galway we played magnificently to emerge victorious by 3-10 to 0-7. All our defenders, especially Willie Doyle, Seamus Doyle and Tom Morgan, performed well. George Glynn and Larry Powell were superb at midfield. The whole forward line was very impressive. Ray Morgan, nephew of my old colleague Brian, scored a brilliant goal. It was a pity that his playing career was cut short by injury. Coming off the field that day I was happy that I had played my part. Though I had not been particularly influential my football adrenalin was certainly flowing again. The rest had done me good. I had put things in perspective. My father had always preached this type of philosophy. He was right.

1966 began well for me when I was recalled to captain the Railway Cup team in my favourite centre half forward position. It was good to be back playing with wonderful players from other Ulster counties like Paul Kelly of Donegal, Jody O'Neill of Tyrone, Charlie Gallagher of Cavan and P.T. Treacy of Fermanagh. In the provincial semi-final we beat Leinster 1-8 to 1-4. In a terrific exhibition of accuracy Paddy Doherty scored all eight points. We beat Munster in the final by three points. This was Ulster's fourth title in a row and my third Railway Cup medal. On the intercounty front things did not go as well. Donegal overcame us again in the Lagan Cup. Cavan beat us in the Wembley Tournament play-off and Antrim, for the first time in years, defeated us in the McKenna Cup. It was good, however, to see a side like Antrim who had experienced so little success progress to the final where they beat Tyrone.

As we prepared for the 1966 Ulster senior football championship there was a prolonged dispute as to who should train our team. In the previous autumn the existing trainer, former Antrim star Paddy O'Hara, asked to be relieved of his duties. This was because he was training Queen's University for the Sigerson Cup campaign. In January, Armagh native Des Farrelly was appointed to replace him. After his Sigerson commitments were completed the county board reappointed O'Hara to the exclusion of Farrelly. For several months this was a bone of contention because many people thought that Farrelly had been unjustly treated. Then, at the beginning of May, Paddy O'Hara resigned. At short notice Joe Lennon was asked to train his fellow players. This was an additional burden for Joe who, because he lived in Gormanston in Meath, was already making a round trip of 130 miles to attend training. Still, along with Brian Denvir as manager, Joe had us in good shape in a short space of time.

We beat Tyrone and Antrim to reach Down's ninth successive provincial decider. Our opponents Donegal were a very good side sprinkled with many star performers. Bernard Brady, Paul Kelly, P.J. Flood, Anton Carroll, Sean Ferriter, Mickey McLoone and Frankie McFeely would have graced any of the top county teams. Another future All-Star and legendary manager to be, Brian McEniff, came on as a substitute that day.

Despite the quality of the footballers on the pitch, this was a sub-standard match. At half time the teams were level with four points each. In the end a fabulous fisted goal by Sean O'Neill was the reason Down edged out Donegal by 1-7 to 0-8. In one sense the game will always be remembered for one remarkable Down substitution. In the second half the Mourne men introduced Colm McAlarney who had won an Ulster minor medal just an hour earlier. Colm made his own piece of history a week later when he played for Down in the defeat to Donegal in the Ulster U-21 final. Thus, within a space of eight days, he had represented his native county in three provincial finals at three different levels. Dan McCartan had the privilege of lifting the cup when he deputised for the injured Patsy O'Hagan.

The Last Goodbye

Another interesting footnote was that it was the first Ulster GAA final to be televised live. The BBC covered it with former Derry captain Jim McKeever as commentator.

In the All-Ireland semi-final Down played Meath. We won a lot of possession in the first half and actually led at the interval on a 0-6 to 0-3 scoreline. The most disappointing feature of that opening period was that our brilliant corner back Tom O'Hare had to retire injured after 20 minutes. Still, we were satisfied enough as we began the second half. However, that initial optimism was soon squashed when a reinvigorated Meath took over completely. In a productive three-minute spell they scored three points to level the score. Not to be outdone Paddy Doherty put us ahead again with an excellent point. The next three minutes swung the match in favour of the Royal County. First, they equalised with a point. Then, twice in rapid succession, they tore our defence to shreds to score two crucial goals. Though Brian Johnston replied with a fabulous goal, it was not to be our day and Meath cruised to an emphatic victory by 2-16 to 1-9.

1967 was to prove a defining season for me. Having lost any chance of qualifying for the latter stages of the National League and having been beaten by Donegal in the McKenna Cup, the signs for a good championship run were not good. Again we proved ourselves wrong by performing brilliantly against both Derry and Donegal to reach the county's tenth Ulster final in a row.

In the final Cavan were much the more dominant team in the first half and led, at the interval, by 1-4 to 0-5. To compound our difficulties our full back Leo Murphy suffered concussion and had to retire ten minutes before half time. Within five minutes of the resumption we conceded another goal. This had a positive, catalytic effect on Cavan and in a real scintillating display they ended the game comprehensive winners by 2-12 to 0-8.

As I left Clones on that July Sunday I knew that I had played my last senior championship game for Down. I also realised that there were many young talented players on that defeated side. Their day would surely come but mine were over. This time there would be no return. My decision was based on a thought process that had occupied my mind since the beginning of 1967. Even though I was still relatively young, 29, I had played a lot of county football since I joined the senior team 11 years earlier in 1956. With the exception of my suspension in the latter half of 1957 and my self-imposed exile in 1965, I had given my complete life to Down football. I had enjoyed every minute of it, except for 1964/65, especially the glorious times of 1960 and 1961. The vast majority of the players with whom

The King of Down Football

I had shared so many exciting moments were now also retired. However, there was a far more significant change about to take place in my life. I was about to get married and I realised it would be unfair on my new wife, Marie, if I were to continue playing county football. My business and farming commitments in themselves were time consuming enough. It would be totally unreasonable if I were to absent myself from our new home for an additional three hours for two or three nights per week in order to go training alone, not to mention playing county matches. County football had been good to me. Luckily I had remained relatively injury free. At the same time and for the same reason I also decided to retire from senior club football with Glenn. Life had taken on a different priority for me.

During those glory years of the sixties I had many brilliant experiences. Prominent among them was our own version of "The Sunday Game" at home on the Monday after a match. Somebody would have been designated to tape the game and on Monday night our house in Donacloney was packed not only to see or hear a recording of the match but also to witness a definitive analysis of our performance. The show did not commence until Maurice Hayes arrived with a carload of players. With my father as presenter and chief critic there was a total and frank exchange of opinions on both individual and team displays! Even though he did not spare anyone, including the commentator, from any mistakes they may have made, the whole proceedings were carried out in a spirit of good humour and goodwill for the success of Down football. Soon after my mother had made tea for everyone the crowd happily dispersed.

I had been part of many playing fields in Down, Ulster, the rest of Ireland and abroad. Each of them, in their own way, made me what I am – a lover of Gaelic football. To see and hear the packed stands and tiered terraces echo loudly as 30 men played their hearts out for the honour and glory of their native county was an overwhelming experience that I will never forget. The tumultuous roar that greeted a wondrous Down goal and the long whistle that signalled a momentous victory will stay with me until I die.

When I arrived back in Donacloney on that last Ulster final night I was happy to say goodbye to my senior intercounty football career. And I was very excited and contented to meet the challenges of a happy marriage with Marie.

9

The Stars of the County Down

Many people are responsible for the successes of any team at any level. However, one constant factor remains at the heart of every triumph. One can have well-structured underage coaching systems, supportive county boards and excellent management teams but have the wrong type of players. It takes a certain calibre of player to put all the sophisticated coaching and preparation theory into practice, especially in pressurised situations. I was extremely lucky to be playing for Down when we had a superbly talented and focused squad of players. All of us had but one singular aim – to win an All-Ireland football title. To give you a flavour of their immense contribution to Down football I have included in the following pages, a short resumé of the careers and lives of my fellow teammates and managerial officials.

EDDIE MCKAY

> *In the 1961 Ulster semi-final against Derry the Oak Leaf County's Phil Stuart blazed through for what seemed a certain goal but the heroic McKay made what must have been the greatest and most spectacular save of his brilliant career. If he had not done so Down would probably have been eliminated from that year's Ulster championship.*
>
> Sighle Nic an Ultaigh, *An Dún, The GAA Story*

Often referred to in the media as Eamon, Eddie McKay was an outstanding goalkeeper. Though small in stature for a custodian – 5'9" – and weighing only 11 stone, he nevertheless carried out his duties with great aplomb. He had a safe pair of hands, fantastic judgment and superb reflexes. He never, surprisingly, played minor or junior county football. His senior championship debut was in June 1957 against Donegal in the first round of the Ulster championship. Eddie's final championship game was against Cavan in the 1962 Ulster final. An injury in the first half of that match effectively finished his career. Thus the end of an illustrious but short period in the Down colours came to a premature conclusion at the age of just 24.

A mechanic by trade, he is now retired and lives in his native Dundrum. Over the decades he coached a number of Down clubs at senior level.

GEORGE LAVERY

> *There's the great Geordie Lavery, the County Down star. His fame on the field is well known near and far. For tackling and catching he stands out supreme. He plays centre full back for the dashing fifteen.*
>
> Poetic tribute to George from the history of St Michael's GAC after Kilwarlin had won the 1955 North Armagh League final.

Known to his friends as Geordie, George Lavery was the most reliable, consistent and experienced member of that Down team. Only 5'9" in height he was very cool under pressure, quietly competent rather than spectacular. Without a shadow of doubt, in my opinion, he was the real man of the match in the 1960 All-Ireland final. George was born in the parish of Magheralin, which is situated in the north west of the county and borders both Armagh and Antrim. Up to 1961 he played for St Colman's Kilwarlin, which was then one of two clubs in the parish. Kilwarlin played their league football in the North Armagh League and their championship football in Down. Consequently very few Down supporters ever saw George playing except when he was playing county football. In 1961/62 the two Magheralin parish clubs amalgamated under the name of St Michael's GAC. At club level George won a county championship runner-up medal in both 1956 and 1966.

George actually made his senior intercounty debut playing for Antrim against his native Down in a Dr Lagan Cup game in 1952 when he marked Barney Carr! It was only then that the Down selectors got to know about him and he made his senior championship debut for them in 1953 against Derry. His last senior championship appearance was in the 1964 Ulster final against Cavan. George was also a talented soccer player and had been signed by the famed Belfast Celtic when he was only 17. The unassuming bricklayer is now retired and living in Belfast where he spent the majority of his working life.

Leo Murphy

> *This young dashing defender gave us a packed year [1960] of impeccable displays on the square. His form in the All-Ireland final topped the lot for its polished skill and tactical assurance.*
>
> Paddy Downey, *The Irish Times*

Leo was an excellent full back and a prodigious kicker of a dead ball. He also possessed a remarkable turn of speed for such a big man. He usually won all the sprints in training. A native of Kilkeel he played as a county minor in 1957 and won a MacRory Cup medal with St Colman's in the same year. In 1958 he was in the junior county team as well as on the senior side in the Ulster final against Derry. His last championship game was against Cavan in the 1967 Ulster final. He played club football for Kilkeel and Rostrevor.

Leo was principal teacher in Killowen Primary School for many years. He is now retired and living in Rostrevor with whom he won a county championship runner-up medal in 1975.

Pat Rice

> *Brave Pat Rice, who was carried off with a badly split thumb, insisted on returning to the fray and put his shoulder to the wheel in heroic fashion.*
>
> *Armagh Observer* report on 1961 final

Pat Rice was a spectacular high fielder and at 6'1" was the tallest player on the team. A very courageous and consistently reliable performer who was also a very long kicker of a dead ball. In 1954 and 1955 he was on the county minor team and he graduated to the junior team that played Monaghan in the 1956 provincial championship. He made his senior championship debut against Donegal in 1957 at midfield. His last major championship appearance was against Dublin in the 1963 All-Ireland semi-final. Pat won two county championship medals with Castlewellan in 1958 and 1965 as well as captaining Down juniors in the 1966 All-Ireland final against Cork.

Pat, a foreman carpenter, worked in the Shetland Islands for many years but came back to spend many happy years helping around his beloved Castlewellan club. He retired in 2000 and died in May 2005 after a long battle with a serious illness at the age of 68 years. A deeply religious man who was a daily massgoer he faced up to his untimely death with the same steely determination and courage that he so often displayed on the football field.

The King of Down Football

KEVIN MUSSEN

> *When all around was a desert of physical effort, Kevin Mussen appeared as a football oasis, as if saying to his men: "Look lads, this is the way we play it."*
>
> "Linesman" in *The Frontier Sentinel* after
Down had beaten Cavan in 1960 NFL final

Kevin Mussen was a class footballer and outstanding captain who was a true diplomat on and off the field. He had a wonderful positional sense and terrific vision. No one deserved the honour more than Kevin to be the first man to carry the Sam Maguire Cup across the border. He played for the county minor side in 1950 and 1951 and made his senior championship debut the following year against Cavan. His last major game was when he played, as a forward, in the 1963 league final. Kevin won league and county championship medals both with his native Clonduff and O'Donovan Rossa in Antrim. He also won MacRory Cup medals with St Colman's in 1949 and 1950. Though only 29 when he retired, he had given 12 years of great service to the county team.

Kevin's uncles, George and Dan, played for Down in the 1930s and his son Damien played for the county minors in 1990. Incidentally, George was the first Down man to captain an adult team in Croke Park when he led the county junior team against Louth in the 1934 All-Ireland junior semi-final. Kevin himself had the rare distinction of captaining his county to three successive senior provincial titles in 1959, 1960 and 1961. A prominent Kerry forward said to Kevin when they were playing against each other in a Railway Cup game in the middle fifties: "It must be terrible to have to play for a county that never has a chance of playing in Croke Park."

Today in St Patrick's Park in Newcastle, not far from Kevin's home, there is a large stone of Mourne granite. Engraved on it, in large ornamental letters, are the names of Down's historic winning team of 1960. Prominently featured is the name of its captain – one Kevin Mussen. I think that plaque answers the Kerry man's rather condescending remark quite aptly.

Kevin who was principal teacher in his native Hilltown for many years is now retired and living in Newcastle.

DAN MCCARTAN

> *Twenty-year-old Dan McCartan was the main barrier to every Kerry advance, not only covering the middle but also going to the flanks to cover off the rare mistakes of his colleagues.*
>
> Michael Cogley in *The Irish Independent* after
> Down defeated Kerry in the 1960 NFL semi-final

Dan was a very good fielder of the ball as well as possessing an innate anticipation of where the ball might land. His greatest asset was his fierce determination and spirit to play to the final whistle regardless of how Down were playing. The winner of two MacRory Cup medals played for Down minors in 1957 and his senior championship debut was against Tyrone in 1959. His last senior championship appearance was in the 1975 Ulster final against Derry. Along with Sean O'Neill he holds the proud record of having played in 16 Ulster finals, including the 1974 replay against Donegal. During his career he played club football for Glenn, Tullylish and Carryduff. At the age of 47, along with his son Mark, he won a Down junior championship medal in 1986. The long-serving Dan played his last club game for Carryduff in 1998, at the ripe young age of 59!

Dan, who is a dentist by profession, made a large contribution towards establishing handball in Down in later years. He won many handball prizes while at St Colman's. In 2004, while in his mid-sixties, he, along with Des McNeill (the former Antrim footballer), brought another All-Ireland to his native county. That year they won the All-Ireland Diamond Masters' doubles 40 x 20 final in Mullingar. Dan's only son, Mark, also played for Down in the late eighties and early nineties and was a member of the 1991 All-Ireland senior winning panel.

When we were training for the 1960 All-Ireland Dan was a dental student at the College of Surgeons in Dublin. Instead of travelling north he did his midweek training with his colleagues who were members of Lansdowne rugby club. Furthermore his examination results were not due until a few days after the final. On the Friday before the big day his professor kindly informed him that he had passed his exams.

Dan is now retired and living in Tyrella, about six miles from Downpatrick. He is still actively involved with the Carryduff GAA club in north Down.

KEVIN O'NEILL

> *Few GAA players could claim to have dominated Paddy Doherty at the height of his brilliance but that was the achievement of Kevin O'Neill when he held the Ballykinlar bricklayer scoreless in the 1960 Down senior championship final.*
>
> Down GAA Yearbook

Despite his slight build Kevin O'Neill was a resilient, skilful player. He was a great reader of the game and his renowned long and accurate kick passes quickly turned a defensive situation into an attacking one. A model sportsman he was also famous for his exceptionally long kick-outs and great fielding ability. He made his debut for Down in the 1958 Ulster senior football championship having played for the county junior and minor teams prior to this – his last major senior championship appearance was the 1964 Ulster final against Cavan. He was a MacRory Cup medal winner with Abbey CBS in 1954. In 1962 he was full back on the UCD Sigerson Cup winning side. Kevin also won four county championship medals with Newry Mitchels and he was their captain in the 1960 triumph.

After a distinguished career as chief executive officer of Newry and Mourne District Council Kevin is now retired and living in Newry.

JOE LENNON

> *Joe Lennon pulled a muscle just before the interval. It was his decision not to return for the second half. This was real captaincy and it was fitting that he took his place on the Hogan Stand afterwards to receive the Cup.*
>
> Raymond Smith, *The Football Immortals*, referring to Joe's injury in 1968 final

Although relatively small for a midfielder, Joe Lennon was a very good catcher. However, it was when he was switched to left half back that one saw the full repertoire of his skills. He played minor for Down in 1951 and 1952 and junior in 1953. In 1954 he transferred to Fermanagh and played for the Erne County, just for one year. His travels as a meteorologist brought him to England, the Shetland Islands and the Persian Gulf. As a result his early intercounty career was badly curtailed. His first senior championship match for Down was against Armagh in 1956 and his last championship game was against Antrim – 14 years later in 1970. The 1968 All-Ireland winning captain played club football for

Aghaderg, John Mitchel's in Birmingham and St Patrick's in Stamullen, County Meath.

Though born in Poyntzpass in Armagh Joe's family later moved a few miles away to a farm in Aghaderg in Down. When he stopped his meteorological duties he qualified as a science, maths and PE teacher. He was appointed to the staff of the Franciscan College in Gormanston, Meath, in the early sixties. He coached the college's team to several Leinster titles as well as a Hogan Cup success in 1973. He organised the first national GAA coaching course in Gormanston in 1964. He has written several well-known books including *Coaching Gaelic Football for Champions* and *Fitness for Gaelic Football*. He won various handball titles both at colleges' and provincial levels as well as managing Down to an Ulster championship and a NFL Division Two title. Joe is now retired and living in Meath.

Jarlath Carey

I taught him all he knows. But not all I know!

A jocular reference by Jarlath about Patrick Kielty when the latter first became a TV personality. Jarlath had been Patrick's principal teacher in Dundrum.

Jarlath Carey was a great midfielder to play with – especially if you were a forward. There was no indecision with Jarlath. He normally caught the ball and sent it up to the forward line immediately. Occasionally he would go on a spectacular solo run and score a great point or notch an opportunist goal. Generally, however, he did what most midfielders should always do, i.e. gave good quick ball to the forward line. Jarlath learned his football in St Malachy's College, Belfast, where Derry's Jim McKeever was a fellow student and played on the 1950 Down minor team. He made his intercounty senior championship debut at centre half forward against Derry in 1953. His last major championship appearance was when he came on as a substitute against Galway in the 1965 All-Ireland semi-final. Immediately afterwards he retired from both club and county football. At club level he played for Ballymartin and Dundrum, winning a championship medal with the former in 1955.

Jarlath was a native of Glenravel in County Antrim and came to Down to serve as a schoolteacher in Longstone, Ballymartin and Dundrum. In the latter parish he taught John and Patrick Kielty who, along with Jarlath's own son Martin, won All-Ireland minor medals with Down in 1987.

A great community activist Jarlath served as an SDLP Councillor for many years. He had an innate love of learning and along with his wife Nuala he travelled to such diverse places as Canada and Peru. Golf, bridge and quizzes were other topics that occupied a mind which was always interested in learning more. Sadly, after a long illness, Jarlath died on 4 October 2006 aged 74 years.

Sean O'Neill

> *Sean O'Neill changed all accepted concepts and convictions in the dying seasons of the sixties – he became the sensitive probing point of balance – the power finish coming from the speed of his reflexes, his deadly anticipation and his way of sizing up an opening, to turn it into a goal or point.*
>
> Raymond Smith, *The Football Immortals*

Sean O'Neill was a footballing genius. There was nothing he could not achieve. He was a superb fielder and excellent passer of a ball. He could score from any angle with either foot. His bodyswerve was particularly deceptive. As a goalscorer he really was unrivalled. He was a member of Down's first provincial winning minor team in 1958 and played his first senior championship game against Tyrone in the semi-final of the provincial championship in 1959. His last championship game was against Derry in the 1975 Ulster final. He played in 16 Ulster finals including the 1974 replay against Donegal. During the course of his career he also won a record number of eight Railway Cup medals as well as two Sigerson Cup medals with Queen's University. He obtained All-Star awards in 1971 and 1972. In addition he managed Ulster between 1976 and 1981 and was selected on both the Team of the Century and the Team of the Millennium. He managed Down to their first All-Ireland minor title in 1977. The Newry Mitchel's stalwart won four Down championship medals.

Sean O'Neill is one of the all-time greats of Gaelic football. Though he played right half forward at the start of his career he is probably best known for the originality he brought to the full forward position with the 1968 side. Sean who is a solicitor in Belfast has been active in cross community work with the Northern Ireland Sports Council.

PADDY DOHERTY

> *If Paddy Doherty is not the greatest forward in Ireland I will do "The Hucklebuck" on top of the Hogan Stand.*
>
> Brendan Bowyer, Irish showband singer, after one of Paddy's masterly displays in Croke Park.

Paddy was an outstanding forward with a naturally instinctive flair for scoring wonderful points both from frees and play. He was the best penalty taker that I have ever seen. In addition he could send very accurate pinpoint passes with his famous left foot. In 44 championship games he amassed the phenomenal total of 15 goals and 158 points. He played for Down minors in 1951 and 1952 before making his initial appearance with the county junior side in 1953. His first senior championship county game was against Derry in 1954. An incredible 17 years later the Ballykinlar clubman made his last appearance in a championship match when he appeared as a substitute against Galway in the 1971 All-Ireland semi-final.

One of the most naturally gifted players ever in Gaelic football, Paddy set scoring records which endured until modern times. He also played professional soccer for Lincoln City in England and Ballyclare Comrades in the Irish League before concentrating once more on his Gaelic career. He managed the Down senior side for a spell in the 1970s. A keen horseracing fan Paddy also served as an SDLP Councillor for many years. A bricklayer by trade, he is now retired and living in Castlewellan.

TONY HADDEN

> *Just after two minutes the roving Tony Hadden received the ball from George Lavery and from 40 yards out he kicked beautifully over the bar to give Down the first score. His speed and lightning thrusts up the middle had Kerry in a tangle and left corner back Tim "Tiger" Lyons could never keep track of his activities.*
>
> Armagh Observer report on 1960 All-Ireland final

Tony Hadden was a very accomplished footballer and could play anywhere from midfield up. A brilliant fielder with a quick turn of speed he was always good for a score. When our midfield was experiencing difficulty Tony was the one asked to act as a third roving midfielder. Another different dimension to his play was his ability to fist the ball over the bar from long range. Fisted points from Tony from 25 yards or more were commonplace. Though naturally left footed he also cultivated his right to devastating effect.

His first championship game as a senior was against Armagh as a midfielder in 1956 and his last major championship outing was in the 1963 All-Ireland semi-final against Dublin. He started his county career as a minor in 1954 before graduating to the junior side in 1955. Tony won two championship medals with Newry Shamrocks in 1956 and 1961, being captain in the former year.

Tony was also a gifted soccer player. For many years he was regional sales manager for Bass Charrington and sales director for Tennents. The man with the distinctive crewcut was also part of Sean O'Neill's minor management team of 1977 and Joe Lennon's senior management team of 1980–82. Tony is now retired and living in Newry.

PATSY O'HAGAN

Patsy O'Hagan raced for a ball that seemed to be going right of the post and, from the end line, sent a curving, rasping and almost incredible shot into the Galway net.

"Fear Ciuin" *Sunday Press* 1959 after Down's Wembley Tournament victory over Galway

Patsy O'Hagan was the most versatile player on our team. He could field, pass and score in equal measure. In one National League semi-final he filled five positions – all with distinction. History will record that Patsy was the first Irishman to score a hat trick on the famed soccer pitch! Indeed his Wembley exploits in 1959 and 1960 attracted soccer scouts, including one from Chelsea FC, but Patsy decided to stay with Gaelic football.

Patsy played at centre half forward for St Colman's College in the 1957 All-Ireland colleges' semi-final. He made his county debut with the Mourne minors in 1956 and in 1958 he played in both the junior and senior provincial championships, winning a medal in the former. His last important game was the 1966 All-Ireland semi-final against Meath. During the course of his county career he played in every position except goalkeeper. He began his club career with Cabra. When they amalgamated with Clonduff in 1959 Patsy joined his fellow parishioner Kevin Mussen on his new team. Incidentally both parish clubs had opposed each other in the 1957 Down senior final that Clonduff won.

A quantity surveyor by profession Patsy moved to Galway in the 1970s. His son Brendan featured on Galway underage teams and his grandson Danny

Cummins is a current member of the Galway senior football panel. Sadly Patsy died unexpectedly on 21 March 2010.

BRIAN (BREEN) MORGAN

> *The Kingdom's tradition never bothered us; once we got to Croke Park, reputations counted for nothing. We raised our game to suit the challenge – and it was very hard to stop us.*
>
> Brian Morgan in an interview with Fabian Boyle in *Down's Unsung Hero*

Despite his small stature and light build, Brian Morgan was often described as the iron or rubber man of our team. No matter how hard the tackles or how difficult the opponent; Brian kept coming back for more. He had a great football brain and always could anticipate what was going to happen. As well as that he took some great points and even more opportunist goals. He made his debut for the county minors in 1953. In 1954 he not only captained the minor side from midfield but played for the juniors and seniors as well. He made his senior championship debut in 1956. The curtain was drawn on his illustrious career nine years later when, along with his nephew Raymond Morgan, he was a substitute on the Down team that were beaten by Galway in the 1965 All-Ireland semi-final. His oldest brother Dan was a member of many Down senior sides between 1935 and 1943.

His name was a byword for passion and commitment on the field. The regard in which he is still held in Down was reflected by the decision of Club Down to christen their top honour as "The Breen Morgan Spirit of Down Award". Regrettably Annaclone's greatest son, who was boss of his own steel erecting business, died in February 2004 after a relatively short illness. He was the first of the team to do so.

KIERAN DENVIR

Kieran was a beautifully balanced skilful footballer. He was probably past his peak in 1960 but still good enough to be a worthy addition to both the 1960 and 1961 panels. He was a member of the St Malachy's College, Belfast, team that reached the MacRory Cup final in 1949. In the 1950s he played in seven successive Sigerson Cup finals including the 1954/55 replay. He was on the winning team on four occasions and captained the 1956 winning combination. Kieran played his first senior championship game for Down against Derry in 1953 at right half forward. Incidentally his UCD club mate P.J. McElroy made his senior Down championship debut on the same day. His last major championship senior start for Down was in the 1960 All-Ireland semi-final replay against Offaly. In the All-Ireland final he came on as a substitute for Joe Lennon. During his club playing career Kieran fielded with UCD, Kilclief, Ballina and Greencastle.

A veterinary surgeon by profession, Kieran is now retired and living in Kilkeel.

P.J. McElroy

P.J. was a great fielder and very difficult to dispossess. Only a serious injury prevented him from making a realistic claim to be a member of the starting 15 for the 1960 final. P.J., who played minor for Down in 1950 and won MacRory Cup medals with Saint Colman's in 1949 and 1950, made his senior championship debut in 1953 before his travels working in Wales with the Forestry Commission prevented him from being regularly available. Having returned to Ireland on a permanent basis he came on as a substitute in the 1959 All-Ireland semi-final against Galway. Though he played in the 1963 league final P.J.'s last championship game in the red and black was the 1962 Ulster final against Cavan. During the course of his club career he played for Castlewellan, UCD, Leitrim and Glenn. As well as being on our winning Glenn championship sides, he also won a county championship with Castlewellan in 1950 as well as a Sigerson Cup medal with UCD in 1954.

P.J. who was employed as a forestry official with the Department of Agriculture is now retired and living in Newcastle. When P.J. joined the Glenn club he became a regular visitor to our house. After completing his week's work in Antrim, where he was stationed at the time, he used to arrive at Donacloney on his motor bicycle on a Saturday and stay with us until Monday morning. The first words which the jovial man uttered on his arrival were: "Show me the *Armagh Observer* to see how good I was last Sunday. Do you know what? I went up so high there was snow on my hands when I came down with the ball!"

Every Monday morning, while the rest of us were in bed, Dad got up, boiled two eggs and made a bowl of porridge for him. P.J. was always a great character.

Eamon Clements

Eamon was a very competent goalkeeper who first came to the notice of the selectors when he used to play with us in our practice games at his home club in Banbridge. The outstanding form of Eddie McKay meant that he rarely got an opportunity to play for Down. Still, he won two Ulster senior championships, one All-Ireland and one National League. Eamon served his apprenticeship with the well known Hendron Brothers engineering firm in Belfast. The outfield club player, who was a top goal scorer and talented soccer player, emigrated in 1963 to Pittsburgh in the United States and was lost to Gaelic football. Tragically he was killed in a traffic accident in the States in February 1973 at the age of 33.

John Haughian

John was a very promising defender who emigrated at the peak of his career, just after he had been a very able substitute in the 1960 and 1961 successes.

He was man of the match in the 1958 All-Ireland minor semi-final against Dublin. Having missed out on further glory for Down, John returned to live in Rostrevor in the early seventies. At club level he played with Longstone and Rostrevor with whom he won a championship medal in 1976. He will be forever remembered as the man whose drainpipe trousers inspired Maurice Hayes to introduce tracksuits into Gaelic football! (See Chapter 10 for further explanation.) An uncle of the late great Ambrose Rodgers, the retired builder now lives in Killowen outside Rostrevor.

Pat Fitzsimons

Pat Fitzsimons was on that historic provincial winning Down minor team of 1958. Along with the magnificent Sean O'Neill, whom he partnered at centrefield, Pat played so brilliantly through that campaign that he was drafted into the senior squad a year later. O'Neill, John Haughian and Pat were the only three members of that successful minor team to actually make the team sheets for the All-Irelands of 1960 and 1961. Pat who owned a civil engineering business played his club football with Kilclief.

John Smith

John Smith was a tremendous fielder of the ball. His long clearances always quickly turned defence into attack. In 1956 he played for the county minor team. His displays on the Down 1961 junior side were so impressive that he was immediately drafted into the senior panel for the Ulster championship. He took over at left half back and remained there throughout the whole campaign. As a result he won one All-Ireland, one league and two Ulster championship medals. In a relatively short intercounty career his last major game in a Down jersey was the 1963 All-Ireland semi-final against Dublin.

A successful building contractor, the Ballykinlar clubman is now retired and lives near Downpatrick.

Eamon Lundy

Eamon was a very strong high fielder. When he came on as a substitute the Dromara native always played very well. He was the type of dedicated player who always seemed to lose out on the big occasion because the rivals for his position were so good. In the Ulster senior final of 1960 he came on as a sub for Joe Lennon. His total commitment to Down ensured that he won two senior All-Ireland, one league and three Ulster championship medals as well as a provincial junior medal.

When I think of Eamon I always recall an amusing incident that happened to him on one of our trips to play at Wembley. It was a lovely sunny day and we went to see Petticoat Lane, which has a famous fashion and clothing market in east London. Eamon spotted a pair of very fashionable trousers at a very reasonable cost. We encouraged him to haggle and bargain for a lower price. Eamon could not believe his luck when the seller agreed to a vastly reduced price. When he came back he could not wait to show off his bargain purchase to family and friends alike. Imagine his surprise and embarrassment when he opened the parcel. Inside there was not London's most up market trousers but instead a pair of boy's pants!

A former building contractor he is now retired and living in Newcastle where his sons play for the local Bryansford Club.

Gerry McCashin

Gerry was a very competent goalkeeper who was unfortunate to be understudy to the splendid Eddie McKay in 1961 and 1962. His most significant appearance for Down was when he replaced the injured McKay midway through the first half of the 1962 Ulster final. Even though his intercounty career was very short he was, nevertheless, a deserved recipient of one All-Ireland, one league and one Ulster championship medal. He played his club football with Ballykinlar. A bricklayer by trade Gerry was also renowned for his love of cricket.

One must also mention the many panel members who did not make the first 15 or indeed the listed substitutes bench in either 1960 or 1961. These players deserve more praise than the rest of us because they did the same work but did not receive the same national acclaim either on the field of play or in the media.

Thus the people of Down will never forget men such as John McAuley, Eddie Burns, Seamus Kennedy and James Fitzpatrick who did such trojan work in those glorious years.

To complete properly the list of stars of Down's great achievements one must also pay due tribute to our three-man management team of Barney Carr, Brian Denvir and Maurice Hayes. Each, individually and collectively, made a massive contribution to the team's success.

Though the role of GAA team manager was not really popularised until the advent of Kevin Heffernan and Mick O'Dwyer in the seventies, Down's Barney Carr was, in actual fact, the first man to be given that defined position. Between 1959 and 1963 Barney was in charge of the Mourne men and he will always be intimately and justifiably associated with those glorious years of 1960 and 1961. He was also an outstanding player in his younger days and played for the county side between 1944 and 1952, captaining them on many occasions. When Down won the McKenna Cup for the first time in 1944, Barney was the side's talismanic centre half forward. In addition he won three county senior championship titles with Warrenpoint in 1943, 1948 and 1953. He was also a freelance Gaelic games journalist of the highest calibre. His weekly feature articles in the *Frontier Sentinel* were always looked forward to with keen anticipation. The former employee of the Education and Library Board is now retired and living in his native Warrenpoint.

Brian Denvir served on the management team during all the years Barney was in charge. When the Warrenpoint man stepped down Brian took up the managerial reins for several years before retiring. His father, James, was Down's first county chairman in 1903 and his brother Kieran, of course, was very much part of our successes. He was one of the best dual players ever to play for the county. From 1940 to 1956 he played for the hurlers. In the midst of that long hurling career he also played eight years for the county footballers between 1943 and 1951. He represented Ulster hurlers in the Railway Cup on many occasions, including the famous time that they defeated a star-studded Leinster team in the 1945 semi-final. The stylish high fielding Kilclief farmer's proudest football-playing moment was when he lined out at midfield in the 1944 McKenna Cup success. Brian, who also won numerous hurling league and championship medals at club level, died in February 2000.

10

Dr Maurice Hayes
The Visionary

It must be said that the All-Ireland successes of the Down team in the 1960s was not just due to the fantastic performances of the players of that era. It was, in my opinion, the ultimate reward for all the work and organisation undertaken by so many people since Down won the 1946 All-Ireland junior football final. One man, nevertheless, did more in that interim period to channel all the necessary and relevant factors into an All-Ireland match-winning formula. That person was Maurice Hayes.

For 12 years he co-ordinated a variety of team building strands. This involved a revision of league structures, the overseeing of club and college football developments, the introduction of proper training methods and the application of appropriate team tactics on the field of play. The implementation of best practice, confidence building strategies, the cultivation of a team ethic and the appointment of suitable personnel at all levels were other key issues, which he addressed both regularly and competently. Underpinning all of these was an emphasis on proper communication skills between all stakeholders, including the media. Backed up by a selection of ideal people Maurice masterminded all the facets of a successful team into a cohesive county team unit. By early 1958 all these elements were in place for a successful assault on the All-Ireland senior football championship.

Maurice Hayes was born in Killough on the east coast of county Down in 1927. His father was a Waterford bank official who had served in World War I in Mesopotamia. His mother was a native of Listowel in County Kerry. After working in Wynnes Hotel in Dublin she moved to Killough to take up employment.

When his father returned from army duties in 1920 he moved to County Down where he joined the petty sessions court service. He finished his working career as Town Clerk of Downpatrick Urban District Council. Maurice went to secondary school in St Patrick's De La Salle High School in Downpatrick before entering Queen's University to study English. After graduating with a PhD in

English he returned to teach in his old alma mater. As hurling was his first love he played for the Down based Kilclief club which then participated in the south Antrim league. He won numerous junior and senior championships with Kilclief and represented Down on many occasions.

His first administrative position was as an officer of the east Down camogie board in 1946. 1947 was to provide the teenager with his first real insight into the political mechanism of the GAA. Two fellow east Down men, Brian Denvir and Alfie Oakes, had been selected as delegates to the annual congress of the GAA in Dublin. However Brian was unable to attend and he asked Maurice to replace him. This congress has gone down in GAA folklore for the impassioned speech by Canon Michael Hamilton of Clare who persuaded delegates to vote for the 1947 All-Ireland football final to be played in New York.

Maurice then became secretary of the east Down football board in 1948 and by the time of the 1950 Down county GAA convention he was ready to make his first major contribution to the development of Down football. His introductory public pronouncement was based on his personal observations that previous to the 1950s there had always been excellent footballers in Down. The 1940s, especially, had produced a plethora of fine footballers including the 1946 All-Ireland junior winners as well as Ulster Railway Cup star goalkeeper John O'Hare.

Up to that time the whole county board selected the county team. Maurice now observed that this system had little to recommend it. There was a lot of jockeying by each member of this unwieldy selection committee to get his own man on the team. Many good players were also kept off the senior championship team deliberately so that they would be available for the junior championship team the following year.

Thanks to Maurice's promptings and to redress this inherent imbalance, a motion was passed at the 1950 convention to set up a county football selection committee of not less than five and not more than seven selectors. Many clubs did not accept the spirit of this motion in its totality and by 1955 the county team was again selected by the whole committee of the county board.

One of Maurice Hayes' greatest achievements was the setting up of the All County League in 1950. He acted as secretary to this body as well as being assistant county secretary to Peadar Barry who had been county secretary since 1927. A feature of this new system was that a yearly fixture list was drawn up in January of each year and strictly adhered to. The advantage of the All County League format was that it got teams from the two GAA strongholds – east Down and south Down – playing against each other. The new system, which consisted of the county's top ten sides, helped to break down divisional barriers and greatly assisted the development of a new, united county team spirit.

Another exciting development helped to encourage Maurice in his future team planning. At this time two Newry secondary schools – St Colman's College and Abbey CBS – were making outstanding progress in colleges' football. Both of them had long-established GAA traditions. First of all St Colman's had won the MacRory Cup in 1949 and 1950, as had the Abbey in 1954. Later, in the fifties, St Colman's notched two senior colleges' titles in 1957 and 1958. Not to be outdone, Abbey again secured another Ulster senior colleges' title in 1959. All of these sides would bring their own special football graduates to the senior county team.

Maurice Hayes would never look upon himself as a supreme organiser or overall co-ordinator of anything simply because that is not the nature of his personality. He does not believe in the cult of the individual. Everything that he did was to promote the importance of a team ethic in all structures within the county. He would look upon himself as more of a facilitator, a man who could persuade others to contribute to the common good. In this regard, the role of the Down county chairman at that time was vital. George Tinnelly from Rostrevor was the chairman from 1949 to 1966. George always enjoyed the highest confidence of all groups within the county. He furthered the consistent policy of team building and he fostered the growth of a fine team spirit not only among players but also between selectors, trainers, officials and anyone associated with the county team. In tandem with this the very efficient underage co-ordinator, Fr Joseph Pettit, and his committee did outstanding work at minor level. As a result a large reservoir of skilful players were regularly coming on stream for county senior availability.

From a club structure perspective another groundbreaking plan was the initiation of the Winter Barony League in the middle fifties. Hayes was also the driving force behind its implementation. All senior and junior clubs within a barony (a traditional historical and geographical division which covered several parishes) amalgamated to form one team. Five or six baronies usually entered a team in this novel competition. This league had a three-fold impact. First of all, it allowed young players to play regular Gaelic football when hitherto, at this time of year, soccer and rugby were the only alternative playing outlets. Second, this imaginative system appealed greatly to spectators and players alike. The third characteristic, however, was the most important of all. In the All County League teams, the best players, regardless of their natural positions, played at midfield. So when you selected the county team you had 15 midfielders who did not know how to play anywhere else. This competition allowed players to play in their best positions. Players from junior clubs who up to now had been largely ignored could now make realistic claims, if they were good enough, for a place on the senior county team.

By 1957, despite various setbacks through emigration, injury, retirements, suspensions and defections, the major parts of a successful Down football jigsaw were now in place. Hayes has often publicly stated that the return of Paddy Doherty, Tony Hadden and myself (all from soccer suspensions) was a wonderful injection as they prepared for the 1958 Ulster championship. It was in unusual circumstances, however, that Maurice Hayes' most famous conclusion was reached. After the disastrous display against Donegal in the 1957 Ulster championship – I could not be blamed as I did not get a lift! – Maurice and Barney Carr met the night after the game. For over four hours they debated at length about the state of Down football. They concluded that if Down were to achieve ultimate success it would not be achieved miraculously overnight. Despite overt evidence to the contrary, they were absolutely convinced that they were on the right tracks. The Holy Grail would only be secured by the implementation of a long-term team plan that would take four or five years to implement and they were determined to see it through.

At the beginning of 1958 Maurice outlined the prototype of his plan to the players:

In the first year we will get to the Ulster final and get beaten (1958). In the second year we will win the Ulster title and lose the All-Ireland semi-final (1959). The third year will see us reaching the All-Ireland final but we will be defeated (1960). The next year we will win the All-Ireland (1961).

What helped Maurice to come to this conclusion was another imaginative initiative that he had introduced. Having become county secretary in 1956, as well as being Down's central council representative, opened up avenues at GAA headquarters. Consequently he formed a very happy working relationship with GAA General Secretary Padraig O'Caoimh. Maurice had now decided that Down should play challenge games outside Ulster. Every effort was made to get games against the best possible opposition but particularly with sides that had different playing styles. Those counties which we subsequently played have no idea as to their intrinsic contribution to Down's eventual success. Counties like Mayo, Carlow, Louth, Dublin and Meath were of immense help to us. Maurice's contacts with the general secretary and other central council representatives were used to arrange these challenge games that were designed to develop our team to its full potential.

Having created the thinking behind the new administrative structures and team planning strategies Hayes was also centrally involved in the popularisation of these ideas in GAA circles. Other talented young men like himself had risen to the forefront of Gaelic games at the same time. People like Paddy O'Donoghue and Barney Carr were foremost amongst them.

O'Donoghue, who subsequently became chairman of the county board as well as an SDLP assemblyman, penned the same modernist thinking in his GAA column in *The Mourne Observer*. Paddy constantly opined that there should be a more coherent team management system. The versatile and ubiquitous Barney Carr was a regular propagandist of the same philosophy from 1957 onwards in *The Frontier Sentinel*. In addition, these articles of Barney's really represented the combined thinking of himself, Maurice and Brian Denvir, all three of whom were destined to lead us to the promised land. The influential eloquence of Canon Hamilton had not been forgotten, especially by the 1947 east Down congress delegate! Earlier in the same paper, in 1953, and masquerading under the name "Fear na Mourna" Barney said the time had come for a manager alone to be in charge of a county team. That really was revolutionary thinking at the time.

While this trio of wise men were plotting and planning their future strategies, the vast majority of the other county board members kept their distance. I believe that some of them thought that Maurice and company were foolish idealists and they were not prepared to take any flak if things went wrong. Be that as it may, we were all thoroughly impressed with Maurice's long-term plan when he submitted it to us. He also kept telling us that we had the talent to win the All-Ireland. This built up our confidence immensely. When it comes to the present buzz phrase "player welfare" he was away ahead of his time. He once wrote:

> *We paid special attention to how players were treated. We were determined to bring together a squad of good players, set up a good organisation for them and then encourage them to train hard. We said to them: "Commit yourselves, you stick by us and we will stick by you. If you are hurt we will bring you to hospital. If you have trouble getting off work we will see to that also."*

The nett result of this was that there was a great sense of solidarity and unity of purpose in our training camp. The message from 1958 onwards about our future timetable was both prophetic in its outcome and exceptionally well planned and progressive in its intent. Psychologically it made us feel totally confident in our ability whilst still respecting the talent and determination of other counties to make life difficult for us on the playing fields. Being told that we were good enough to win an All-Ireland made all of us absolutely determined to win every game that we played in.

When we achieved our aim a year ahead of target in 1960 was not Maurice just a little cautious in his forecast? No is the answer. His reasoned response to this question is entirely logical. We had drawn the 1960 All-Ireland semi-final against Offaly. The extra game, the replay, was the same as another tough championship match in the concluding stages of the All-Ireland series. This fast-forwarded our 1961 intended win to the reality of a 1960 triumph.

Before the 1959 Ulster senior championship began two of our key players made themselves available again for senior duty. Joe Lennon who had worked abroad in the Persian Gulf was now a meteorologist based in England. P.J. McElroy who had been working with the forestry commission in Wales had now returned home to play with Dan and myself on the Glenn club team. Again the stamp of Maurice Hayes was on P.J.'s decision to return. In 1956 he had written to him and told him to keep training, as he believed the team was going somewhere and that he would have a central role to play.

In the same year Kevin Mussen had told Hayes that a younger brother of Kevin O'Neill's was the best young footballer he had ever seen. When Maurice saw the youngster playing for the Abbey CBS he came home excited that another exceptional talent would soon graduate to senior ranks. That young player was of course the multi-talented Sean O'Neill. During this period also Paddy Doherty was occasionally working in England. Both Lennon and Doherty had to be flown home for games. The management team always believed that all of the county's best footballers should be available at all times, even challenge matches. As the county board were operating on a shoestring budget this, initially, was not possible. On one occasion Hayes made a rather flippant comment that they could not afford to bring home these two English-based players any longer. The next morning, after this casual comment, two fanatical but very loyal Down supporters marched into Maurice's office in Downpatrick. (He had resigned his teaching post in 1954 to take up the position of Town Clerk.) One of them, my father Briney, lambasted Maurice for his remarks.

"Here is a £50 note to cover the extra travelling expenses for this game," he said.

Charlie Carr from Warrenpoint, who was with my father, said that he would pay the flight expenses for the next game. Both Charlie and my father continued with this alternating arrangement until the two men could return to Ireland on a permanent basis.

At the beginning of 1959 the county board finally decided to appoint a three-man selection committee to be totally in charge of the county team. Barney Carr would be the manager and Brian Denvir and Maurice Hayes would be his selectors. Barney would be in charge of tactics. Maurice was the chief scout who would go to see potential opposition teams playing and assess their strengths and weaknesses. The sort of question that occupied his mind was how does one deal with an outstanding midfielder like Mick O'Connell. The players then teased out the implications of the question. In this case they came to the conclusion that Joe Lennon or Jarlath Carey, if required, would box the ball away from O'Connell. Our half forward line would know this so they would always be ready to race in and get possession of the broken ball. If the midfielders were still experiencing difficulty Tony Hadden would roam outfield and act as a third midfielder. How to counteract the strength and height of Offaly's sterling full back Greg Hughes was another poser. That was why P.J. McElroy, normally an outfield player, was placed at full forward to negate Hughes' likely dominance in that sector in the 1961 final.

Hayes was always alert as to how the game could be improved in any area, no matter how trivial it may have appeared initially. When he watched John Haughian take almost four minutes to remove his drainpipe trousers before he could enter the field of play as a substitute in an important match, he was not impressed. A game could be lost in such circumstances, he reckoned. So next day Maurice began the process of buying tracksuits for all Down sides. They were the first Gaelic county team to have such modern gear. John Haughian should be canonised for this innovation and Maurice should receive royalties for life!

After our 1960 success Maurice had another brainwave. He and Brian Denvir always wore black togs when they were both playing in the forward line for Kilclief hurlers. This helped them to spot each other, especially when they were stooping down to pick up the sliotar. Maurice reasoned that if the Down football team wore black togs it would considerably speed up their natural combination style of play. In addition it gave the whole side a separate identity in the fashion stakes. Thus black togs were purchased and every Down side have worn them ever since.

There is one funny story that I distinctly remember about Down wearing black togs in the 1961 All-Ireland semi-final against Kerry. After Down had totally outclassed Kerry a disgruntled and well known Catholic theologian priest came over to Maurice and loudly and publicly accused him of introducing "soccerising" tendencies to Gaelic games. The unflappable Maurice did not bat an eyelid. He merely told the rest of us he did not see any point in discussing, with the biased clerical Kerry supporter, the merits of peripheral vision, especially at ground level!

When Down won the 1960 All-Ireland, Maurice Hayes did not travel homewards to take part in the team celebrations. His job was done so he left the revelry to others. Instead, the modest Maurice retired for the remainder of the week to enjoy Listowel Races and visit his mother's maternal home place. Shortly after our own festivities took a short break, during that same week, Sean O'Neill, Tony Hadden and myself, amongst others, also went down to Kerry and joined Maurice at the races. We had a right royal time and we were warmly received by hundreds of Kingdom supporters. One night six or seven of the Kerry players – Tom Long, Seamus Murphy and Paudie Sheehy were among them – invited us out to dinner. They very generously paid for our meals from their own personal resources. Despite playing so determinedly against each other a few days earlier, both sets of players had tremendous mutual respect.

On the Friday night we were the guests of the legendary playwright and short story writer Bryan McMahon. Bryan was a great GAA man and his son Gary had played for Kerry against us in the final. It was fascinating to listen to the two literary intellectuals Bryan and Maurice (Maurice was equally gifted in this department) along with several of the players from both teams discussing not football but the merits and demerits of certain aspects of Irish drama! Then Bryan paused for a moment and suddenly started to chuckle to himself as he sat in the corner of the room. Just as quickly he resumed his storytelling in his own inimitable way. He recalled being at the Abbey Theatre in Dublin the previous week and a fierce argument raged amongst the acting fraternity at the end of the night's proceedings. This was not a literary dispute but a serious conversation about the respective pros and cons of the current Kerry and Down Gaelic football teams! Those two stories highlight for me the massive appeal that exists for both Gaelic games and Irish literature in the Irish psyche.

Pressure of work forced Maurice to step down as county secretary in October 1964. T.P. Murphy was eventually appointed to succeed him with Maurice acting as his assistant for 1965. Furthermore, when he was not re-elected as Down's central council delegate he bowed out entirely from GAA administration. He had given 17 years of dedicated and wonderful service to the GAA in his native county. Since then he has continued to support Down as an ordinary supporter. No-one in Down, however, will ever forget his extraordinary contribution to our historic success.

Maurice Hayes has had a distinguished career as a public servant. From 1954 to 1973 he was Town Clerk in Downpatrick. He was also a former Northern Ireland Ombudsman, Boundary Commissioner and Permanent Secretary of the Department of Health and Social Services. In the 1973 Power Sharing Executive he was assistant to Sir Kenneth Bloomfield. He was also Chairman of the Community Relations Council, Chairman of the National Forum on Europe as well as being a member of the Commission on Police Reform. This led to the formation of the PSNI in Northern Ireland. He is justifiably proud of the fact that he was responsible for creating the duties and responsibilities of the role of Police Ombudsman. The first ombudsman, Mrs Nuala O'Loan, has praised his efforts in this regard. The multi-talented Down man is also a prolific writer, having written several books and numerous articles on a host of topical subjects. One of these publications, *Sweet Killough, Let Go Your Anchor*, is a particularly well-written and lyrical memoir.

Since 1992 he has been a regular contributor on current affairs in the *Irish Independent*. He has also served as a director of Independent News and Media PLC as well as being a member of various other public and private bodies. He was European Person of the Year in 2003. From 1997 to 2007 he was a Taoiseach's nominee in Seanad Éireann. His insightful contributions to a variety of Seanad subjects added greatly to the standard of debate in the Upper House of the Oireachtas.

After Down had won their first Ulster senior championship title in 1959 and their subsequent defeat in the All-Ireland semi-final against Galway, Maurice Hayes penned the following sentiments in that year's *Cuchulainn Annual*.

> The present Down team is young, average age 23, and will not reach its peak for some time yet. The selectors set out to win an Ulster championship this year and that object has been accomplished. The team is a two year old and like all two year olds is rather unpredictable. With the maintenance of the present rate of progress and with the experience gained from meeting top class teams there is no reason why consistency should not be attained and further honours garnered within the next two seasons.

Those prophetic words heralded the imminent arrival of two All-Ireland senior football titles for Down in those very same years. No one did more to effect this than Maurice Hayes – sweet Killough's most famous son. All of us in Down are eternally grateful that he turned our dreams into a wondrous reality.

11

My Clubs – Glenn and Tullylish

When my cousin Seamus brought me to Glenn in 1954 he introduced me to a parish steeped in a love for the GAA. That parish, Donaghmore, has a population of over 1000 people and is situated just north of Newry near the Armagh county border.

After I joined Glenn I had a dream start to my club career. Before the last game of the season we were leading Castlewellan by two points in the All County League. To make matters more interesting the top two teams faced each other in that game. We only required a draw to ensure our first senior league title. In an exciting first half we played very well and led at the interval by 1-3 to 0-2. Shortly after the restart we scored another goal and an easy victory seemed assured. However, Castlewellan came storming back to snatch a draw just before the final whistle. Nevertheless the day belonged to Glenn. After many years of striving they had won their first senior league. It was a very proud day for my cousin Seamus McCartan who captained the side. In addition, my other McCartan cousins, Fr Daniel, Gervase and Dominic, were also on the team. I played at right corner forward and, just a few weeks after my 17th birthday, I had won my first club medal.

On the following Sunday night, in the AOH hall in Glenn, the whole parish of Donaghmore assembled for a presentation céilí. The county chairman, George Tinnelly, presented us with our medals. That was the night I first realised the importance of a local community spirit and how success achieved by the people they knew meant so much to the parishioners.

For the next four years the club made steady progress and in 1958 we again won the senior league. It was, however, 1959 before we made any significant championship advancement. In that season we played Newry Mitchel's in the opening round of the county championship. A thrilling hard-fought game followed with the issue in doubt right up to the final whistle. In the end we won by the narrowest of margins.

The next round saw us pitted against Annaclone and the mighty atom Brian Morgan. The traditionally fierce rivalry between the two teams was exemplified by another tough contest. At half time we were comfortably ahead but Annaclone made a fantastic comeback. With two minutes remaining we were only leading by a point. Then hesitancy in our defence allowed the ever-alert Morgan to pounce for an opportunist goal to put them two points in front. Soon afterwards young Tom Maguire grabbed the ball at centre field and soloed upfield before parting the ball to one of our forwards who hammered it to the net. I was relieved to hear the final whistle sound moments later to signal another slender victory for us.

In the semi-final we met an experienced Clonduff side that included my county teammates Kevin Mussen and Patsy O'Hagan. Patsy scored a brilliant goal that day and we were lucky to escape with a draw although we had led by four points as the game neared its end. Even though we had a player sent off after only ten minutes in the replay, we played well and emerged victorious to meet Rostrevor in the final. At last we had broken our semi-final hoodoo and all of us were looking forward to our first county final.

The final was played in driving rain, aided by a gale force wind. Rostrevor, surprisingly, elected to play against the elements in the first half. We took full advantage of this and by half time we were leading by 3-3 to 0-3. With victory in sight our defence played heroically during that second period. In the process they restricted Rostrevor to two points from frees while we added another. Thus the final score read Glenn 3-4, Rostrevor 0-5. My brother Dan, who had also joined Glenn, had a great game at centre half back and our captain Aidan Conlon, Gerry Bagnall and goalkeeper Sean Gallagher ably supported him. Mick Jennings and I managed to dominate the midfield sector, while Seamus Kennedy, Fr Anthony Davies, Dominic McCartan and Ciaran Conlon starred in the forward line.

It was a day of distinction for all associated with the club particularly Aidan Conlon who was not only team captain but club chairman as well. When we arrived back in Newry, Fr Davies and Aidan Conlon brought the cup to Daisy Hill hospital where one of our greatest supporters, James Murtagh, was recovering from illness. His brother Harry, who was an outstanding motivator, had been our long serving manager. No one had worked so long and so hard to make our victory possible.

After Down won the All-Ireland in 1960 we attended many receptions in various parts of the county. One of the most joyous homecomings was to the Glenn club. Presentations were made to club members such as P.J. McElroy, Dan and myself who were players on the listed winning squad. There were two other

Glenn men who had been reserve panellists on that Down side. It was only fitting that these players, Seamus Kennedy and Fr Fergus Conlon, should also receive souvenir mementoes of that historic occasion.

It was not until three years later, 1962, that the Glenn side reached another county final, this time against Castlewellan. Playing in a torrential downpour did not deter us from performing well. In the first half both Ciaran Conlon and P.J. McElroy at midfield gave sterling displays. Conlon, particularly with his penetrating runs, caused panic in the Castlewellan defence. By the end of the first quarter this midfield dominance allowed us to score five successive points without reply. By half time we were leading by eight points to one. After the magnificent Conlon and Seamus Kennedy scored points apiece shortly after the resumption, we knew the title was ours to lose. When the final whistle sounded we had recorded a convincing 1-12 to 0-4 triumph. Our half back line of Fergus Conlon, Dan McCartan and Dominic McCartan were superb. Our whole forward line performed excellently as a cohesive unit. The young elusive Val Kane and the ever-reliable Seamus Kennedy sublimely flanked me at centre half forward. The full forward line of Gervase McCartan, Mick Jennings and John Lennon certainly played a pivotal role in a magnificent team performance, as did the full back line of Hugh Kennedy, Pat Hurley and Gerry Bagnall. Seamus Kennedy top scored with 1-2 and John Lennon and myself shared eight points between us with Ciaran Conlon also notching two superb scores. This was an especially happy occasion for me as I had the honour of captaining Glenn to their second senior championship title.

The following year we again reached the county final where we faced Downpatrick. Incidentally my brother-in-law, Felix McKnight, who was a GP in Downpatrick at this time, was full back for the East Down side. In a very close contest the game finished in a draw. As a sporting spectacle the replay was essentially destroyed as a fierce crossfield breeze made scoring extremely difficult. Thus defences were generally on top. In the first half we gained a lot of possession but, with the exception of Ciaran Conlon at full forward, our forward line was not as dangerous as usual. Despite our outfield superiority we only led by a point at half time on a 0-4 to 0-3 scoreline. Shortly after half time Downpatrick equalised before Gervase McCartan placed Seamus Kennedy to give us the lead once more. Again Downpatrick levelled with a magnificent point by Gerry McGuigan. At the end of the third quarter the classy Ciaran Conlon soloed up field and passed the ball to Seamus Kennedy who accurately steered the ball over the bar to restore our lead on a 0-6 to 0-5 scoreline. Five minutes from the end my heart was in my mouth as Downpatrick, in a clever movement, worked the ball up field. It was quickly transferred to Downpatrick substitute Eugene Russell who seemed certain to score a decisive winning goal. However, our goalkeeper Sean Gallagher brilliantly smothered his kick and the ball was cleared to safety. Finally, just before the end, Gervase McCartan, who had an excellent match, swung over a terrific point to leave the final score, Glen 0-7, Downpatrick 0-5. I had won my third and what was to prove my last senior county championship medal with my adopted club.

The whole team played well with Fergus Conlon, Hugh Kennedy and P.J. McElroy being particularly effective. Dominic McCartan, who was switched early on to partner me at midfield, had an outstanding game. Gervase McCartan, Joe O'Donnell and Seamus Kennedy were very prominent in the forward line and were always available to take a pass from the ever dangerous Ciaran Conlon. This was one of the best games that I ever played for Glenn. One press report stated that "my fielding was immaculate, my kicking crisp and my every move brought panic into the opposition's ranks". That sounds nice but I keep stressing football is a team game, any individual is only as good as the men around him, and I had great players alongside me that day. During that sequence of success many club members, too numerous to mention, had played their part in Glenn's achievements. One man, however, should be singled out for his extraordinary commitment – our manager, Harry Murtagh. Harry was very quick to spot a weakness in the display of any player. If a defender missed a couple of tackles he was either immediately moved to a different position or replaced. He had an immediate solution for any problem he saw. He had also some very simple and straightforward philosophies. For example: "Do not worry about Paddy Doherty or Sean O'Neill. Just concentrate on the man who is going to give them the ball." His most famous advice to us was when we were trying to retain our county championship title: "If you are the champions you must win the game early. The longer the opposition stay in the game, the better they become."

In 1967 the Glenn club decided to grow potatoes to generate some much needed revenue to develop our football field. A contract was entered into for the sale of the crop to a Newry firm of potato exporters. All went well with the project until harvest time arrived. The weather was so bad that there was no opportunity to dig the crop until November. The last Saturday in November was the appointed day for harvesting. However, there was a low turn out and nothing was done. At a hastily convened meeting it was decided to hire a potato digger and potato gatherers at the field on the following day, a Sunday.

In those days unnecessary physical work on a Sunday was not looked kindly upon by the Church authorities. Nevertheless it was decided that God would really understand Glenn's predicament and so everything went ahead! At 1 p.m. 12 tractors with diggers were ready for duty. To make things even better, over a hundred gatherers were waiting and primed for action. At four o'clock the whole six and a half acres were dug and harvested. When the bags were filled they were taken and loaded on to Mick Murphy's lorry and brought to the factory in Newry. Our treasurer, Gerry McNally, was very happy. That day's phenomenal work epitomised for me what can be achieved with a proper community spirit. No organisation is better at this than the GAA.

Another outstanding feature of the Glenn club was the magnificent contribution made by the local religious order – the Society of African Missionaries which was based in Dromantine in the heart of Donaghmore parish. They had arrived in the area in 1926. From the formation of Glenn GAC in 1931 right up to the present day they have enhanced and enriched both parish and club life. Many of their community, such as Brother Tunney, Tom Maguire, Fr Fergus Conlon and Paddy Hurley, played for Glenn during my playing days. All of them won county championship medals except Brother Tunney who was a member of the 1954 league winning side. Due to their generosity, in the intervening years the Glenn club were afforded the use of their playing fields and training facilities, the availability of their spacious hall for Scór competitions and, in the early days, the luxury of showers.

In the winter of 1967, after I had retired from playing with both Glenn and Down, some members of my native parish club, Tullylish GAC, approached me to see if I would become part of their management team for the coming year.

The first club in the parish was Laurencetown St Patrick's which was founded in 1944. St Patrick's changed its name to Tullylish GAC when they amalgamated with another club in the parish, Geraldines of Gilford, in 1961. The following year the new Tullylish minor team reached the county final but were beaten by Downpatrick. This was a fantastic achievement considering the limited number of players at their disposal. In 1966 the minor side were again in the county final only to be beaten by Castlewellan.

So, when I finally decided to join the club in early 1968, I was happy to take on the dual role of both player and management official. The talent was there and I reckoned that with proper organisation and a collective approach to training and discipline we could go places. As the pitch was near our home and as Tullylish was a junior side, I felt that this would be a good opportunity to try a new challenge.

In addition I owed it to the club that gave me my first taste of football. Also, after we had won our two All-Ireland titles, Tullylish had not forgotten Dan or myself. A double presentation was made to us on behalf of the club and the parish in Gilford Catholic hall in 1962. Paddy MacFlynn, who was then chairman of the Ulster Council, made the presentation. Maurice Hayes, Barney Carr and T.P. Murphy were among a host of dignitaries present, including representatives of the Armagh and Derry county boards.

The response to our training schedule was very good. The team performed so well that we qualified to meet Drumaness in the county junior final of 1968. Played at Newcastle, this game provided a very exciting and entertaining hour of football. We had a nice blend of youth and experience. Despite my original intention not to play anymore I was glad that I had changed my mind. The fact that my brother Dan had also transferred his allegiance to Tullylish made the experience all the more enjoyable. Drumaness took an early lead when Jim Wray goaled. Then county star John Purdy, who had just won an All-Ireland medal with Down, added two superb points for Tullylish. Shortly afterwards John Brown and Dan Purdy also raised two white flags for us. At the end of the first quarter we thus held a slender one-point lead. Playing against the breeze in this period did not prevent Drumaness from regaining the initiative. They were rewarded when Hugh Rice placed their outstanding player Tom McGlennon for an excellent goal. Two minutes later the same player scored a penalty. From this until the interval we reasserted our authority and John Purdy and myself each had points. Just before the short whistle Dan McCartan scored a goal to leave the half time score Tullylish 1-6, Drumaness 3-0.

During the second half the spectators witnessed an enthralling contest as both sides matched each other point for point. Then Drumaness went four points clear with a well-taken goal by Sean Mooney and another point from McGlennon. I will let the local press take up what happened next: "James McCartan then conjured up former moments of glory when he scored two brilliant goals similar to those great scores which were a hallmark of his play when wearing the county jersey."

In between these goals Tom McGlennon and John Purdy exchanged points. During the final minutes Sean Mooney and Sean Murphy of Tullylish swapped points to leave the final score Tullylish 3-10, Drumaness 4-5. I was delighted that we had won our first junior championship title. My rookie managerial involvement had got off to a winning start. More importantly, however, the people of the Tullylish club had something of substance to celebrate.

My Clubs – Glenn and Tullylish

For the next five years I continued in my dual capacity. Indeed, in 1972 I had sole control of the team. Both scenarios appealed to me especially because, during those years, Tullylish experienced the most successful playing period in their history. We annexed division three, division two and division one league titles as well as qualifying for senior league and senior championship status. Three winter leagues were also won.

At that time Bryansford were the dominant team in Down senior club football. One of the highlights of my involvement with Tullylish was to play in the senior championship and to reach the county final in 1971. Though beaten by Bryansford we were not too despondent, as we had come a long way in a very short time.

In January 1974 we turned the tables on that famous Bryansford side. In a league match, in what was considered to be one of the best club matches ever seen, we defeated them by a single point. A subsequent 2-8 to 1-5 victory over Downpatrick meant that we were crowned senior league champions for 1973.

That achievement was the culmination of six years of unprecedented success for Tullylish. Many great club people had done trojan work during that time. In 1968 Fr John Sinnott was club chairman, Plunkett Campbell was team trainer and Leo McEvoy was team captain. Jimmy Larkin, Kevin Murphy, Billy Byrne, Ron Egan, Dan Purdy, Harry Convery, Con Murphy, Greg McCartan, Pat McEvoy and Eamon Burns were just some of the members who played a significant part in that golden era. Indeed Harry, Kevin, Plunkett, Pat, Con, Greg and Eamon are still loyal club supporters.

Having retired several times I now knew it was time to draw the final curtain. I would like to think that I made a contribution to my native place. So it was with a sense of parochial pride that I finished with the club where I had started over 20 years earlier.

Tullylish have provided many fantastic footballers for Down teams over the years. John Purdy won an All-Ireland senior medal in 1968 and my son James did likewise in 1991 and 1994. Dan had also won another one in 1968 to add to the two he and I had won in the early sixties. Joe Byrne won a National League medal in 1983. "Wee" James and my eldest son Brian were members of the Down minor side that won the 1987 All-Ireland title. My brother-in-law, Seamus Murphy, was a member of the Down minor side that beat Armagh in the 1962 Ulster final. Our other sons Charlie Pat, Daniel and Eoin also began their football careers in Tullylish before we moved house in 2002.

Another well known Gael associated with Tullylish is Paddy MacFlynn who has had a very long and distinguished administrative career. He was born in Magherafelt in County Derry in 1918 and became a founder member of the local O'Donovan Rossa club, becoming its first secretary at the tender age of 16 in 1934. Paddy, who was a member of Derry's first county minor team, won a senior club championship medal with Magherafelt in 1942. After representing Derry at Ulster and central council levels he moved to Ballynahinch in Down to take up a teaching post in the late forties. In 1953 he was appointed principal of Gilford Primary School in our parish. As well as that he helped to form the Geraldines GAA club. When the latter amalgamated with Laurencetown he threw himself wholeheartedly into the development of Tullylish GAC.

In quick succession he became chairman of the East Down District Board as well as Down's representative on the Ulster GAA council. From 1961 to 1963 he was chairman of the Ulster Council. Between 1955 and 1973 he was Down county board treasurer. In 1964 he was selected as Down's representative on the central council and he remained in that position until he was chosen as the first president-elect of the Association in 1978. The following year saw him assume the illustrious office of President of the GAA. To date he has given over three quarters of a century of total commitment to every level of Ireland's premier organisation. He epitomises what loyalty to the ideals of the founding fathers of the GAA is all about. The Tullylish club is extremely proud that Paddy MacFlynn, their past chairman and now their esteemed president, has spent well over 50 years in their midst furthering those same ideals. It says much for the man's ability and endurance that a person of almost 92 years of age could make such a valuable contribution to the annual GAA congress, which was held in April 2010 in Newcastle, County Down.

Both Glenn and Tullylish clubs were good to me and for me. Both were rewarding and fulfilling experiences. Silverware of historic proportions, at different levels was attained. More significantly I gained a host of friends for life.

12

The Glory Days Revisited

When 1968 came around there was a complete sea change in my Gaelic football life as far as the county team were concerned. After 12 years as an intercounty player I had to adjust to the trials and tribulations of an ordinary supporter. Unlike my previous "retirement" two years earlier, there was no difficulty in resisting the lure of returning to intercounty football. I was definitely at ease with myself about the finality of my decision. However, initially I found it difficult to watch from the sidelines and remain detached from the action on the playing field. When Down were playing well everything was all right. However, if there was a misplaced pass or slack marking by a Down player, things were different. In the beginning, in such circumstances, I felt that if I were on the field these mistakes could be rectified. This was not arrogance or cockiness on my part, just an inability to cope with what other more experienced supporters had always been able to do. Still, I was lucky that such moments of sheer frustration were limited. Down were now showing distinct and promising signs of a return to the glory days of old.

After that crushing defeat in the 1967 Ulster final, hopes were raised a little when Down beat Kerry in the Gaelic Weekly tournament final in Croke Park in the autumn. In a new National League format they convincingly defeated Antrim and Louth in the opening games. Their good form continued with a fantastic draw with newly crowned All-Ireland champions Meath at Newry. In the replay they produced a scintillating performance to dethrone the Royal County. This qualified them for the divisional semi-final of the league against Dublin. Again they emerged victorious to once again face the Meath men in the divisional final. A brilliant performance by Sean O'Neill and an equally impressive display by young Ray McConville in defence gave the Mourne men a one-point victory. In another superb achievement they overcame Galway by a five-point margin in the league proper semi-final.

For the first time, in five years, they were now in a league final. Before a crowd of 47,000 Down faced Kildare in the decider. Though Kildare made a determined late comeback Down were fully deserving of their eventual 2-14 to

2-11 success. Four of my old All-Ireland winning colleagues were still playing. Dan McCartan was now a very competent full back and captain. Joe Lennon was a very accomplished left half back. Paddy Doherty and Sean O'Neill, at centre half forward and full forward respectively, gave an imposing sense of solidarity to the forward line. Those great veterans dovetailed perfectly with rising stars such as Tom O'Hare, Brendan Sloan and Ray McConville in defence. Colm McAlarney was an exceptional midfielder and Mickey Cole, John Murphy, John Purdy and Peter Rooney were all livewire forwards.

After witnessing the "new" team playing so well, many friends, including my father, wondered was I sorry that I had retired. My answer was an emphatic "No". I had my years of county football triumphs and was eagerly looking forward to a new generation of Down heroes helping the old stagers to another All-Ireland senior football title.

Just a fortnight after the league final, Down met Derry in the first round of the Ulster championship at Ballinascreen. This was a tough bruising encounter often referred to as the Battle of Ballinascreen. Though two players from each side were sent off I always thought that it was not as dirty a game as some sections of the media made it out to be. Mick Higgins, who refereed the contest, was criticised for being too lenient. However, I think he did a fair job in what was, admittedly, a difficult task. From a Down perspective I felt that they were brilliant at stages and the physical aspects of the encounter stood them in good stead for the remainder of the season. A point blank save by Down goalkeeper Danny Kelly from Derry danger man Sean O'Connell in the last quarter was the decisive factor in Down's 1-8 to 1-6 victory.

Another narrow two point success over Donegal in the provincial semi-final meant that the Mourne men would be contesting their 11th successive Ulster final. For the seventh time in that sequence Cavan were once again their opponents. After our heavy defeat to the same opposition the previous year I was hoping for a much better performance. Thanks to points from Paddy Doherty (2), Sean O'Neill (2), Mickey Cole, Colm McAlarney and John Purdy, Down went in at the interval ahead by 0-7 to 0-5.

Shortly after half time Cavan scored two points to bring the sides level. It now appeared that a close, tough match was likely. However, Down suddenly began to play with more authority. After Paddy Doherty pointed from play Down became completely dominant. The unerring Doherty, both from free and play, added a further six points. The excellent John Murphy nonchalantly popped over another two points. In the meantime Cavan had only scored once point since their early scoring burst immediately after the resumption. Near the end Charlie Gallagher scored a consolation goal for the Breffni men. The final score, Down 0-16, Cavan 1-8, did not reflect Down's superiority. Colm McAlarney at midfield was superb. He was ably assisted by Jim Milligan and later by the very impressive John Murphy. Joe Lennon had another terrific game in the half back line. Up front my two former colleagues Sean O'Neill and Paddy Doherty oozed pure class. Their skill, style and supreme accuracy were a joy to behold.

Watching Down prepare for the All-Ireland semi-final made me realise that there was a nucleus of another good side in the making. They were performing with real confidence and no little skill. That game against Connacht champions Galway was a wonderful advertisement for Gaelic football. Galway opened the scoring with a pointed free by John Keenan. For the remainder of the first half Down played splendidly with Sean O'Neill, Colm McAlarney and Mickey Cole particularly outstanding. At half time Down led by 1-5 to 0-3.

After the interval they suffered a couple of crucial blows when Galway got two quick goals. The first occurred when goalkeeper Danny Kelly was harshly adjudged to be behind his own goal line when he caught the ball. The second was as a result of a very dubious penalty. It took a masterclass in all round skilful attacking football to enable the immaculate O'Neill and his fellow enterprising forwards to eventually snatch a 2-10 to 2-8 victory.

Down were now in their third All-Ireland senior football final. An interesting footnote to the match was that it was the first All-Ireland semi-final to be televised live by the BBC. In a team of stars, corner back Tom O'Hare was awarded the Telefís Éireann trophy for man of the match. What made the final more intriguing was the fact that Down once again had to face their old adversaries – the mighty men from the Kingdom of Kerry.

In a repeat of the 1960 final, the Kingdom, like Down, had just four survivors from that historic occasion. They were Mick O'Connell, Mick O'Dwyer, Seamus Murphy and Johnny Culloty. Within 13 seconds of the commencement of the game, Sean O'Neill scored a point from a Jim Milligan pass. Then Milligan punched over another Down point before Mick O'Connell opened Kerry's account with a free.

After six minutes, Sean O'Neill scored one of the most unique goals scored anywhere. When corner forward Peter Rooney had hit the post, about five feet above the crossbar, the onrushing O'Neill managed to stab the rebound into the corner of the net. If a player of lesser quality had scored the shot it may have been put down as a fluke. However, given O'Neill's tremendous reflexes and his instinctive talent for the impossible, most commentators concluded that his goal was the hallmark of a genius. Now playing with supreme confidence, Down continued to attack.

A minute after Paddy Doherty had pointed a free, left half forward John Murphy lobbed the ball into the Kerry goalmouth. Goalkeeper Johnny Culloty appeared to have it covered but the alert O'Neill ran in and palmed the ball right back to the inrushing Murphy who slammed the ball to the net. Thus, within eight minutes Down had established an eight-point advantage. Within the next five minutes Kerry stormed back with three points, two frees from Mick O'Dwyer and an effort from play by Pat Griffin. Brendan Lynch and Paddy Doherty then exchanged scores before Down's corner back Tom O'Hare slotted a 50 over the bar four minutes before the interval. A minute later Doherty fisted another point before O'Hare again scored a 50. When the referee signalled the end of the first half, the scoreline read Down 2-7, Kerry 0-5.

The first half will always be remembered as the day a new Down star on the national stage was born. The young midfielder Colm McAlarney, not only with his superb fetching but also with his galloping strides, made life extremely difficult for a hard-pressed Kerry defence. Another star of that first half was team captain Joe Lennon. His positional sense and accurate passing to better placed colleagues were truly outstanding. Unfortunately, the Aghaderg man had pulled a thigh muscle just before the interval. Courageously, Joe himself made the decision not to resume and Larry Powell replaced him. Larry's promising career had been badly curtailed by injury so it was good to see him come on. However, his long-term injury affected him and he had to come off in the last quarter to be replaced by my brother-in-law, George Glynn.

Sean O'Neill fisted over the first score of the second half before Mick O'Dwyer pointed two frees. Shortly afterwards Doherty and Lynch exchanged points to leave the score 2-9 to 0-8. At this stage Kerry became dominant and they were rewarded with two points from Griffin and a long range point from Mick O'Connell. There were only 12 minutes left and four points between the sides. Everyone, including myself, expected the Kingdom to cut the deficit even further. Peter Rooney then eased our anxiety with a point before Dan McCartan cleverly intercepted a dangerous movement that seemed destined to result in a Kerry goal.

Six minutes from the end Mick O'Dwyer landed a point. Then George Glynn gained possession at midfield and sent a long pass to Paddy Doherty who was fouled. He converted the free himself to increase the margin to five points. Peter Rooney then slotted over a delightful point to make matters safe for the Mourne men. In the dying moments Kerry completed the scoring with a point from D.J. Crowley and a consolation goal from Brendan Lynch, whose 14-yard free hit off Brendan Sloan and landed in the net. When referee Mick Loftus sounded the final whistle Down had won their third All-Ireland title on a scoreline of Down 2-12, Kerry 1-13.

Immediately Croke Park became a scene of red and black as our supporters raced on to the famous stadium. Joe Lennon was carried shoulder high to the victory rostrum in the Hogan Stand. It was a great moment not only for Joe, Dan, Sean and Paddy but also for all of our young players and supporters. Except for the four veterans, the rest of the team was incredibly young. Brendan Sloan, Ray McConville, Colm McAlarney, Mickey Cole, John Murphy and John Purdy were only 20 years of age. Peter Rooney was the babe of the side, just a month short of his 19th birthday. Of all the teams that have won All-Irelands, that Down side of 1968 was surely the youngest.

In 1968 Gerry Brown was the manager and Des Farrelly the trainer. They had a magnificent back-up team of Paddy O'Donoghue, T.P. Murphy, Dan Rooney and my old playing colleague George Lavery. Gerry Brown had originally made his name as an outstanding coach with Abbey C.B.S. in Newry. Gerry was a master tactician, who always emphasised the need to play the game in a positive, sporting and skilful manner.

On the Monday after the game the Down victory cavalcade first stopped at De La Salle College in Finglas. This was in recognition of Colm McAlarney's Dublin origins. At Gormanston College a guard of honour and trumpet fanfare welcomed their teacher Joe Lennon. (Joe had left his meteorologist job and qualified as a teacher. He had joined the staff of Gormanston several years before this.) Civic receptions followed in Drogheda and Dundalk. At Newry a massive crowd greeted the new All-Ireland champions. Finally they arrived at the Slieve Donard Hotel in Newcastle at 3 a.m. on Tuesday morning, just two hours behind schedule.

For me personally it was a thrilling experience to be among so many excited and happy Down supporters. To know that my brother Dan and my other three former colleagues had gained their third All-Ireland medal was a source of particular satisfaction. I was especially happy for my sister Gay who has always been a real loyal Down supporter. Now her husband George Glynn was bringing a Celtic Cross medal to their home. George had had a major knee operation on the Friday, in the Mater Hospital in Dublin, just before the first round of the Ulster championship against Derry. As he listened to the match on the radio the tension of this enthralling contest unnerved him. His blood pressure went so high that a nurse had to pacify him by threatening to remove the radio. More importantly he recovered so well that he was able to contribute handsomely to Down's victory. Substitutes like Dickie Murphy, Patsy McAlinden, Hilary McGrath, Larry Powell and my cousin Val Kane had also played their part in this successful campaign.

As in other years there were a lot of receptions and presentations for the winning side throughout the whole county. It would be remiss of me not to mention a very welcome ecumenical gesture. The unionist Lord Mayor of Belfast, Alderman William Geddes, gave the team an official civic welcome in Belfast's City Hall. Some extreme unionists, however, felt that this was a betrayal of their British heritage. Consequently, a small group of protestors led by Mrs Eileen Paisley (wife of the redoubtable Ian) voiced their disapproval outside. William Geddes will always be remembered for stretching the hand of friendship across a divided community.

Given the age profile and the quality of the football that they played I was certain that this Down side had the ability to secure further major honours in the coming years. Only time would determine whether or not this would happen.

13

A Voice From The Sideline

After Down's All-Ireland victory with a talented team in 1968 it was presumed that the future of football in the county was exceedingly promising. Whether it was bad luck, lack of commitment or some other reason, the following ten years proved to be very disappointing. True they won an exciting Ulster senior final against Derry in 1971, but by and large the flair, commitment and determination of former years seemed to be missing. When then manager Jackie Fitzsimmons resigned just before the start of the 1977 Ulster senior championship the outlook was even bleaker.

One morning after Jackie's retirement, county secretary T.P. Murphy arrived at my workplace in Tullyraine Quarries and asked me to take over as manager. At first I was reluctant to do so, but eventually agreed provided certain conditions were met. First, I would have to be free to select my own management team. Second, and more pertinently, I requested that the club league programme should be modified to facilitate intercounty challenge games if they were considered necessary for county team preparation. I then chose Val Kane, my brother Dan and Dominic McCartan as team selectors. Val would train the side and Dan McCartan from Saval would act as liaison officer with the county board. Later Sean Sands would join our backroom staff. The county board ratified both of my requests.

Little did I then realise that the challenge game provision would cause so much difficulty in the ensuing years. However, I was happy with the agreement and put my heart and soul into restoring Down's past glories. I did not promise success, but did add that pride in the wearing of the county jersey would definitely be enhanced. We were also put in charge of the county's under 21 team.

As we had only a few weeks to prepare for the provincial championship we set to work immediately. A team panel was quickly assembled and regular training schedules established. In the first round we defeated Fermanagh but were beaten by a very accomplished Derry team in the Ulster semi-final.

The U 21s fared a lot better. We overcame Tyrone and Antrim on our way to a provincial success against Cavan. After the first match, at Newry, was drawn we beat Offaly by 2-8 to 0-9 in the All-Ireland U 21 semi-final at Tullamore. However, a Kerry side that included Charlie Nelligan, Mick Spillane, Captain Ogie Moran, Jack O'Shea, Eoin Liston and Sean Walsh proved too strong for us in the final.

Nevertheless, as we prepared for the commencement of the National League in the autumn, I was happy enough. Players from our U 21 team like Paddy O'Rourke, Liam Austin, John and Jim McCartan (my cousin Seamus' sons) and Tommy McGovern were serious contenders for the senior team. As well as that, the minors had just won Down's first All-Ireland in that grade. Paddy O'Rourke and John McCartan were central figures in that success. Paddy Kennedy and Ambrose Rodgers were other special talents in that history-making team. I reckoned that these players, along with very good established senior players such as Colm McAlarney, Brendan Sloan, Peter Rooney and Mickey Cunningham, would form the nucleus of a promising championship outfit for the 1978 season.

At this time Down were in Division Two of the league. Though we lost the first game to All-Ireland finalists Armagh, we played well to beat Westmeath, Louth and Monaghan. Eventually, after a complicated play-off system, we qualified to meet Kildare in the league quarter-final on St Patrick's Day 1978. It took a replay and extra time before Down, inspired by the magnificent Colm McAlarney, edged through to a semi-final meeting with Mayo. Though we fought hard, luck was not on our side and we lost by two points.

Given the peculiarity of the National League system at that time, we were still in the home final of Division 2 which was played in the autumn of 1978. We beat Laois in that contest. In the final proper we easily beat Warwickshire at Birmingham in England.

In the first round of the Ulster championship we overcame Fermanagh by a point before recording a three-point victory over Derry in the Ulster semi-final at Casement Park.

However controversy ensued when, at an informal meeting with the county chairman after the Derry game, we asked that a series of club league fixtures arranged for Wednesday, 5 July 1978, be rescheduled to an agreed date. He consented to do this provided the Down hurling board would facilitate such an arrangement. The hurling board subsequently agreed to this alteration. However, the club fixtures were played on 5 July. The chairman, for his part, stated that his understanding of our request was that it was for another date. On a point of principle we, as a management team, decided that we had no option but to resign. The county team announced that they were not willing to train or play under any other management team for the Ulster final, which had been fixed for Clones on 23 July.

After many informal meetings had failed to resolve the impasse, a meeting of all parties to the dispute was arranged for 9 July. After a marathon and often heated session, which began in sunlight and ended in sunlight the following day, an agreement was finally reached. As a result we agreed to return. This was not ideal preparation for an Ulster final which was only two weeks away. We were now more determined than ever to leave no stone unturned to win Down's first Ulster senior title in seven years. The implications of that dispute would hopefully not arise again.

In the decider Down started well but Cavan stormed back to take an interval lead of 1-6 to 0-8. In the second half, with Colm McAlarney now playing superbly at midfield, the whole team gained in confidence. Colm not only scored four points himself but also laid on a perfect pass for corner forward Joe Byrne to score a brilliant goal. After that great second half display Down emerged victorious on a convincing scoreline of 2-19 to 2-12. Mark Turley was outstanding at full back and was ably supported by Brendan Sloan, Brendan Toner and Cathal Digney in defence. Liam Austin ably assisted McAlarney at midfield. Joe Byrne, Mickey Cunningham and Jarlath Digney were the best of a very impressive forward line. It was only fitting that team captain Colm McAlarney should receive the man-of-the-match accolade. Deep down both players and management knew that they had a point to prove. That day the players did us all proud.

In the All-Ireland semi-final Down met a splendid Dublin team that had won the two previous All-Irelands. Again Down started well but the Metropolitans soon began to exert their dominance throughout the field. With only a minute to go before half time, Down's right half back Cathal Digney was sent off for retaliation. It was hard luck on Cathal as he had been subjected to some very rough treatment by a Dublin forward. At the interval the Mourne men were 1-7 to 0-4 in arrears. The second half was anticlimactic as Down found it extremely difficult to cope with the extra man. When the final whistle sounded, Dublin had won comfortably by 1-16 to 0-8.

Our U 21 team again reached the Ulster final. They narrowly defeated Cavan before meeting Roscommon in the All-Ireland semi-final. They only lost thanks to a dramatic last minute point from the westerners. In the autumn we resumed our National League activity, this time in Division One. In the pre-Christmas games we beat Mayo, Roscommon and Antrim, drew with Tyrone and lost to Cavan. This enabled us to qualify for the quarter-final of the league. This was to be against Kildare and was scheduled for 8 April 1979. When we played our last league game on 10 December 1978, we did not realise what obstacles we would face. A rude awakening lay ahead.

In most counties there was and there is one ongoing central problem. How does one ensure that regular club football is provided while at the same time the necessary needs of county teams are also addressed? As a management team we had always ensured that all members of the county panel had been available to fulfil all club league and championship engagements. Members of the county panel had also been released from county training so that they could be with their clubs. The following is a summary of the main sequence of events that occurred in the next few months.

After county training at Burren on Tuesday, 20 February, I requested a meeting between the members of the county committee, the county chairman, the county secretary and the chairman of the Activities Committee and ourselves. The purpose of this was to discuss a proposed club fixture and county programme for 1979. We requested that one Sunday, 25 March, should be made available so that a county challenge game could be arranged. As we had not played a competitive game since 10 December, we felt that one challenge game was required to prepare us for the league quarter-final on 8 April in Croke Park. After a lengthy discussion it was agreed that this request should be granted and that the series of club games planned for 25 March should be transferred to Monday, 23 April. It was also agreed that the county chairman and county secretary should attend the Activities Committee meeting planned for the following Thursday, 22 February. This was to make sure that the whole Activities Committee, which had overall responsibility for fixtures in the county, would ratify the recommendations of 20 February.

At the Activities Committee gathering in Newcastle on 22 February, it was decided on a vote of four to three not to sanction our agreed proposal of two nights earlier. The county chairman did not attend this meeting. As this was the second occasion that an informal agreement with us had not been ratified we, as a management team, felt we had no option but to resign. We felt it was reasonable and fair to ask just for one Sunday's club programme to be rescheduled. In addition, since September 1978 (a period of six months) we had not made any other requests for the readjustment of the club league programme.

When I learned of the result of the Activities Committee vote, I immediately informed the county secretary of the management decision to resign with effect from the following Tuesday night, 27 February. In order not to interrupt the team's preparations and to explain to the players our reason for resigning, we decided to take training on that Tuesday night. We met the players in front of the county secretary and the chairman of the Activities Committee. We then urged the players to accept whatever management the county committee would appoint and withdrew from the meeting.

On Tuesday, 6 March, at a meeting in Burren the county committee briefed the players of the situation as it was from their perspective. The players through their captain stated that they would not train or play under any management team except ourselves.

Two nights later on Thursday, 8 March, we met the players, at their request, in Warrenpoint. We reiterated to them our reasons for resigning before withdrawing from the meeting.

After failing to reach an agreement with the players, the county committee invited Barney Carr to take over as team manager. Barney was an iconic figure in Down football thanks to his success in leading us to two All-Ireland titles in 1960 and 1961. Presumably the county committee reckoned that Barney's appointment would help to change attitudes. However, the players remained totally loyal to our management team. Originally the county committee agreed when Barney went ahead and picked an alternative squad of 24 players. Nevertheless, it appears that a majority of the county committee then thought that this would not be a good idea. They feared that it might lead to an irreconcilable split in the county.

The next main stage in this whole saga saw former GAA President Con Murphy of Cork being asked to chair an extraordinary meeting between county committee, clubs, players and our management team. This was held in Newcastle and the objective of this exercise was to seek a solution to the whole controversy. Some progress was made after four hours of heated debate. This resulted in the players (pending a final resolution) agreeing to return to training with county secretary T.P. Murphy as acting manager.

The controversy rumbled on for several weeks with many unpleasant things being said and done. A further county committee meeting took place on 2 April. Again, after many bitter exchanges, it was agreed to ask our management team to be put back in charge of the county team. This we accepted and we immediately set about preparing the team for the quarter-final of the league on the following Sunday.

Barney Carr was always a man of integrity. His only wish, as I understand it, was to see a Down team play in a National League quarter-final that April. After learning the full story of what had happened in the previous weeks he was naturally upset. The details of what occurred at the meeting with Con Murphy made him hit out strongly at the Down county committee's role in the team management crisis. In a statement issued to the *Irish News* on 30 April 1979 he said, "It's a matter of deep regret that I allowed myself to be used by the county committee in the interests of the Association." He added, "It would seem that the county committee was bluffing me and it was the reality of the new panel which brought its somersault. I wish to assure the 24 players who responded that I was not bluffing and I express my appreciation for their response."

Barney Carr, in my opinion, had been an innocent victim caught in the crossfire between the county committee and our management team.

Following all these events, four executive members, the chairman and treasurer and two ordinary members of the county committee, resigned. All were asked to reconsider but only three agreed to withdraw their resignations. Whereas our management team appeared to have good support in the wider GAA community, it was obvious that at executive level there was a very definite split in views as regards our return. Subsequently the county committee asked the chairman of the hurling board, Benny Crawford (uncle of future Meath star, Nigel), to act as county chairman with Sean Murdock and Pat Magee replacing the other two officers who had resigned.

At the following year's county convention in 1980, Benny Crawford called on everyone within the county to refrain from recriminations over past disputes. He received a standing ovation from the delegates. Thanks to Benny, a year of bitterness and internal strife was at an end. Every GAA person in Down was now speaking with one voice.

Now I return to that much talked about National League quarter-final against Kildare. All of this dissension was far from an ideal preparation for such an important fixture. To add to our woes we were missing star player Liam Austin. On a day of heavy rain and gale force winds, we went in at the interval behind on a scoreline of 0-7 to 0-3. The team bravely fought back in the second half but was always chasing the game. In the end we lost by 0-11 to 0-9. Then, in a rather tempestuous encounter two months later, we also lost to Monaghan in the first round of the Ulster senior football championship.

I was still optimistic that our U 21 side would do well. They showed their true worth in disposing of Donegal, Monaghan, Derry and Tyrone to claim their third provincial title in a row. In the ensuing All-Ireland semi-final against Galway they played excellently in the first half to go in at the interval leading by 0-8 to 0-2. Paddy O'Rourke at centre half back, Paddy Kennedy at midfield and Liam Austin at centre half forward were very impressive in that opening period. Gervase O'Hare was our outstanding forward and when he again scored on the resumption it looked as if we were going to win easily. However, Galway assumed the ascendancy in the second half. It took some heroic defending from our backs before we eventually won by 0-11 to 0-9. We were now in the All-Ireland U 21 final against Munster champions Cork.

During that year Liam Austin had been our U 21 captain. However, in the week prior to the final I replaced him as captain with right corner back Ned King. This caused some controversy and indeed Liam himself was not pleased. I had a rule that if any player did not turn up for training or did not offer me a reasonable excuse for doing so he would be disciplined. As I felt Liam had transgressed on both accounts, I relieved him of the captaincy. I know that may sound tough but I always believed that rules must be applied right across the board regardless of the player's status within the team. As it panned out, Liam eventually, though reluctantly, accepted my decision.

In football terms that year's All-Ireland U 21 final was somewhat disappointing. Though the final scoreline was 1-9 to 0-7 in Down's favour we were much superior in terms of winning possession. In that first period, John McCartan was unfortunate to have two goals disallowed. Cork opened the scoring with a point before Jarlath Digney replied with an opportunist goal. Gervase O'Hare added a point but Cork replied with two of their own. Shortly afterwards Liam Austin rose magnificently to bring off a fantastic catch and soloed upfield. He found O'Hare with a clever pass and Gervase added another point. A Cork point just before the break left the interval score 1-2 to 0-4.

Shortly after the resumption Cork equalised. Then a young man called Greg Blaney stepped up to the plate. Taking over the free taking duties from the injured O'Hare the 16 year old shot three brilliant successive points, two from frees. In what was undoubtedly the score of the game John McCartan landed a terrific long-range point. Ned King, who was particularly impressive in the second half, scored a great point from a 50. Another great fetch by Austin followed by a lengthy clearance gave corner forward Peter Donnan an opportunity to notch a point. With 17 minutes gone Down were now leading by 1-8 to 0-5. Ger Mulcahy added a Cork point before the classy Blaney had Down's last point. Just before the final whistle Jimmy Kerrigan, who was later destined to become a Cork senior star, scored a consolation point. Down had won their first All-Ireland U 21 title. All of us were absolutely delighted.

Those U 21 players were responsible for leaving me with a multitude of pleasant memories. One, in particular, stands out above the rest. After we had finished training in Burren one night Paddy O'Rourke came into the shower and threw a bucket of cold water over me. He quickly disappeared and I ran after him, out through the doorway and around the pitch outside. Suddenly another player switched on the training lights. There was Paddy and I, now in full view of all the hastily assembled players, chasing each other round in our birthday suits! As they roared with laughter I rapidly retreated into the anonymity of the shower again.

After our exit from the 1979 Ulster senior championship, I had informed the county board that I would resign my position as team manager when our U 21 side had completed their campaign. It had been a very frustrating year for all of us on the management team. I now felt that I did not need any more hassle. I just wanted to be an ordinary Down GAA supporter again. Happily a great U 21 squad had provided us with an ideal parting gift.

For the next three championship seasons I happily watched from the sidelines as others took up the management baton. The 1968 winning manager Gerry Brown took over for the 1979/80 season but experienced little success as Monaghan eliminated Down in the first round of the Ulster championship. Then my old playing colleague Joe Lennon agreed to take charge of the side. After a replay, they beat Monaghan in the first round and Derry in the semi-final of the 1981 Ulster championship. In the provincial decider against Armagh, they played superbly and beat the Orchard County by eight points. Tommy McGovern was a colossus at full back and John McCartan received the man of the match award for a truly imperious display.

Luck was not with them in the All-Ireland semi-final against Offaly. They were forced to field without ace midfielder Liam Austin and Colm McAlarney played despite sporting a heavily bandaged leg. When the full time whistle went, Offaly had won by six points. After Tyrone eliminated the Mourne County in the 1982 Ulster championship, Joe Lennon decided to step down. The county was immediately rife with rumours as to who the new manager would be. I, too, wondered. I did not have long to wait.

Some weeks before the commencement of the National League, county chairman Dan McCartan from Saval asked me to again assume the managerial reins. Initially, given my previous experience, I was reluctant to do so. However, I finally agreed. Dan was a honourable straightforward person who always saw the bigger picture and I would have no difficulty working with a county board under his control. Again I selected Val Kane as trainer. I also brought in Sean Murdock and Danny Murphy as selectors along with Val. Danny was a very able, respected GAA person who was also in charge of club fixtures. The thinking behind appointing Danny was that he would be able to create a balance between the mutual interests of club and county.

As Joe Lennon had led Down again to Division One of the league, we were scheduled to play the top tier of county teams. We had a very successful league run beating both Dublin and Derry and drawing with Cork and Armagh. After Christmas we had a terrific win over newly-crowned All-Ireland champions Offaly in Newry. After beating Mayo and drawing with Kerry in Killorglin we had qualified for the semi-final of the league against Kildare.

On a day of torrential rain and high winds we lost the toss so Kildare had the wind advantage in the first period. Heroic performances by Paddy O'Rourke, Paddy Kennedy, Liam Austin and Brendan Toner helped to curtail Kildare in that first half. As a result we went in at the interval only two points adrift, 0-4 to 0-2. We really dominated the second half with Brendan Mason, in only his second game for the county, scoring a spectacular goal. Donal Bell, John McCartan and Liam Austin all played well as we cruised to a 1-9 to 0-4 triumph.

In the final we were scheduled to meet our close neighbours Armagh who had defeated Meath in the other semi-final. Armagh were hot favourites. They had a capable goalkeeper in Brian McAlinden and talented defenders in Denis Stevenson, Paddy Moriarty and Brian Canavan. Joe Kernan was a top class centre half forward. Their two corner forwards, John Corvan and Mickey McDonald, had wreaked havoc in every defence during the whole league campaign.

Armagh began strongly and were four points up before Donal Bell opened Down's account with a pointed free. Then Down came good and thanks to a goal by Ambrose Rodgers and two further points we retired at the interval leading by 1-3 to 0-5.

Shortly after the resumption Corvan equalised. Armagh dominated the third quarter but, owing to superb performances by Brendan Toner and Liam Austin at centre field, their overall superiority was negated. Our corner backs Ned King and Mark Turley were also fantastic in curbing the effectiveness of Corvan and McDonald. Two great points by Ambrose Rodgers and two magnificent frees by Brendan Toner enabled our forward line to build up a four-point lead. An Armagh goalbound effort was brilliantly tipped over the bar with only four minutes to go. Despite repeated Armagh attacks our defence held firm. When the final whistle went, Down had won by 1-7 to 0-7. I was delighted when team captain Mark Turley went up to receive the cup. A good all round team performance had delivered Down's fourth National League title in a more emphatic fashion than the final scoreline suggested.

Before the National League final I cleared it with the county board that all 31 members of our panel would receive league medals if we were lucky enough to win the final. They agreed to my suggestion. However, after the final they said that only the 21 players listed on the official match programme would receive medals. The other ten players would instead receive a lesser quality NFL memento. After much hassle it was decided that I would personally pay for the extra ten proper medals myself and that the county board would deduct the price of their own proposed NFL mementoes from my bill. This to me is an example of what I term GAA meanness at official level.

The same type of attitude also prevailed in 1958 when Down won the Ulster junior football championship. If there was more than one member of the same family, in the squad, the county board only allocated one medal per family. Thus Paddy Doherty and myself who played on the team got medals and our brothers, Harry and Dan respectively, who were substitutes, did not. For years I complained about this discrimination to several county board officials but nothing was done. Ulster council secretary Danny Murphy eventually obtained the two medals for Harry and Dan about two years ago. When I presented Harry Doherty with his missing medal he cried tears of sheer joy. It was the only intercounty medal he had ever won and he had to wait 50 years for it.

Similarly, 1968 All-Ireland senior medal winner Tom O'Hare did not receive a medal despite being a substitute on the Down side that won the 1962 league final. Instead his Dr Lagan Cup and league medals were given to another player who was not even in the country at the time. The ridiculous reason given for this was that if he had been here he would have been on the team. It was not until 1999 that Tom actually received his missing intercounty medals. This is miserliness and injustice personified. After all, it is the talent and work of our players who make our games such great sporting spectacles. No one has the right to treat players in such a mean-mannered way.

On the field of play we were soon brought back down to earth when we met Fermanagh in the first round of the Ulster senior championship at Irvinestown. Unfortunately two of our leading players had been injured in a club game and were missing for this contest. Fermanagh who had reached the previous year's Ulster final against Armagh were a good team. We started well with a point by Donal Bell in the second minute but incredibly that was our only score of the opening half. Despite the dominance of the classy Peter McGinnity and John Rehill at centre field the Ernesiders could only muster three points. Though we improved somewhat in the second half we were still below par and Fermanagh went on to win by 0-10 to 0-8. To say that we were devastated by this performance would be an understatement.

When the National League resumed in the autumn we drew with Kildare, lost to Armagh and defeated All-Ireland champions Dublin and Offaly. In the two league games after Christmas we beat Meath and drew with Kerry to qualify for a league quarter-final playoff against Tyrone. Brilliant displays by Brendan McGovern, Liam Austin, Brendan Mason and a youngster by the name of Mickey Linden paved the way for a 2-8 to 0-6 triumph over the O'Neill County.

In the league semi-final against Kerry we were missing the injured Liam Austin who was now playing the best football of his career. In spite of a spirited resistance, Down just could not cope with the talented Mike Sheehy, Pat Spillane and Eoin Liston. The Kingdom deservedly defeated us by three points.

Before the start of the Ulster championship we travelled to Pearse Park in Longford for a Centenary Cup game to commemorate the 100th birthday of the GAA. We shot 27 wides in that game before succumbing to a surprise one-point defeat to Longford after extra time. However, in the first round Ulster championship match against Fermanagh we emerged victorious easily enough even though we were missing Paddy Kennedy, Brendan McGovern and Greg Blaney.

On a day of heavy rain and dangerous underfoot conditions we played Tyrone in the semi-final of the Ulster championship at Casement Park. Playing against the wind we managed to be only two points behind at the interval. We thought everything would be all right with the elements in our favour after half time. It was not to be. Tyrone, with the majestic Frank McGuigan in top form, were the better side and won by five points, 0-10 to 0-5.

When that 1984 championship campaign ended I decided to retire from my managerial duties. This time there would be no going back. Despite all the ups and downs of my active involvement on the sideline I had enjoyed the experience immensely. However, the body was less willing and the spirit of old was declining. During my two terms a National League title, an Ulster senior title, three Ulster U 21 championships and one All-Ireland U 21 honour had been accomplished. The silverware in itself was most welcome. In May 1977 I had promised T.P. Murphy to restore pride in the Down jersey. Along with my two management teams the Down players during my tenures had certainly done their utmost to fulfil my promise.

14

A New Generation of Heroes

From the time I retired as Down senior football manager in 1984 until 1991 there was a barren spell in the fortunes of the senior football team. During that period they only reached one Ulster final, in 1986, when they were beaten by Tyrone who went on to unsuccessfully contest that year's All-Ireland final against Kerry. However, from a personal point of view, I was delighted with the football progress of our two eldest sons, Brian and James Junior. Both won Hogan Cup medals with St Colman's College, Newry (Brian in 1986 and James in both 1986 and 1988). As well as that, Brian was at midfield in Down's All-Ireland minor winning team of 1987 and James played at corner forward in that historic triumph. Nevertheless, in spite of Brian's undoubted ability it was our younger son who now appeared to have the greater chance of senior glory. Unfortunately, a serious knee injury prematurely curtailed Brian's career. Though James was comparatively small in stature he had a lot of skill and pace. More importantly he possessed a tremendous will to win and always wore his heart on his sleeve. From 1989 onwards I was really looking forward to James getting the opportunity to make the grade at senior level.

In September 1989, after several others had refused the position, Peter McGrath became manager of the Down senior team. Morale in the county was at a low ebb at this time. McGrath's detractors, though admitting that he was a good minor manager (he had been the man in charge of the 1987 All-Ireland minor winners) questioned his suitability for the job. However, the shrewd McGrath realised that there was a lot of young talent in the county. He reckoned that they, along with such established players as Greg Blaney, Mickey Linden, Liam Austin and Ambrose Rodgers, might form a winning combination. With this in mind he set himself a target of three years to achieve the ultimate goal of an All-Ireland senior football title. In his first National League campaign Down reached the 1990 final. Though defeated by a star-studded Meath 15, they gave a brilliant performance, only losing by 2-7 to 0-11. What made the whole league so personally satisfying was the fact that James had been called into the squad at the beginning of the season and was now established on the starting side.

Some weeks after the league decider Down played Monaghan in the first round of the Ulster senior championship. In an excellent performance the Mourne men won by five points and James marked his championship debut with a well-taken goal. In the semi-final they drew with Armagh before losing by a point in the subsequent replay.

Although disappointed at Down's exit to their arch rivals, McGrath reasoned that Down had a potential championship winning side. This prognosis was based on the fact that Down had a player sent off and that two very capable and experienced players, Paddy O'Rourke and Greg Blaney, were missing. As well as that, the Orchard County had been awarded a very dubious penalty.

From my point of view I was very content with James' displays in the two games against Armagh. In the drawn match he scored two marvellous goals. One of them was later voted BBC championship goal of the year. The International Rules selectors were so impressed with his performances that he was picked to represent Ireland in Australia in the autumn of 1990. His room mate on that tour was one of the best footballers that I have ever seen, Jack O'Shea. Though quiet by nature, James was always good for a quick riposte when it came to replying to a question from a sports journalist. When asked what it was like to be sharing a room with a legendary GAA figure, James swiftly retorted: "You should ask Jacko that question!" To complete an exciting year he also gained an All-Star award at left corner forward at the annual GAA banquet in December.

Despite my personal satisfaction with James' individual progress, I, like many others, was not at all pleased with Down's poor league results that autumn. Indeed since their championship exit to Armagh there had been a lot of pessimism around. This was a view shared by some of the more established players who had refused to join the pre-Christmas league squad. This winter of discontent was compounded when Down were officially relegated from Division One of the league. Later the league groupings were rearranged on a random basis.

Still, to be fair, McGrath kept his nerve and continued to experiment with the positioning of players. By the time championship preparations for 1991 began in earnest all wayward players were back in training. Significantly McGrath had now introduced a new talismanic figure to the panel. The man in question, Peter Withnall, gave extra strength and direction to the forward line. His surprise selection was to prove an inspired choice as the season developed.

In the first round of the Ulster championship against Armagh at Newry, Down, after a dismal display in atrocious conditions, eventually scraped home by two points. So unhappy was McGrath with his team that he even replaced team captain Paddy O'Rourke at half time This insipid performance reflected a mood of uncertainty and lifelessness among the players. So poor was their general outlook on the team's development and attitude that three players had decided to do something.

Prior to this game, D.J. Kane, Liam Austin and Ross Carr had identified five Down supporters who were willing to sponsor the purchase of boots for the players. However, this unilateral decision did not go down well with either the team management or the county board. After the Armagh match the "Down Three" were brought before the county board. They were threatened with suspension and accused of having a hidden agenda. This was the type of dictatorial attitude that I always detested. Some members of county boards invariably seem to thrive on this type of unnecessary confrontation. In this case, however, there was a satisfactory outcome. The net result of this needless squabble was that although the players refused to apologise for their actions they agreed that in future all such matters should be left to the county board to organise. For their part, the latter withdrew their suspension threat.

Ironically, this whole saga had a positive outcome. The team that faced Derry in the provincial semi-final was now a much more determined and cohesive unit. Training attendances that had been a source of concern for team management had improved dramatically. Everyone was now totally focused on winning some badly needed silverware.

In the match against the Oakleaf County, Down completely controlled the first half with continuous quick interpassing movements which inevitably ended in a score. At the interval they led by 0-9 to 0-4. However the sending-off of Down's Greg Blaney and Derry's Fergal McCusker, in separate incidents, changed the trend of the game. Down missed the guile and leadership qualities of playmaker Blaney more than Derry felt the loss of McCusker. When Derry introduced Anthony Tohill (his first competitive game in a senior Derry jersey) and Joe Brolly, the match definitely swung in their favour. Deep into injury time Derry were leading by a point. I felt it was not to be our day. Then Down, rather surprisingly, were awarded a free 55 yards out from the Derry goal. A man with a proven footballing pedigree, Ross Carr, took a final look at the posts and stepped back five paces. He hit the ball as hard as he could. It sailed straight and true over the bar for a dramatic equalising point. The full time whistle sounded almost immediately. All of us in Down were desperately relieved.

In the replay Derry's ploy of trying to man mark every Down player backfired and Down scored seven points without reply during a period in the first half. Their tactic of bringing back their playmaker Damian Barton to centre half back to curb Greg Blaney proved counter productive. As a consequence the Derry forward line had no shape. By the time the Oakleaf men had changed their players back to their normal positions the game was effectively over. The only scare for Down occurred four minutes from the end when Derry substitute Gary Coleman hit the crossbar. However the ever-alert half back John Kelly grabbed the rebound for the Mourne men. He passed the ball to the equally vigilant Mark McCartan (Dan's son), who had come on as a substitute for Peter Withnall. He quickly transferred it to his first cousin, the overlapping James. He, in turn, found Greg Blaney lurking on the edge of the square. Derry goalkeeper Damian McCusker had no option but to foul him. It was a penalty. Nonchalantly Mickey Linden tapped the ball over the bar to leave the Mourne men comprehensive and deserving winners on a scoreline of 0-14 to 0-9. Down were back in the Ulster final for the first time in five years.

In the provincial decider they faced a fancied Donegal side. For the first 25 minutes a rampant Down played some of their best football ever. Between the tenth and 25th minutes they scored 1-6 without reply. During the interval McGrath warned his players about the need to avoid complacency. After all he had played on the 1974 team against the same opposition. On that occasion Down had led by nine points but lost the game. In the second half Down continued to dominate. A worrying factor, however, was that they shot a total of eight wides in the first ten minutes.

The game's decisive moment came midway through the second half. Donegal's Barry McGowan bore down on goalkeeper Neil Collins' goal. A green flag looked imminent but the athletic netminder dived brilliantly to smother the shot. D.J. Kane collected the loose ball and sent it up to James McCartan. Having avoided many heavy tackles he soloed at speed past several Tir Conaill defenders before slipping the ball to Greg Blaney. Greg found Barry Breen who had come storming up the centre with an astute pass. He sent it over the bar for a truly magnificent score. There were now five points between the sides when it easily could have been only one. It was a very impressive Down that finally cruised to an emphatic 1-15 to 0-10 victory.

I knew that day that all the necessary components for a winning team were coming together. An extra bonus was that most of the forwards could score from distance. In addition they had Greg Blaney. He was a class footballer who orchestrated every move from the traditional centre half forward position. Peter Withnall, at full forward, provided space for the speedy and elusive Mickey Linden and James McCartan in the corner forward spots. The swagger was now back in Down football. The omens looked good for a serious assault on the destiny of the Sam Maguire Cup for 1991.

To make matters even more intriguing was the fact that Down once again were to meet Kerry in an All-Ireland semi-final. In the 1960s Down had defeated Kerry in all three of their All-Ireland senior successes This time, however, they would be meeting a Kingdom side that had won eight senior All-Irelands in the previous 16 years. Nevertheless, only two of their great team of the seventies and eighties, Pat Spillane and Jack O'Shea, were still playing. As it panned out this would be Spillane's last senior championship game and O'Shea would retire the following year. McGrath also reckoned that with Withnall at full forward against full back Tom Spillane, the Down man could win enough clean possession to supply his more dangerous scoring colleagues.

After a pulsating first 20 minutes from both teams, Down seemed to lose their way and by half time they were trailing by a point. One redeeming feature of the first half performance was that Peter Withnall was looking really threatening. To confirm this view he had scored a very good left-footed goal in the tenth minute of the opening period.

In the third quarter, scores were hard to come by. It was not until Withnall scored another goal, ten minutes from the end, that Down actually began to play their normal, fluid game. Showing panache, determination and flair they knocked over three unanswered points to leave the final score Down 2-9, Kerry 0-8. For the first time in 23 years Down were back in an All-Ireland senior football final.

The final was to be against Leinster champions Meath who had made all the summer headlines with their marvellous four games against Dublin in the provincial championship. Including a quarter-final replay against Wicklow, Meath had played nine games to reach the final. Down had played five. Having analysed the capabilities of each Meath player, McGrath and his fellow selectors, Barney Trainor and John Murphy, concluded that each Down man could win his personal duel with his opposite number. If this were to happen it would ensure a good supply of quick ball to a very fast and accurate forward line.

All-Ireland fever gripped the whole county. Overenthusiastic supporters decided that the omens of history repeating itself meant that there could only be one result. Down had always won titles with the number one featuring in the year of success. Ulster titles had been accrued in 1961, 1971, 1981 and 1991. They had won an All-Ireland in 1961. Furthermore, in 1961 Tottenham Hotspur won the F.A. Cup in England, Tipperary won the McCarthy Cup and a Cork Rose won the Rose of Tralee festival. Now, 30 later, all of the foregoing three were waiting on Down to make up the foursome. Bob Beamon set a new world long jump record in 1968 and, like Down's barren spell over the same period, it had not been broken until 1991.

Peter McGrath and his backroom team ignored such unscientific thinking as they meticulously prepared for the greatest day in their lives. Their only selection dilemma was whether to play Eamonn Burns or the fit again Liam Austin in partnership with Barry Breen at midfield. Austin who had been the number one choice at the beginning of the campaign had been injured in the drawn match against Derry. In the end McGrath decided to keep faith with the existing pairing. Prior to the match Meath suffered a body blow when Colm O'Rourke was declared unfit to start because of a viral infection. Down management, nevertheless, planned for O'Rourke's possible introduction to the game if things were not going well for the Royal County.

The opening period was very physical but Down refused to become embroiled in this type of play. Instead they concentrated on their own running game. Meath tackling intensified as first a Royal defender knocked out one of Mickey Linden's teeth and another Meath player then bodychecked Brendan McKernan. Frustration set in amongst the Meath backs. As a result they resorted to fouling the buzzing Down forwards. The deadly accurate wing forwards Ross Carr and Gary Mason each duly pointed three frees. 20 minutes had actually elapsed before the Mourne men managed their first score from play, a terrific effort from Eamonn Burns. Before half time James McCartan put over a well-taken point. At half time a confident Down led a rattled Meath by 0-8 to 0-4.

For the first 14 minutes of the second half Down played brilliantly. Their spellbinding movements tore the Meath defence asunder. During this time they scored 1-6, all but one from play. James, in particular, was having a wonderful game. Despite a heavy challenge from Meath full back Mick Lyons, he dodged several other tackles before curling over a left-footed point in the fourth minute. Ross Carr and Mickey Linden then added further points before the best move of the game. James, in spite of conceding several inches in height, leapt above a cluster of Meath defenders to securely take a crossfield ball. He gave a short pass to Peter Withnall who quickly transferred the ball to Greg Blaney. Showing superb vision, Greg neatly delivered the ball to Mickey Linden near the end line.

Mickey drew the Meath defence before landing a perfect pass to the inrushing Barry Breen on the edge of the square. He palmed the ball to the net to score his first goal for Down. With 26 minutes left, Down led by 1-11 to 0-5.

Within the next five minutes Ross Carr (from a 50 yard free), James McCartan and Greg Blaney added three further points to a solitary white flag for Meath. It was now 1-14 to 0-6 and the Mourne men seemed to be on their way to another All-Ireland title.

Then that stalwart Meath footballer Colm O'Rourke entered the contest. The great comeback that all Meath supporters and neutrals were hoping for was about to happen. Though Down had anticipated this move they were powerless to stop the inspirational O'Rourke. Thanks to his promptings, Meath scored 1-8 to Down's 0-2 in the remaining 20 minutes of the game. It was nailbiting stuff and I feared the worst.

In the final minutes McGrath introduced two wily, veteran campaigners, Liam Austin and Ambrose Rodgers, both of whom had given years of loyal service to Down. Both helped to steady their team that was now under incessant pressure. As a result Down just held on to notch another memorable All-Ireland victory on a scoreline of 1-16 to 1-14. Down's proud unbeaten senior decider record was intact. For the fourth time since 1960 Croke Park was enveloped in a blanket of red and black as fans raced across the green arena.

I was overcome with joyous emotion. As well as being a wonderful occasion for all Down supporters it was a particularly uplifting experience, not only for myself, but also for our whole extended GAA family. 1960 and 1961 had been terrific for Kevin and Sean O'Neill, Dan and myself. 1968 saw Dan and Sean O'Neill joined by my brother-in-law George Glynn and my cousin Val Kane on the winners' rostrum. Now Val's younger brother D.J. and his first cousin Greg Blaney were to become All-Ireland senior medal recipients. My nephew Mark McCartan was also a member of the winning panel. However, James Junior took pride of place in my affections when that final whistle rang. Marie and our other six children were there to share in the triumph of a son and a sibling. The little boy who had so often sat on my knee in Croke Park on other All-Ireland final days was now a central figure in Down's latest glorious success. James had displayed the full repertoire of his playing talents on the greatest stage of all.

Though there were many individual stars on that team, the success was really the culmination of a massive, co-ordinated and structured approach by everyone concerned. Peter McGrath had surmounted all the tests that he encountered. He and his management team deserved great credit for their contribution to a fantastic triumph. At the end of the day, however, it is the players who must perform and this they did in style. The capable Neil Collins in goal was fronted by an excellent full back in Conor Deegan and ably supported by corner backs Brendan McKernan and Paul Higgins. Team captain Paddy O'Rourke showed his leadership qualities in the pivotal centre half back position. His wing colleagues John Kelly and D.J. Kane literally ran themselves into the ground. For three quarters of the game, before they tired, Barry Breen and Eamonn Burns controlled the midfield sector. At centre half forward Greg Blaney was playmaker extraordinaire. On either side of him, Ross Carr and Gary Mason converted their frees with considerable aplomb. Full forward Peter Withnall kept the powerful Meath full back Mick Lyons at bay. Both corner forwards, Mickey Linden and James McCartan, were constant thorns in the Meath defence.

As the Sam Maguire Cup was paraded around the county in the ensuing weeks Peter McGrath was rightly fêted with chants of "Ooh Aah, Pete McGrath". In our bar, at home in Donacloney, there were lovely evenings of joy and celebration. Our other children, Brian, Delia, Charlie Pat, Maria, Daniel and Eoin, justifiably basked in the glory of James' achievement. Meanwhile, James himself, who had been named the man of the match for his magnificent display in the final, just kept smiling that pleasant smile of total satisfaction.

I was particularly happy for my wife, Marie. She was the unsung heroine of the whole scene in our household. She was the person who ensured the football gear was always ready and that the many injuries over the years were consistently treated. I am sure all players everywhere can identify with that caring, maternal instinct of mothers, wives, sisters and girlfriends. This All-Ireland win was really Marie's reward for a lifetime of service to the GAA.

Owing to the delicate political climate in Northern Ireland at that time we did not want to offend our Protestant neighbours by putting up GAA flags or bunting on our house or bar before the final. Indeed, Daniel and Eoin, who were then very young, did not wear the Down colours until they arrived in Slane in County Meath on the way to the final. There we bought two hats with the number 15 on them so that they could honour their older brother. However, many people from across the religious divide came to congratulate and celebrate with us after Down's great victory. On the Friday night after the game some of the Down players and officials appeared on the Gerry Kelly show on UTV. When we heard that the whole team and officials were going to come to our bar in Donacloney after the show, two of the barmen, Aidan Barry and Trevor

Walker, went to Banbridge. There they bought flags and bunting and came back and decorated the house and lounge. We had a terrific night of singing, craic and general entertainment. Everyone stayed all night. People slept everywhere, including the bathroom. The local policemen came and shared our hour of glory with us. That was a lovely gesture by them. It was early the following afternoon before the last of the late night revellers left.

One man for whom I was particularly pleased was team captain Paddy O'Rourke. From the moment he won an All-Ireland minor medal in 1977 he had become, in the interim, an integral part of all Down teams. When I was manager he had played a leading role in all our U 21 successes and National League accomplishments. 1991 was his 14th consecutive year in a Down senior jersey. Every All-Ireland victory has its own wonderful stories and unique anecdotes attached to it. 1991 was no exception. Fittingly, my favourite story of that year's homecoming has Paddy O'Rourke as its central character.

The mood of the players that engulfed Down at this time is best illustrated by Paddy's visit to his own Burren club in the early hours of the Wednesday morning after the All-Ireland. After a night of festivities, O'Rourke decided at 7 a.m. that it was time to go home. Finding the exit roads blocked with cars belonging to club supporters inside the clubhouse, Paddy chose to go through the fields, up Burren hill and down the far side to his own house. With dawn breaking, his only company as he traversed the rough terrain was a group of rabbits scampering through the habitat of their normally peaceful surroundings. With the Sam Maguire Cup in hand he soon reached the top of the hill. Looking back at the clubhouse he saw a crowd of happy supporters peering out through the windows. In the cool, morning air Paddy O'Rourke raised the cup aloft while the men of Burren cheered.

Paddy thought as he turned around: "What a fabulous feeling, just me and the rabbits. I am the only person in the whole of Ireland that can do this now."

15

Red And Black Come Again

When Down went on holiday to Tenerife in January 1992 the strained relationship between the county board and the players, which had surfaced a year earlier, began to raise its ugly head again. This centred on the type of accommodation the players were booked into as well as the amount of pocket money allocated to each player. In addition, there was further hassle as to whether or not the players' wives or girlfriends should join them. The county board maintained that because of the excessive financial expense incurred in winning the All-Ireland they were not in a position to fulfil all the demands of the players. Even though agreement on these contentious issues was finally reached, there still remained a residue of distrust between both sides.

At Easter 1992, thanks to sponsorship from the GAA and the Bank of Ireland, Down went on a tour of the main cities in America that had substantial Irish populations. As this trip took place just six weeks before the beginning of the Ulster championship there were mixed views, even amongst the players, as to the wisdom of the venture. Team captain Paddy O'Rourke felt that the main focus should be on the retention of the Ulster and All-Ireland titles. As a result, Paddy stayed at home and vice captain John Kelly led the team Stateside.

All of these events seemed to have a disturbing effect when Down played poorly against Armagh in the first round of the Ulster championship. In a robust game Down eventually won by six points. Only some expert free taking by the very accurate Gary Mason and an opportunist goal by James McCartan enabled the Mourne men to snatch a rather unconvincing win.

Prior to the Ulster semi-final against old rivals Derry, James injured himself when jumping over an iron gate at our farm in Donacloney. However, he took his place on the starting 15, as did Ross Carr who was not fully fit. The match was a fantastic occasion as it pitted the All-Ireland champions against the newly-crowned National League victors who had defeated Tyrone, in dramatic fashion, in the decider at the beginning of May.

35,000 people crammed into Casement Park on a beautiful sunny afternoon to see two of the country's top sides. A highly motivated Derry team played tremendous football against a rather lacklustre Down side. Powered by the dominant midfield pairing of Brian McGilligan and Dermot Heaney the Oakleaf men took control. Thanks to the superb free taking of Enda Gormley and some classic points from play by Damian Cassidy, Derry won by 0-15 to 0-12. In fairness to Down it must be said that they fielded without the injured Barry Breen, and Paul Higgins had to go off injured ten minutes into the game. Also, shortly after the resumption, Peter Withnall was sent off for dangerous play. However it should be mentioned that, on this occasion, the Derry defence kept the Down forwards at bay. In the final analysis it is questionable whether a fully prepared Down could have matched the more positive approach of the Derry men.

Despite this setback I still felt that the mistakes of 1992 would not be repeated and that 1993 would see Down reassert their supremacy. Once again, for the third consecutive year, Down met Derry in the Ulster championship, this time at Newry. From the very beginning of the match Derry's new midfielder Anthony Tohill showed his true greatness and Down were given a football lesson. A Dermot Heaney goal allowed the Oakleaf men to lead at half time by 1-6 to 0-5. When Down's John Kelly was sent off 12 minutes from the end, Derry pulled away with goals by Richard Ferris and Eamon Burns. On a very wet day Derry emerged thoroughly convincing winners by 3-11 to 0-9. This was a dark day for Down football as they had suffered their heaviest Ulster championship defeat since 1952. On a brighter note, that Derry team was a magnificent side that went on to deservedly win a first All-Ireland.

Peter McGrath was furious with his side's woeful display: "I think Down fans are owed an apology from everyone connected with the team. I think the players will have to sort it out in their own minds exactly what went wrong."

Many of the players, and indeed supporters, resented these televised comments by McGrath. Nevertheless, the undaunted St Colman's teacher turned this adversity on its head as he planned for the next season.

When Peter McGrath reassembled his squad for the National League in the autumn of 1993, some players had become disenchanted with the way the management team was handling matters As a result, Greg Blaney and James McCartan refused to join the new panel. Personally, I felt, like many others, that if Down could get their act together another All-Ireland title could be won. This thinking was based on the fact that two other Ulster counties, Derry and Donegal, had won their first senior All-Irelands in the two years since Down's 1991 success. Thus the Sam Maguire Cup had come to Ulster for an unprecedented three years in a row. While I was naturally pleased for my fellow Ulster men, I knew that with proper preparation Down could make it four in a row.

In a patchy league campaign Down initially struggled. However, manager McGrath was then seen at his diplomatic best when he appointed D.J. Kane as captain for the 1994 season. D.J. was a cousin of both Greg Blaney and James McCartan. The nett result of this was that Greg and James settled their differences with the team management. Both of them returned to the squad in February. Furthermore, McGrath introduced Pat O'Hare as county team trainer. Pat was a very enthusiastic and dedicated trainer who maximised the fitness of the players. Everyone had a singular ambition in mind as they prepared diligently for the first round of the Ulster championship on 29 May. What united them more was the fact that they were meeting their recent nemesis and new All-Ireland champions Derry in their own back yard in Celtic Park.

The meeting of the 1991 and 1993 All-Ireland champions caught the imagination of the press and supporters alike. The whole GAA population were eagerly looking forward to a potential classic encounter. It did not disappoint. This game has gone down in folklore as one of the greatest football matches of all time. A beautiful sunny day, a packed stadium and two wonderful exponents of Gaelic football was the backdrop to this titanic struggle. The Down side that had started so badly in the league had gradually improved. Derry, on the other hand, possessed some of the country's finest footballers. Kieran McKeever and Tony Scullion were top defenders. Their centre half back and captain Henry Downey was an inspirational attack minded leader. In Anthony Tohill and Brian McGilligan they had a powerful midfield pairing. Enda Gormley was a deadly accurate free taker and Joe Brolly could destroy any defence. Nevertheless, I felt that if Down could gain parity at midfield our forward line would unhinge the Derry defence.

The game began at a ferocious pace. What made the first half so special, from a Down perspective, was the scintillating display of corner forward Mickey Linden. His five points from play in that period were simply outstanding. When the teams left the field at the interval the whole arena burst into a spontaneous round of applause. Down went to the dressing rooms leading by 0-10 to 0-8.

Shortly after the resumption Anthony Tohill and Eamon Burns both scored for Derry to bring the sides level. Then the magnificent Linden notched his sixth point to edge his team ahead. Both contestants exchanged points before the lively Joe Brolly found Fergal McCusker with a neat pass. The overlapping wing half back had travelled 60 yards upfield. When he drove the ball to the back of the

Down net Derry supporters went delirious with joy. It was 1-11 to 0-12 in favour of the Oakleaf county. There were 17 minutes gone.

I now thought that with home advantage Derry might build up more momentum and take control of the game. However, my son James had other ideas. He gained possession about 60 yards out before rounding Derry defender Karl Diamond. Showing pace and fierce determination he soloed forward to put the ball over the bar for an inspirational score.

Then Anthony Tohill scored a marvellous point to again give Derry a two-point advantage. Down required a goal to win the game as time edged ever closer to the end. And it happened. In a fantastic movement, initiated by Greg Blaney, Mickey Linden received the ball in the Derry danger area. The Mayobridge man spotted Down substitute Ciaran McCabe who was not long on the pitch. In an instant he rammed the ball to the corner of the Derry net to give the Mourne men the lead by the slenderest of margins, 1-13 to 1-12. Down were a point ahead as the field stewards gathered around the pitch perimeter. Just before the end Gregory McCartan scored a free to put Down two points in front. When the final whistle sounded the new stars of the county Down had won one of the all time classic Gaelic football encounters by 1-14 to 1-12. Only eight months after Derry had clinched their first senior title they were out of the 1994 All-Ireland series.

Credit must go to Peter McGrath for his team formation and tactics. His 1991 midfield pairing of Eamonn Burns and Barry Breen had now been repositioned in the half back line along with the dynamic D.J. Kane. James McCartan was given a more flexible role at left half forward. Former full back Conor Deegan had been placed at centre field alongside a new star, the powerful Gregory McCartan. This partnership provided a terrific launching pad for quality ball into the forward line, enabling Greg Blaney and Mickey Linden to pulverise the Derry defence.

After the end of the game there was good humoured banter amongst both sets of supporters. However, there was some unnecessary pushing and shoving between very small groups of people. One overly disappointed Derry official had a petty altercation with me as I mingled with a section of the many joyous Down fans. Shortly afterwards the Derry official had regrets about his involvement and rang a good Derry friend of mine wondering what he should do. Our mutual acquaintance advised him to ring me. The next day the man, bearing the surname of a great Derry football clan, telephoned and offered me his sincere apology for his minor indiscretion. For the next hour and a half we chatted excitedly about all the fantastic matches between Down and Derry for the previous 40 years. And we came to the same conclusion that the preceding day's encounter was the finest of all. That honest Derry GAA man's courtesy call sums up what I like about the Association when one is dealing with the vast majority of ordinary supporters. Once the day of the game passes, all personal animosity disappears.

Coming out from Celtic Park after that superb match I knew that, barring some unforeseen circumstances, Down should win that year's All-Ireland. Derry had been great champions but Down possessed something extra thanks to the innovative play of their forwards. The Mourne County was now scheduled to meet Monaghan in the Ulster semi-final on Sunday 19 June. I could not wait. However, little did we then know that a tragic event would soon put the real importance of a sporting occasion into perspective.

For the previous 25 years Northern Ireland had been in a state of political turmoil and civil unrest. Since 1920 there had been a history of discrimination against Catholics, especially in the areas of public housing and equal job opportunities. Successive governments, all of which were unionist in political terms and mainly Protestant in religious affiliation, had perpetuated these malpractices. This had led to the establishment, mainly by the nationalist minority community, of a civil rights movement in the late 1960s. When the moderate unionist Prime Minister of Northern Ireland Captain Terence O'Neill attempted to introduce some basic reforms many extreme unionists, often referred to as loyalists, refused to accept his recommendations. These loyalists considered Catholic businesses and personnel as legitimate targets for indiscriminate bombings and killings.

On the other hand a previously dormant extreme nationalist organisation known as the republican movement resurrected itself and targeted the police and British army with equal ferocity. As a result, many members of both were killed or wounded by the republican movement's paramilitary wing, the IRA. This tit for tat activity continued through the seventies, eighties and nineties. Fear stalked the land and many horrible atrocities were carried out in the name of unionism or republicanism. This is a subject I will return to later, in much more detail, in chapter 17. Suffice for now to say that one of the cruelest events during this period known as "The Troubles" occurred on Saturday night, 18 June 1994. This was on the eve of the Ulster semi-final.

On that night a crowd of mainly Catholic patrons watched the Republic of Ireland play a World Cup soccer match against Italy in a small public house in Loughinisland. This is a quiet village situated near Downpatrick in the heart of County Down. At 10.20 p.m. a group of loyalist gunmen entered The Height's Bar.

They opened fire on the occupants with automatic rifles. 30 bullets were dispatched before the assailants sped away. The Ulster Volunteer Force had killed six people, five of them Catholics, one a Protestant, and injured another five. Those murdered included an 87-year-old man. Nine children had lost a father. Five people died at the scene while the sixth passed away a short time later in hospital. A normally peaceful community had been infiltrated with evil. The whole local community, both Protestant and Catholic, were numbed into a sense of hopelessness.

It was against this surreal background that the footballers of Down and Monaghan took the field the next day. The attendance was poor and a sense of eerie darkness filled both the ground and the hearts of the spectators. The competitive edge of the contest had been dulled by the previous night's terrible event. Still, a match had to be won and Down did so rather convincingly on a 0-14 to 0-8 scoreline. One player stood out that day. Loughinisland's Gary Mason was the man in question. Gary would have known all the people whose lives were brought to a premature end. As Down's normal free taker from the right hand side, Ross Carr, was missing through injury there was extra pressure on Gary to take all the place kicks within scoring range. Showing immense courage and strength of character he scored six excellent points from frees. No one likes winning more than I do but I must say the victory that day felt meaningless compared to the suffering of so many innocent people.

In the Ulster final against Tyrone, Down recovered much of the skill, sharpness and resilience that they displayed in the Derry game. In a strong defence D.J. Kane gave a man-of-the-match performance. Newcomers Brian Burns and Micheal Magill, in the full back line, also starred. As in previous matches the midfield pair of Gregory McCartan and Conor Deegan were superb. Consequently the forward line took full advantage. In the opening period Tyrone conceded many needless frees which Ross Carr and Gary Mason duly punished. Though Mickey Linden missed a penalty, Down still led at the interval by 0-9 to 0-5.

Shortly after the resumption, two Tyrone players pulled down James McCartan, who had temporarily lost his boots, as he bore down on the goal. This time Ross Carr took the resultant spot kick and converted it to leave the score 1-10 to 0-5. Two pointed frees by Peter Canavan and a palmed goal by Adrian Cush helped Tyrone to stage a mini revival but Down soon regained the initiative and they cruised to a 1-17 to 1-11 triumph.

The Mourne men then met Munster champions Cork in the All-Ireland semi-final. Down began playing the much superior football and after 12 minutes they were 0-3 to 0-1 ahead. They continued to press forward and by the 25th minute they had doubled their advantage. Mickey Linden was once again demonstrating the tremendous variety of his considerable skills. Right half back Eamonn Burns sent a long kick downfield. Mickey smartly grabbed the ball and dummied the goalkeeper before passing it to the new, unmarked full forward Aidan Farrell He coolly flicked the leather to the net. However, Cork then took over completely. Within minutes their excellent target man Colin Corkery had scored a sequence of fantastic points to reduce the deficit to a single point. Before half time Down added another point. Despite having controlled the match for long periods they only had a narrow two-point lead. Hopefully the second half would see that gap widen in their favour.

In the third quarter the whole team played superbly with Conor Deegan giving a towering performance at centre field. This ensured a plentiful supply of the ball to the forwards. Between the third and 17th minutes they registered six unanswered points. Frees by Colin Corkery then eased Cork back into the game but by this stage the contest was effectively over Though Down did not score for the last 18 minutes they were never in any real danger. The final score of 1-13 to 0-11 was not really a fair reflection of their superiority.

Down were now in their fifth All-Ireland senior final. For the second time in four years, Peter McGrath and the players had proven their detractors wrong. The feelings which I had when I left Celtic Park at the end of May were still the same. It was Down's All-Ireland to lose.

In the other All-Ireland semi-final Dublin beat surprise packets Leitrim who had just won their first Connacht title since 1927. I was delighted that Dublin had qualified for the decider because all the media hype would centre on them winning the All-Ireland for the first occasion since 1983. Meanwhile, Down could go about their preparations in a much more relaxed and media free manner.

In a tension packed first quarter, on a very wet surface, Down were in the ascendancy. Mickey Linden exploited his pace over Dublin's Paul Curran. Many felt that Curran was not suited to corner back as he was used to playing in the half back line. I believe that the Dublin management made a serious error in how they positioned their defenders. After 15 minutes Down were leading by 0-5 to 0-3. Two minutes later Gary Mason intercepted a Dublin pass and sent the ball downfield to Mickey Linden who raced towards the goalmouth. As he drew the goalkeeper he unselfishly laid it off to James McCartan. James gratefully sent the ball to the corner of the net. This was typical of Mickey's total belief in team play.

He never sought glory for a spectacular score if he deemed another player was in a more advantageous position. Both counties then scored three points each before Dublin's Jack Sheedy shot a point just before half time to leave the interval score, Down 1-8, Dublin 0-7. At this stage I was a little worried as Dublin had more possession in the first half. The only difference between the sides was that Down had maximised their scoring opportunities and Dublin had not.

Down were much the better team in the third quarter and by the fiftieth minute, after a wonderful point by Mickey Linden, they led by 1-12 to 0-9. Nevertheless, in the remaining 20 minutes the Mourne men failed to score. Instead an excellent display by Dublin saw them gradually whittle down the Northerners' lead. Charlie Redmond pointed two frees for the Leinster men and when Sean Cahill added another from play only a goal separated the sides.

I was really getting anxious. The momentum was with the Dubs and I feared a goal was imminent. My worst fears were realised after Dublin sent a long ball into Down's goalmouth. A Down defender fouled the skilful Dessie Farrell in the parallelogram. It was a penalty. Charlie Redmond stepped up to take the kick. If he had scored I have no doubt but Dublin would have won. Down goalkeeper Neil Collins brilliantly parried the spot kick only to see it go back towards the inrushing Charlie. My heart was in my mouth. Thankfully Down captain D.J. Kane detected the danger. His pressurised tackling forced the unfortunate Redmond to drive the ball wide.

For the remaining seven minutes Dublin continued to attack but could only manage one further point before referee Tommy Sugrue of Kerry blew the full time whistle. We had won by 1-12 to 0-13. D.J. Kane was now the Mourne County's fifth All-Ireland winning captain. In the process he became the fourth successive Ulster man to lift the coveted Sam Maguire Cup. I was extremely relieved yet exceptionally happy. The whole side had performed well. 11 of the 1991 team had started the game. The four newcomers Micheal Magill, Brian Burns, Gregory McCartan and Aidan Farrell had all played significant roles in another glorious year for Down football. Winning in 1994 was even more satisfying than 1991 because of all the disappointments in the intervening years. This Down team had proven to everyone, including themselves, that they really were a marvellous team.

As in other years, celebrations continued around the county for many weeks. All of us at home in Donacloney were naturally delighted that James had won another All-Ireland medal. Unlike 1991 Down were very well represented when the annual All-Star awards were announced. Seven players – Micheal Magill, Paul Higgins, D.J. Kane, Gregory McCartan, Greg Blaney, Mickey Linden and James McCartan – were among the deserving recipients.

One player, however, stood out above all the others during that season's success. Mickey Linden had made his senior championship debut with Down in 1982. Here he was 12 years later not only picked as an All-Star but chosen as Footballer of the Year as well. During the course of the 1994 campaign Mickey scored 17 points from play. All of these were created with skill and finished with aplomb. Mickey continued to play for Down until 2003. It was an exceptional career, by any standards, covering 21 years of unbroken service and spanning three decades. It can justifiably be said that Mickey Linden was one of the best and most loyal players ever to wear any county jersey.

Down – National League winners of 1983. We beat neighbouring rivals Armagh in the final.

The day I won my second Railway Cup medal in 1964.

Back row (L to R) – Leo Murphy (Down), Gabriel Kelly (Cavan), Sean O'Neill (Down), Bernard Brady (Donegal), Joe Lennon (Down), P.T. Treacy (Fermanagh), Dan McCartan (Down) and Sean Ferriter (Donegal).

Front row (L to R) – Seamus Hoare (Donegal), Jim McDonnell (Cavan), Paddy Doherty (Down), James McCartan (Down), Jimmy Whan (Armagh), Frankie Donnelly (Tyrone) and Tom Maguire (Cavan).

Marie and myself with Eoin on his Graduation day from Queen's University, Belfast.

James Junior "Man of the Match" in the 1991 All-Ireland final against Meath.

I won three SFC medals with the Glenn club. The majority of the players in the photograph won county medals in both 1962 and 1963.

Tullylish G.F.C.

**All County Division 1 Winners, Winter League Winners
County Championship Runners Up 1971**

back L-R: T Argue J McCartan P Byrne E Fitzgerald D Purdy T McCartan E Morgan P McEvoy R Egan D McCartan
middle L-R: M Purdy G McEvoy S Murphy M Brown B Murphy S Savage J Byrne J Brown A Byrne
front L-R: P Mackin J McShane H Convery G Murphy

The successful Tullylish side of 1971 of which the highlight was reaching that year's senior county final. Winning the 1968 county junior title with them was another great occasion.

Playing foreign games! I was introduced to rugby at Greenmount Agricultural College. I loved it and was the college's fullback. That's me, third from left in the front row.

St Colman's College, Newry, is a supreme Gaelic football nursery. To date they have won seven Hogan Cups and 18 MacRory Cups.

Our two eldest sons played in the 1986 side, which is shown above. Brian is the second player from the left in the back row and "Wee" James is first from the left in the front row. Also included on the extreme left is legendary college coach Raymond Morgan. The then president of the college Fr Malachy Finnegan is behind him. On the extreme right is another talented manager, Peter McGrath.

The St Colman's team which won the MacRory Cup for the 16th time beating keen rivals St Patrick's Maghera in the 1993 final. Our third son, Charlie Pat, who had an outstanding game in the decider, is fifth from the left in the back row.

The Shelbourne Leger. One of my best dogs was "Fancy Joe". He won the Shelbourne Leger in 1995. Shown above are: Back row (L to R) – Tom Egan, Paschal Taggart, Imelda Egan (who made the presentation), Noel Hynes (then General Manager of Shelbourne Park), myself and Ger McKenna (trainer).

Front row (L to R) – Luke Kilcoyne, Owen McKenna (Ger's son) and Cathal Curley.

Down v Cavan, May 2006. First occasion that our two youngest sons – Daniel and Eoin – started an Ulster senior championship match together for Down. Eoin is third from left in back row. Daniel is second from left in middle row.

Pictured before the 1960 All-Ireland final.

Our last walk before immortality. Walking in perfect harmony as we wonder what the next hour will bestow upon us.

Players in order, from left to right – Patsy O'Hagan, Dan McCartan, Leo Murphy, Pat Rice, yours truly and Tony Hadden.

A replica of that picture appeared on the 2009 All-Ireland football championship ticket which celebrated the 125th birthday of the GAA.

Down's Gala GAA Banquet. Pictured at a banquet to commemorate Down's five senior All-Ireland title wins were (L to R) – Leo Murphy, President Mary McAleese, Martin McAleese, Eddie McKay (partially hidden), Marie and myself.

Down Under! James Junior and myself with Australian Prime Minister Bob Hawke at an International Rules Series reception for the Irish team in 1990.

Queens' Sigerson Triumph. Our five sons Brian, Daniel, James, Eoin and Charlie Pat at a function for the successful Queens University, Belfast, Sigerson cup winning team of 2007. James was the manager, Daniel was captain and Eoin a team member.

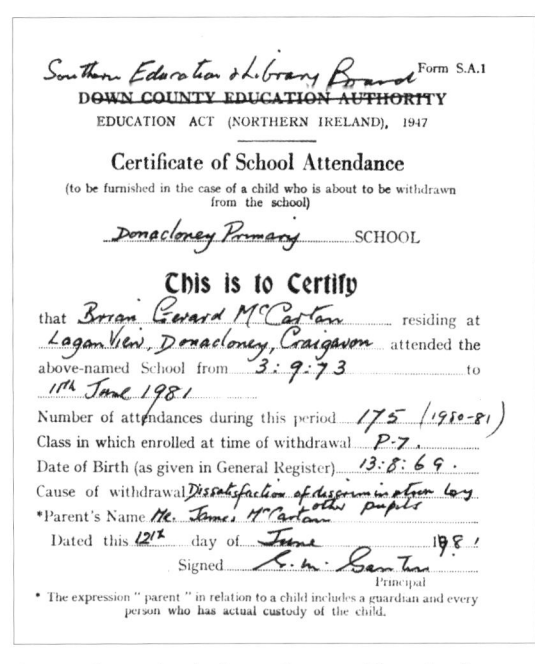

A copy of Brian's school attendance certificate by the principal of Donacloney Primary School, explaining why he was forced to leave the school (see Chapter 17). A similar certificate was issued to each of our five school-going children at that time.

Our son Daniel about to clear his lines for Down.

16

Going To The Dogs

For three weeks before the 1960 All-Ireland senior football final Down trained at Celtic Park on Belfast's Donegall Road, the ancestral home of Belfast Celtic soccer club. It had a magnificent playing surface and was floodlit. This was because it had a well established dog track that was used regularly for greyhound meetings. As the evenings became darker it provided a perfect setting for our training sessions. One evening, after we had finished practising, I was standing watching the greyhound racing when a small, friendly man approached me. He was a native of Kerry and he asked me could I get him a couple of tickets for the final between our two counties. Immediately I struck up a good rapport with him and informed him that I would do my best. When he heard of the Kerry man's request a good, personal friend presented me with two precious tickets. Just after our last practice, before the final, I gave the surprised man the tickets. The man, Ando Moriarty, then offered to pay for them. I told him that they were complimentary. Before I left his pleasant company he assured me he would put the value of the tickets on a couple of good dogs during the next few weeks.

I had totally forgotten about this until just after the following Christmas when Ando walked into our bar at home in Donacloney. Smiling from ear to ear he produced an envelope. Inside it was two twenty-pound notes, the proceeds of Ando's voluntary investments on my behalf! I could not believe it. Here was a man I did not know, except for two brief meetings, giving me forty pounds, which was a colossal sum of money in those days. His sheer honesty became the gateway to a deepening, personal friendship. Prior to this I had no knowledge or indeed interest in greyhounds or the whole racing scene. Eventually, thanks to Ando's encouragement, I decided to buy a greyhound. Ando had been born in Killarney and then moved to Dublin to train dogs before moving to a similar position with the well known Rice Bookmakers in Belfast. He had taken up residence in Derrymacash outside Lurgan in County Armagh. This was only a short journey from my own home. Thanks to Ando a new and exciting pastime was about to unfold for me. I was now a greyhound owner and Ando would be my trainer for the next 25 years.

Ando Moriarty selected my first dog, which he purchased for me in Tralee in his native county. It was called Ballyard Bomber and it enjoyed modest success. In the ensuing 25 years Ando trained all my dogs at his home in Derrymacash. Most Sundays, when our children were small, Marie and myself would visit Ando's house to get an update on the progress of whichever dogs I owned at the particular time. During the course of our partnership I would have stabled over 40 greyhounds in Ando's kennels. I would never have owned more than five dogs at any one time. I ran all my dogs under my wife's maiden name, Marie Mulholland. We had really enjoyable fun and excitement bringing our dogs to all the tracks around Ireland. Visits to Shelbourne Park and Harold's Cross in Dublin, Galway, Limerick, Tralee, Longford, Mullingar, Waterford, Youghal, Clonmel, Enniscorthy, Kilkenny, Navan, Lifford, Newbridge, Thurles, Belfast, Dungannon and Dundalk became a regular occurrence for a quarter of a century. Many new friendships were established and maintained. Money was won and money was lost. Yet, I would have to say, in all honesty, that I enjoyed every minute of it.

From a racing perspective we had some superb trackers. The first really good dog that I had was Count Five which I sold to former Monaghan footballer Cathal McCarthy. I have always had mixed feelings about this as he went on to contest both the English and Irish Derbys. Our best dog was, undoubtedly, Newpark Arkle, which won the Easter Cup at Shelbourne Park and the Ulster St Leger at Celtic Park. Newpark Arkle was so good that it was once named Northern Ireland Dog of the Year.

Then there was Gullion Lad and what a fantastic performer he was. He won the Guinness Puppy Stakes at Mullingar and then the Sprint Cup at Celtic Park in 1977. The following year he landed the Cesarewitch at Navan. In that Navan final Gullion Lad was all of ten lengths down at half way but came with a massive run that saw him catch Solitary Aim in the final strides for a neck victory. My favourite memories are of Gullion Lad landing me a financial coup at Celtic Park. My good friend, the well known Tyrone bookmaker Des Fox, was at the receiving end of my windfall.

Matt Ryan from New Inn in Tipperary was a tremendous man for continually breeding good quality pups. Every year Ando and myself would visit him and he would supply us with wonderful dogs that were always successful in terms of winning races. They all bore the name Hymenstown. Hymenstown Owl proved to be the best of Matt's long list of top class trackers. However, it always took the skill and guile of Ando Moriarty to maximise the performance of each dog that I bought.

Like horse racing, betting is an integral part of the greyhound scene. As long as it can be kept under control it can be a fun exercise for all involved. During the course of my active participation in owning and racing greyhounds it is true to say that I made a lot of money on some occasions. Equally it would be realistic to admit that I also lost plenty of cash at other times. However, at the end of the day, on a countrywide basis, the real winners in this type of scenario are always the bookmakers.

After Ando retired as a trainer I brought my dogs to another excellent trainer, Ger McKenna who lived in Borrisokane in County Tipperary. Ger is a legend of the greyhound world. He was a very helpful and considerate man who knew how to bring the best out of a dog. I have many happy memories of all my dealings with him. For several years everything went well with this arrangement. However, as I got older, the strain of long distance travelling and the general hassle involved made me eventually decide to leave the greyhound scene. I had a great innings but it really was a long, long way from Donacloney to Tipperary. Besides I had also, at this time, made up my mind to retire from my business and farming activities as well. It was time to create a more leisurely existence for Marie and myself.

I had witnessed a total revolution as regards facilities right across the spectrum of the complete greyhound industry. The meagre, almost non-existent, amenities for owners and punters alike when I started were now replaced by corporate hospitality and general top class comfort for all concerned. Nevertheless, all good things must come to an end. As in my football days I knew the time had come to stop. Old father time was taking its toll. What had been a very fulfilling pastime was now beginning to feel like work.

Greyhound racing has provided me with some unusual stories. Two, in particular, I vividly recall. The first one relates to my dentures which I have a habit of losing, misplacing or even breaking. About ten days before the wedding of our daughter Delia who is a dentist I went to a greyhound meeting in Dublin. Near Balbriggan I stopped the car to let the dogs out for a run. Meanwhile, as was my normal habit, I placed my dentures on my knees while I ate a sandwich. It was not until I arrived in Shelbourne Park that I remembered that I must have let the dentures fall on the grass when I went to bring the dogs back into the car trailer. As it was now dark there was no point in looking for them on the homeward journey.

Exactly a week later I returned for another greyhound meeting in Dublin. On the way I stopped at the same spot outside Balbriggan where I had let the dogs out the previous week. I found my beloved dentures on the grass verge, intact and undamaged. Happily for Delia her dental expertise was not required and she was able to concentrate fully on her own wedding preparations!

The second story concerns a good friend of mine, Cathal Curley. He is a keen greyhound enthusiast and is a native of Derry City. Formerly an executive member of Bord na gCon, Cathal was also a very famous rally car driver. He won numerous top class events, including the 1974 Circuit of Ireland. We often went to greyhound meetings together. The craic was always good and Cathal's main fixation was to see how many rats he could kill with his car on any given journey! Returning from Shelbourne Park one night, near Collon in County Louth, I shouted to him that he had missed a rat. Without thinking of the possibility of any oncoming traffic he quickly and expertly turned the car around in the manner that only a talented rally driver could do. At the same time he kept screaming, "Where is the rat?" Unknown to the unfortunate Cathal, another car was speeding from the opposite direction. The vehicles crashed headlong into each other. Luckily no one was injured but both cars were effectively written off. That obsession to kill a rat proved to be a very costly hobby for one of Irish sport's true characters.

Of all the people that I met in over 40 years of greyhound involvement, three special men have always stood out in my mind. Paddy Owens, from Lurgan, is a fantastic Down supporter. Paddy, who used to own Drumbo Park Greyhound Stadium, regularly came to races with me and is still a great friend.

Ando Moriarty was unique for his intimate greyhound knowledge, his integrity and his unwavering friendship. Ando and his Kerry-born wife Peggy had two sons, Ando and Paddy, as well as two daughters, Margaret and Mary. One of his sons, Paddy, became a household name. He was an outstanding sportsman, playing both hurling and football at all levels for Armagh. He made his senior intercounty debut in 1970 and he won four Railway Cup medals in a sparkling career. Just 18 months after making his senior intercounty debut he was picked at left full forward on the 1972 All-Stars team.

> *The voice is now silent, the heart now cold,*
> *The smile and welcome that met us of old,*
> *We miss you and mourn you to sorrow unseen,*
> *And dwell on the memories of days that have been.*

The above lines are taken from the memoriam card of another great friend, now sadly departed. Des Fox was a native of Edendork, near Dungannon in Tyrone. He was a teacher before he turned to bookmaking. Des was a natural at the odds.

Form and figures were his forte. He enlivened the ring and had acquired some of the best pitches at both our major greyhound and horse racing tracks. His business was carried out very efficiently and very honestly. He had a perpetual smile, even when he was paying out. The whole betting community admired him. Regardless of the circumstances, no one had a bad word to say about him. To the people of Edendork he was the driving force behind St Malachy's GAC. No one was more proud than he when Edendork opened their splendid, new GAA facilities in May 1990. In his address, as the club's esteemed chairman, he epitomised his modern thinking with the following words: "Things have changed all over Ireland. We are saying goodbye to the rush bush, to the zig zag sidelines and the chair and the table at the gate. Clubs realise that modernisation is a necessity and presentation of our games must compete with TV and other sports."

Sadly, a few months later that distinctive voice of progress, of friendship, of that all-embracing smile would be no more. We had to say our earthly goodbyes to one of nature's real gentlemen.

On 30 September 1990 Des Fox was driving to the Curragh for one of the last flat race meetings of the season. Just a few miles from the track, near Clane, a gang of armed robbers ambushed his car. As Des tried to escape they fired a shot at one of the car's front tyres and punctured it. They then cruelly shot him dead before grabbing a substantial amount of cash from his car. A criminal gang had deprived his lovely wife Bernadette and his three young children of a marvellous husband and a great father. Des and Bernadette, who is a native of Newry, were dear friends of all of us in the greyhound and horse racing industries. It is particularly disappointing to realise that after all these years no one has been charged for this terrible atrocity.

In the spring of 2008 I became an inductee into the Hall of Fame for my contribution to the greyhound industry. It was a great personal honour and I will always be grateful for those who sponsored the award. I would also like to acknowledge another outstanding greyhound patron and sports commentator, Michael Fortune, for his kind words on the night. However, the real winner of that personal honour was an absent and deceased friend. After all, it was Ando Moriarty whom I have to thank for providing me with such pleasure since the night he asked me for those All-Ireland tickets over 50 years ago. I can honestly say, without fear of contradiction, that he was the nicest and most gracious person that I ever met. All of us need an interest outside our family, our work and our normal hobbies, sporting or otherwise. Ando certainly supplied me with that in great abundance.

17

Loyalist Intimidation and Extreme Republicanism

After my mother died in 1968 my father gradually withdrew from active involvement in the family quarry business at Tullyraine, which is about five miles from Donacloney and two miles from Banbridge. After this, three first cousins who were all sons of the original three shareholders now controlled the quarry business. Xavier was a son of my uncle Charlie, Seamus was a son of my uncle Jimmy, and I inherited my father's share. Xavier, Seamus and I worked together for the next 30 years and developed the quarry into the thriving concern that it is today. Sadly Xavier passed away some years ago and Seamus and I have now retired. Seamus' son John and my son James Junior are now responsible for the day to day running of the enterprise. All of us had really enjoyable times working in the business. People who worked along with us like Jimmy McClorey and Davy Andrews were not only great workers but tremendous characters and lifelong friends as well.

The quarry was also the setting for a very informal and unusual gathering every Monday morning after a county match. This "Monday Morning Game" lasted for over 40 years, from the late 1950s to the late 1990s. Our morning tea break was usually from ten o'clock until a quarter past ten. However, such was the intensity of the post match analysis and the variety of opinions expressed, work often did not commence again until eleven o'clock. In the early years my father and my uncle Joey Murphy (my mother's brother, who also worked in the quarry) were the main discussion facilitators. We were very democratic as to whom we allowed to take part. Lots of people who had no association whatsoever with the quarry came, not only to listen to a lively discussion about Down football, but also to actively participate. It would have been great if all those conversations, especially regarding Down's All-Ireland and provincial successes in all grades, had been recorded. That would have meant that the Tullyraine archives could have been used for the GAA's national oral history project!

Tullyraine Quarries were incorporated in 1954 for the purpose of carrying on the business of quarry masters and civil engineering contracts. The company today produces high quality products which are sold locally as well as in the Republic of Ireland. The company also produces bitmac and asphalt materials for sale and for its own surfacing contracts. Our customers have included the Department of the Environment, Louth County Council, the Water Service and many other construction firms both north and south. When Seamus and I were involved he was in charge of the production work in the quarry. It was my job, as foreman, to ensure that our staff carried out our surfacing contracts to agreed specifications.

On the farming front we started off with a dairy herd but by the mid-fifties we had changed to a suckler herd. Gradually we expanded our livestock and bought two additional small farms to supplement its growth. Everything progressed very satisfactorily for the next 45 years. There were two main reasons for this. First, we had a succession of very able and hardworking farm managers who took control of the daily running of the farm. Trevor Walker, Paddy Doran, Seamus Mallon and Paddy Convery always made sure that all farm work was carried out to the highest possible standards. Second, the man who was mainly responsible for buying our stock had a great eye for selecting top class cattle. That man, Brian Mullan, was a constant source of support and advice. Brian was a native of Ballerin in north Derry and was a celebrated member of a noted GAA family. Brian himself played for Derry in the 1958 All-Ireland final against Dublin. In latter years Declan McQuaid from Loughbrickland also contributed immensely to ensuring that our livestock needs were always met.

There were three components to my working life – the quarry, the farm and the bar. Even though I adopted a hands-on approach to all three, my daily quarry duties meant that my farm and bar activities were limited to evening and weekend work. The first two presented no difficulty. However, it was the bar that would present Marie and myself with the greatest challenge from the early seventies onwards. It was in the bar that my wife Marie deserves all the plaudits. She worked unceasingly and built up a great rapport with both customers and staff alike. Along with Marie, the staff, who emanated from both sides of the religious divide, made our premises a place of conviviality and hospitality. People like Aidan Barry, Mickey Browne, Gary Knox, Eamon McCusker, Geraldine McCusker and Kevin Robinson were all magnificent workers.

Nevertheless, external forces soon contrived to make our home and bar a place of increased tension and unhappiness. I have never had any involvement or interest in party politics. It would be true to say that I believe in the concept of a united Ireland. However, that thinking would be based on a consensus only arrived at by democratic and constitutional means amongst ordinary nationalists and unionists. The idea of either IRA or loyalist paramilitaries forcing their separate agendas of national unity or a sectarian statelet would be totally repugnant to me. It is easy to express republican ideals from the relative safety of south Armagh. When the IRA campaign of killings and bombing escalated from 1969 onwards it was the innocent Catholics living in unionist strongholds such as Donacloney who suffered most. Similarly, innocent Protestants living in largely nationalist areas felt under threat after horrific killings and intimidation of Catholics by loyalist extremists.

Our parish of Tullylish had more than its fair share of terrible deaths during the period of the Troubles, particularly between 1972 and 1994. During this time nine people from our parish were cruelly killed, most of them simply because they were Catholics. The first parishioner to meet a violent death was Joe Fagan in August 1972. 28-year-old Joe was working at the Custom Office in Newry when an IRA bomb exploded prematurely. The next casualties were John Michael Feeney and Joe Toman who were shot dead in a gun attack at Bleary Social Club in the far end of the parish in April 1975. A group called the Protestant Action Force admitted these killings. Three other parishioners were killed in their own home on 4 January 1976. They were Joseph O'Dowd and his nephews Barry and Declan who were shot by the Ulster Volunteer force (UVF). 32-year-old Patsy Feeney, who was a Catholic security man at Liddell's factory in Donacloney, was killed by the Ulster Freedom Fighters (UFF) on 20 February 1988. In 1993 two masked men burst into the family home of two brothers, Gerry and Rory Cairns, at Bleary and gunned them down.

It was against this background of anti-Catholicism, fear and tension that we lived for 30 years. Prior to the troubles the picturesque village of Donacloney was a place of peace where we lived in harmony with our Protestant neighbours. Its adherence to Protestant values was evidenced most clearly in the 1960s when July came and the colours of red, white and blue bedecked the village. These few weeks of triumphalism were adequate to remind us for the rest of the year that "we were different". This never maintained itself beyond the marching season or into violence until the early 1970s, coinciding with the Troubles. To give the reader an exact understanding of what we, as a family, went through I have in the following pages itemised the more significant incidents and facts that occurred during the period 1970–2000.

1. On the day that Princess Anne of England was married in 1973, a coursing event had been planned for Ballymena in County Antrim. As most hotels were under threat of bombing either by the IRA or extreme loyalists, a coursing judge asked me to put him up for the night. I duly obliged. Some time later I noticed a large, suspicious looking object placed at the entrance of our lounge bar. I immediately alerted the police and brought Marie and our three young children, Brian (3), James (2), Delia (1), to a friend's house about a mile from our home. I then got a towrope and put it around the suspicious package. I had intended to tie the rope to my Massey Ferguson tractor before dragging it away to a safer place. Luckily the police and an army bomb disposal team arrived. They did what I had planned and then carried out a controlled explosion. It was a powerful bomb, which would have killed all of us. It had been planted by a loyalist paramilitary organisation. After it was all over I was trembling with fear as I wiped the cold sweat off my forehead. The prompt action of the security forces had saved our lives and our home. In the midst of all of this commotion the startled coursing judge, a Kerry man, ran out, put his luggage in his car and drove off at speed. I never saw or heard of him again!

2. On 3 January 1976 a group of regular customers, the O'Dowd family, who lived a few miles away in the townland of Ballydougan, were having a night out in our bar. The parents were looking forward to their 25th wedding anniversary party which was to be held the following night at their house. The O'Dowds who were prominent members of the mainly Catholic and moderate nationalist party the SDLP were looking eagerly forward to a family reunion.

One family member, Seamus, was helping to prepare the food for the party on the night of 4 January when he decided to go to a neighbour's house for another carving knife. When he returned 20 minutes later, he found their Alsatian dog lying in the gateway obviously poisoned. As he entered his homestead a scene of total mayhem and desolation awaited him. In his brief absence a group of gunmen had come to the house, killed the dog and shot all the male occupants. Three of them were dead and several others were seriously injured. It later transpired that the men, who had carried out the killings, were members of the loyalist Ulster Volunteer Force.

Three of the victims, Joseph O'Dowd and his two nephews Barry and Declan O'Dowd, had been killed instantly. All of them had been in our bar the previous night. The next day the South Armagh Republican Action Force that was alleged to be a cover name for the Provisional IRA retaliated with the killings of ten Protestant civilians at Kingsmill between Whitecross and Bessbrook in South Armagh.

Fear now continually stalked us as to what we could do to minimise the danger to ourselves. We asked the RUC to keep a close watch on our premises and our movements. To their eternal credit they did so in a very fair and unobtrusive manner. However, my most abiding memory of that January in 1976 is of the three coffins being brought up the road from the O'Dowds' house and then up the aisle for the funeral mass in the local Catholic church. In my mind's eye I still see the trauma of the whole congregation as they watched a distraught family trying to come to terms with the horrific end that their loved ones endured. As with so many other victims, the O'Dowds were not just our customers, they were also our friends.

3. Our children attended the local Protestant primary school because the nearest Catholic school was over five miles away. Everything was ok at first. Still, as the atrocities and the tension between the two communities in Northern Ireland increased, so did the intimidation of our children from their Protestant peers. They did not allow them to play football or take part in any schoolyard games during breaktimes. They were continually taunted and called unmentionable names. They experienced a sense of total isolation.

Despite our protestations most of the teachers washed their hands of this intolerable situation. Basically they did not want to offend the rest of the children, most of whom were Protestants. One teacher, a Mrs Judd, was an honourable exception. On one occasion she was called to the phone. When she was taking the call she heard a catalogue of sectarian abuse and jeering directed at our children. She tried to reprimand the culprits but they would not listen. Afterwards she came to Marie and apologised for the nasty behaviour.

By 1981 we could take no more. We transferred our five school-going children to the nearest Catholic school in Laurencetown. The Education and Library Board eventually agreed to transport them to Laurencetown for the remainder of their primary school careers. Every school principal must state in writing the reason for any pupil's transfer. In his honest report the principal of Donacloney Primary School stated that the McCartans left because they were being discriminated against by their fellow pupils. There is something terribly wrong with a society that allows children to be treated in such a manner. Though annoyed we were now happy that our children could enjoy the innocence and fun of childhood in a happy environment which Laurencetown School certainly provided.

4. As we were the only licensed premises in Donacloney, we prepared rather diligently for the local 12th of July district demonstration of Orangemen, which took place for the first time in our village one year in the mid-eighties. We purchased more stock and set up a mobile bar in our yard to facilitate our projected extra trade. However, a small group of our erstwhile friends and neighbours stood at the bottom of our avenue on the morning of the twelfth and told would-be customers not to drink in our bar. If they did so they would really be drinking Barry's Holy Water, they sarcastically remarked. This was a cynical reference to the Minister for Foreign Affairs in the Republic, Peter Barry.

   What made the protest more galling was the fact that one of the main protestors was a local businessman who had a facility in the Republic to export goods to Northern Ireland! In other words he did not mind making money out of the Republic, which was a foreign country as far as he was concerned. Yet he would not let us earn our own livelihood in our own village. The local cricket club to whom we occasionally transferred our liquor licence was not patronised either as they were considered collaborators with "The Fenian McCartans". I had always a good relationship with both the local cricket and soccer clubs. Indeed, I regularly sponsored both organisations and had installed showers for the soccer team in an old outbuilding on our farm in 1977, as well as allowing them to use one of our fields for their matches. As the day finally panned out, we sold very little alcohol.

   More frightening was our conviction that the depth of antagonism towards us by the local Protestant population had dramatically increased.

5. During all these tortuous years graffiti was constantly scrawled on the walls of both the bar and our dwelling house. Local young fellows were responsible for this but no one was ever charged. After discovering these slogans I would paint over them. Then the loyalists would repeat their actions and I would erase them again. This was a regular pattern of activity that seemed to last for an eternity.

Every night we had our own security routine. We would drop the blinds, draw the curtains and then jam a chair against the bottom of the window. As most serious injuries are caused by flying glass this process was designed to limit the damage to ourselves should we be attacked by either bomb or bullet. We carried out this procedure in every room, every night, for almost 30 years. That is a cold statistic that I can hardly believe when I look back on what we went through.

We often had to sleep in tracksuits in case we had to leave prematurely because of an attack. The saddest part of all of this was that many of the younger people in the village had no loyalty or respect for us. This was in direct contrast to most of their elders who were very decent God-fearing Protestants. Despite the hooliganism of many of the younger neighbours, our original Protestant customers still kept coming to us. Our customers were our friends.

Outside of my visits to greyhound stadiums, Marie and myself rarely went anywhere. So our social life was the nightly chat of friendship with our Protestant patrons. I am happy to say that today I can still call many of them good and decent loyal friends.

6. One night in October 1985 I attended a greyhound meeting in Dunmore Stadium in Belfast. After racing my dog, Hymenstown Joe, I put it into a reserved kennel. When I went to collect it at the end of the night, the greyhound was gone. The police informed me that a loyalist extremist had probably stolen it.

Having signalled my intentions to the police, I decided to contact a well-known Belfast loyalist paramilitary leader. I knew him not in any political sense but rather as a fellow greyhound aficionado. I phoned this man whom I will refer to as Mr X and told him of my plight. Mr X knew I had no interest in politics. All that I wanted was peace for my family and myself. He arranged to meet me at a house on the unionist Shankill Road.

The house was full of loyalist emblems and paramilitary paraphernalia. I was really scared and wished I had not come. Led by Mr X I went to several similar houses searching for the elusive greyhound. I prayed for my safety and that of my family back in Donacloney. Eventually we found the greyhound. The terrified dog was absolutely delighted to see me! I thanked Mr X and hastily drove out of Belfast. The sweat poured off me as the images of bigotry gratefully disappeared from view. I was never so pleased to see Marie and the children. Regardless of the circumstances, I would never take such a risk again. Good health, safety and happiness should never be compromised.

7. We were constantly being asked to subscribe money to various loyalist organisations such as prisoners' dependent funds. At all times during these years we kept the police informed of any suspicious behaviour or unusual phone calls. On one scary occasion in July 1986, Marie answered the phone to such a request. Two days later the original caller rang back and asked to speak to me. I was told to leave £12,000 Sterling in an envelope inside a named locker in Portadown Swimming Pool, at a specified time and date. We did not respond or react to these calls.

Shortly afterwards, a suspicious looking man came into the bar and ordered a drink. After taking just a sip he got up, left an envelope on the counter and departed the premises. Inside the envelope was a note demanding the £12,000. It also said that they knew our children, which schools they attended and the routes they travelled. The unsigned note concluded with the chilling, terrifying message: "James' end will not be quick. It will be slow and painful."

All of us were now at breaking point. I felt awfully sorry for everyone, especially Marie who was totally stressed out. Desperate problems require desperate solutions. So, I decided to go for broke. I phoned Mr X and informed him of my terrible anxiety and overwhelming fears. He phoned me back a few days later and told me everything would be okay.

However, much to my disillusionment, the original protection racket man phoned me three days afterwards to say that he knew I was talking to certain people in high places. "That does not work for us. You need not think that Mr X is going to save you," he added before hanging up the phone.

I was in a real quandary. I wondered was I being double crossed? After all, I knew that Mr X was really the phone caller's boss. Nevertheless, when I again phoned Mr X, I knew he was straight with me, especially after his surprised reaction to the latest instalment of the phone saga.

"Put me over that again," he defiantly pleaded. I reread the initial letter as well as recalling what had been said on the phone. Three nights later Mr X called once more. "I think you will have no more bother," he said curtly. "These people have been taken care of."

He was right. We never saw or heard from that protection man again. Mr X had saved our lives from being regularly subjected to such outrageous ransom demands.

8. During that fortnight of misery the police inserted a bugging device on our telephone. The arrangement was that we could not answer any phone message until the phone rang three times. Marie was to answer it. I was not to answer it, as I was the perceived target to be killed. The army and police special branch officers were now placed strategically and constantly in the fields around our house. We had to make a promise to Mr X that if the police did find out the identity of the loyalist protection visitor, we were not to press charges. For example, under police instructions, Marie had carefully placed the drinking glass that the "protection messenger" had left on our counter into a brown paper bag. She then brought it to a named newsagent in an adjacent town from where the police collected it. From the fingerprints on the glass the police were able to identify the name of the loyalist responsible for bringing the envelope into the bar. However, we kept our pledge to Mr X and we did not press charges against the suspected individual. We were now relieved to be alive and happy to resume some semblance of normality in our lives.

9. During the spring of 1987 there was much speculation among the greyhound fraternity about a matter which was especially disturbing for me. There was repeated conjecture that the loyalist paramilitary organisation the UDA was demanding protection money from the bookmakers who manned the greyhound track at Dunmore Stadium in Belfast.

Furthermore, it was widely circulated that if the bookmakers did not pay, two prominent GAA personalities who regularly attended Dunmore would "be taken out". To the best of my knowledge there were only two people that fitted this description and I was one of them.

Even though there was no initial proof concerning the validity of these remarks the whole scenario was very upsetting for my family and myself. As we approached Easter Sunday the stories intensified and I became increasingly apprehensive. It emerged that a Sunday newspaper was going to publish an account of the alleged protection racket on the Sunday and that I would be named as a target for assassination. On Holy Saturday night I went, as normal, to the greyhound meeting in Dunmore. Just before the first race, my loyalist acquaintance Mr X informed me that he wanted to have an important discussion after the last race. To say that I was worried would be an understatement.

When we met afterwards Mr X confirmed the substance of the proposed newspaper article. However, he assured me that in no way was my life under any threat. For whatever reason the next day's paper did not publish my name and a very sanitised version of the saga was printed. Nevertheless, the whole episode evoked a terrible sense of unease. Everywhere I went I was conscious of the possibility of someone trying to bring my life to a premature end. It was many months before I could relax properly. In fairness to Mr X, as far as I was concerned, he always kept his word.

10. On the night before the first round of the 1991 Ulster senior championship match between Armagh and Down there was a huge bomb explosion at Clover Brea, just across the River Lagan on which Donacloney village is built. It was an IRA bomb that caused the explosion. Apparently it was planned to go off in Lurgan, six miles away. The bombers could not get it transported in time so they were forced to abandon it and it exploded prematurely. All of the doors and windows of our house and the neighbouring houses were blown out. We brought all the affected people into our bar and lounge and made them as comfortable as we could for the night. Our whole family, including James Junior, helped to block the doorways and windows with boards. Ironically, all the people who we willingly gave refuge to were Protestants. James helped all night. When he togged out for Down the next day he had not been in bed for over 30 hours.

11. On 28 October 1993 two good family acquaintances that were neighbours of the O'Dowds were killed. Brothers Gerry (22) and Rory (18) Cairns were gunned down by two masked gunmen who burst into their family home at Bleary, just a few miles away from Donacloney. There were many suspicious circumstances surrounding the deaths of these two innocent young Catholics.

In the hours before the terrible deed, the British Army and the police had set up roadblocks in the area surrounding Bleary. Helicopters also hovered overhead. The question most ordinary people asked was how did the gunmen pass through the roadblocks unhindered. This highlighted the suspicion of collaboration. No one has ever been charged with these murders. Among the chief suspects were men who were believed to have committed many heinous crimes. From our viewpoint we just prayed that this mad cycle of violence would end and that the ordinary people of Northern Ireland would be allowed to live in peace.

12. In the late 1990s, one night I went to a greyhound meeting in Shelbourne Park in Dublin. Marie and our youngest son Eoin were in the bar with the staff. There was a pre-arranged function for a party of people in our lounge. Suddenly Marie received a frightening phone call from an agitated caller to say that our pub was a UDA pub and not a UVF establishment.

The UDA were a leading loyalist paramilitary group who were often in conflict with another loyalist paramilitary grouping known as the UVF. Apparently on that day there had been a bloody feud between the two groups in a public house in Belfast and several people had been shot. The voice said, "You have UVF men in your bar. I want to tell you that the people who killed Robert Hamill are in your bar at the moment."

This was a reference to a 25-year-old Catholic man who had been beaten unconscious by a loyalist mob in Portadown in 1997. Robert had died 11 days later in hospital. The RUC had arrested six men and charged them in connection with the killing. All were released after the charges were withdrawn.

Marie wisely remembered the advice of Mr X: "Never confront a loyalist phone caller. If you do so you automatically become a target for them to shoot you." She did not go into the function room.

A short while later the man rang back. "I told you to get them out," he angrily shouted before adding, 'If you cannot get them out we will get them out. We will have no problem doing it. We have already done it in the Shankill Road today."

Eoin, who was only 14 at the time, was terrified. "They are going to come here and have a bloodbath," he cried. A Protestant friend who was in the bar that night and who used to work as a barman with us came to Marie's assistance. He told Marie not to go into the function room. He would go in himself and shout "bomb scare". He told the party in the function room that the staff had received a phone call that there was a bomb on the premises. The party wanted to know what the caller's password was. Marie did not have a password.

The brave ex-bar manager shouted "I do not know, just get out!" The party knew that there was something unusual. If there had been a bomb Marie and Eoin would have left the bar. So they went outside and kept hammering the front door as Marie rang the police for help. "Please come quickly. They are going to kill us," she pleaded. The police arrived within minutes.

The remainder of the customers had now gone home. The police stayed comforting Marie and Eoin for over three hours until I arrived back from Dublin. The police were terrific that night. They had become our friends because they knew the constant threats and intimidation that we were experiencing were really terrifying.

Most people who lived in pubs in similar situations had experienced the same type of trauma during the course of the Troubles. There were many unsung heroes and heroines right across Northern Ireland. Marie had been at the coalface of fear and tension for 25 years. That night she proved herself a real heroine.

13. The police often told us that the vast majority of the people in the village admired us for our constant stance against the threats of violence and intimidation. Understandably they were afraid to publicly admit this because of a certain unruly element in their own midst. Still, they respected us for the consistency of our approach towards all people of violence regardless where it emanated from. We never closed the pub to accommodate loyalist threats or to facilitate republicans who, for example, wanted us to close because of the deaths of IRA hunger strikers in 1981. Our only duty as we perceived it was to accommodate our customers and thereby earn a livelihood for the upkeep of our family of seven children.

14. On another 12th of July, over 200 posters with the slogan "It is unhealthy to drink in McCartans" were posted on all telephone and electricity poles throughout the village. Young ruffians came up our avenue and painted all our kerbstones red, white and blue. Next morning I repainted the offending stones with grey paint.

15. We were often called an IRA pub by loyalist extremists. One anecdote highlights the total inaccuracy of these bitter comments. Marie's sister is married in England to a man who was a serving officer in the British Army at the time. She and her husband used to visit us every year for a short holiday. As per normal, the police were always aware of this visit and would keep a close watch on our premises when they were staying with us. This was done to prevent the IRA from attacking us! The loyalists were taunting us about our non-allegiance to their British heritage while inside our house a serving officer belonging to the same heritage was happily holidaying.

16. As the years progressed the intimidation increased both in its frequency and methodology. For example a crowd assembled one year and threatened to burn

us out. I was able to hold them at bay as I pretended to assemble a gun for my protection. In the meantime Marie had phoned the police. Again they arrived in time to save us from another catastrophe. Very often when Marie walked through the village, young locals would spit on the ground as she passed. Regularly, when our Protestant customers came out of the bar at night each of their cars would have a black rose attached to the windscreen. This action was designed to intimidate them from ever returning to the bar. Still our brave neighbours remained undaunted and kept returning. They enjoyed our hospitality and we appreciated their custom. We were good for each other.

17. One afternoon four strange young men came into the bar. They were drinking very heavily. They quickly downed double vodkas mixed with Buckfast. Marie was serving them. She alerted me to their suspicious behaviour. I was in the kitchen.

    I walked out of the front door and entered the bar where they were drinking. I pretended that I was a customer and started to read a newspaper. We knew that they were strangers and therefore did not know who I was. Eoin went outside and took the numbers of their cars. This was a regular activity which all of our family in turn, but especially Eoin and Daniel, did over the years.

    Marie phoned the police with the information. They told her that our unwanted visitors were leading paramilitary activists. They told Marie not to confront them, as they would arrive within ten minutes. When the gang spotted the arrival of the police they immediately ran out and made their escape across the river. The police then seized their abandoned car. The boot was packed with baseball bats and balaclavas. Our dodgy customers had obviously been preparing to carry out a punishment beating on some unfortunate individual(s) in another town.

On 10 April 1998 a political settlement for the people of Northern Ireland known as "The Good Friday Agreement" was finally concluded. It set out a plan for devolved government in Northern Ireland and provided for the creation of human rights for all as well as an Equality Commission. Both the British and Irish governments as well as most of Northern Ireland's political parties with the notable exception of the hardline Unionist party, the DUP, signed the Agreement. Since then, both the DUP and Sinn Féin, who were the political allies of the IRA, have come together to form a historic Power Sharing Executive. This is a welcome change from both parties' previous intransigent positions. It is just such a pity that most of these people did not listen to the voice of moderation as espoused by SDLP leader John Hume over 25 years earlier. After all, if his 1972 proposals had been adhered to the ordinary people of Northern Ireland would have been spared much death, destruction, violence and intimidation.

From our own perspective, I initially thought that the Agreement would make our lives in Donacloney a little more peaceful, a little less tense. Unfortunately this was not the case. The seeds of bitterness and hatred had been deeply implanted in the new generation of our Protestant neighbours. They just saw us as soft targets for continuing sectarian abuse and intimidation.

This Orange triumphalism was particularly evident towards us in the weeks preceding the 12th of July every year. So bad was it that all our family felt compelled to stay with us to protect us from this annual vitriol. Gradually Marie and I came to the reluctant conclusion that it was time for both of us to step down from our regular working lives. Our family was effectively reared. Each of them in their own way had charted a career path or was in the process of doing so. None of them had any interest in carrying on the traditional farming and bar business in Donacloney.

So the hard decision was taken. We would retire from work, sell our home place and move to a quieter area. The farm and business were advertised for sale by private treaty.

The highest bidder for the property was a local and exceptionally decent Protestant man. However, the twin forces of Orange bigotry and hardline Unionism raised their ugly heads again. A small caucus of extreme Unionists visited the bidder and tried to prevent him from paying us the agreed price. They wanted us to get as little as possible for our property. It was bad enough to be forced to sell your ancestral home without the added burden of trying to get a just price for it. Courageously, our Protestant purchaser stood firm and paid us the market value. To him I will always be eternally grateful for his sense of honesty in the face of unadulterated anti-Catholic bigotry.

It was very much a time of mixed emotions when we drove away from our home in Donacloney for the last time. It was 16 January 2002. Four generations of the McCartans had been reared in that beautiful village which nestles on the banks of the River Lagan. There had been times of hardship, of laughter and fun. Through sheer hard work each successive generation had provided a comfortable livelihood for their offspring. Luckily all of us always possessed a tightly knit sense of family spirit and unity of purpose. However, none of our forefathers had experienced the trauma, challenges and difficulties that Marie and I endured. During those 30 years of constant fear and unnerving intimidation, we were often asked, "Why do you stay here? Why not sell out and buy a different place in a safer location?" Both Marie and I were blessed, or some might say cursed, with a steely inner determination. We would not be bullied out of a home and a livelihood that others had worked and striven for. It was only when we had done our duty for our children that we decided to move.

When I looked in the mirror of our departing car I shut out all thoughts of negativity. I fondly remembered the words of my grandfather when I innocently hammered the nails into his kitchen unit all those years ago. I thought of my father and his games of football with Dan and myself in the yard when he came home from work every evening. Playing football with the O'Neills in the hayfields of those far off sunny summer days evoked a sense of pride. It certainly was a long way from Donacloney to Croke Park but the four of us had made it many times and with great results.

Marie and I looked at each other as our homestead finally disappeared from view. It was time to say farewell to the past but not to each other. After all we had just celebrated 34 years of a very happy marriage. For the present it was more important to say hello to our new life and our new home. It was 23 miles away from the madding crowd in the south of the county Down. We could not wait to start our lives all over again.

18

A GAA Family Dynasty

My greatest supporter during my playing days was, undoubtedly, my father. He had always yearned for the day when Down would win an All-Ireland senior football title. What made that breakthrough all the more enjoyable for him was the fact that he himself had played for Down for nine years between 1924 and 1932. Then expectations were limited and victories extremely rare.

He was the team's regular centre half back as well as captain. He made his championship debut at left half back in 1924 against Antrim. Despite a spirited performance the Mourne men were defeated. In a preview of the 1925 championship match, also against Antrim, the *Frontier Sentinel* described him as "a splendid half back who played a glorious game in the 1924 contest". The paper added that "he has a very strong kick and is a great shot from the 50 yard line".

Again, however, Down lost as they did the following year against Monaghan. Nevertheless, 1926 was to provide us with a story highlighting the amateurish nature of arrangements at that time. The championship contest with the Farney men did not begin until one hour after the appointed time. Incredibly both sides had forgotten to bring a football and, to make matters worse, the Down officials had neglected to bring a set of jerseys. Consequently a man was commissioned to ride a bicycle from the match venue, in Hilltown, to get a ball several miles away in Rathfriland. At the same time, and by the same mode of transport, another messenger was despatched three miles in a different direction to get the jerseys.

1927 was the most significant year during Dad's intercounty days. On three successive Sundays in March, Down played a county match. Down and Tyrone met for the first time in an intercounty competition when they played in a National League encounter at Dungannon. A one-point victory gave the Mourne side encouragement to face Armagh on the following Sunday in the first round of the new McKenna Cup knockout competition. However, defeat was their lot on this occasion.

A week later they overcame Monaghan in the league. This was one of Dad's most impressive displays. He was also now the team captain. Sighle Nic an Ultaigh, in her excellent book *An Dún – The GAA story*, states: "Brian McCartan was the outstanding man on the Down team. Tumilty saved well. O'Hare was a steady back while Gribben and Mussen played classic football."

A fortnight later that side made their own bit of history when they became the first team from the county to travel overnight for a fixture. The game was against the Lilywhites in Kildare. It was also the first time that they wore their new red and black jerseys. That was an outstanding Kildare team that had lost the previous year's All-Ireland final against Kerry only after a replay. Furthermore they were destined to win both the 1927 and 1928 All-Irelands using the same 15 players. So, to be beaten by only six points represented a very creditable performance. An interesting footnote to all of this was that the county board had placed a levy of five shillings on each club to pay for the new jerseys.

When the National League resumed in October, Down defeated a star-studded Dublin 15. The Metropolitans included eight All-Ireland medal holders who were all survivors of Croke Park's infamous "Bloody Sunday" which had occurred seven years earlier in 1920. Again Sighle Nic an Ultaigh refers to my father: "Briney McCartan outshone all afield in speed, artistic tackling and accurate long shots."

From then until the end of his intercounty career Down did not achieve anything of note at senior level, though the county did win a junior provincial football title in 1931.

During this time GAA clubs were not as well structured or as efficiently organised as they are today. In fact my father had no natural home club. At different stages he played for Mayobridge (a Cabra and Rathfriland amalgamation), Hilltown, Annaclone and Clonduff. His work in the family quarry business took him all over the place. This usually meant living in a hut wherever he was working. If the local club in that area was playing a match the following Sunday, Dad would automatically "sign on" for them. His friendship with well known Armagh interprovincial footballer and county secretary Padraig "Poppy" Fearon also brought him to clubs not only in Armagh but as far away in Monaghan. He did not mind where he played as long as he could get a game.

My father loved all sports and was a great follower of Irish League soccer club Belfast Celtic. They were a famous team, founded in 1891, that became one of the most successful sides in Ireland until they suddenly withdrew from the league in 1949. Even though they were an all-inclusive side, the vast majority of their supporters were Catholic and nationalist. On the other hand their fiercest rivals,

Linfield, did not allow, at that time, Catholics to play for them. Their support emanated totally from the Protestant and unionist traditions.

The end for Belfast Celtic came on Boxing Day in 1948. In a match against their greatest opponents, Linfield, at the latter's home ground at Windsor Park, Celtic led for most of the game. After Linfield had equalised in the last minute their fans invaded the pitch and attacked several Celtic players. Celtic's magnificent centre forward, Jimmy Jones, who incidentally was a Protestant, had his leg broken by the mob. The directors of Belfast Celtic felt that the police were unable to protect their players so they withdrew from the league at the end of the 1948/49 season.

When Belfast Celtic folded, their ace forward Jimmy Jones transferred to the Lurgan-based Glenavon club. Dad instantly became a Glenavon supporter and remained so until his death. Jimmy became a goalscoring legend. Dad was one of his greatest fans as indeed were many other people from the greater Donacloney area. Watching so many soccer games on Saturdays and Gaelic football on Sundays provided my father with a feast of sport every weekend. Incidentally, my son James played a few matches with Glenavon during the mid-nineties.

My mother was a very kind, hardworking person who attended to all our needs and indeed much more. She was an absolutely outstanding homemaker. In truth she spoiled all of us, including my father. When Dad went with us on our American trip in 1962 she thrived on the extra responsibility of looking after the farm as well as the bar. During our absence she supervised, meticulously, the building of a new hayshed and was especially proud when it was completed before our return. Thanks to her, our home was always a very hospitable place. Very often it was packed with visitors. Footballers and GAA mentors or supporters were especially made welcome. None of them ever left without being well looked after, particularly in the tea and food departments.

Each year after a Railway Cup match, Maurice Hayes would arrive with four or five players in his car. At her own insistence she would make dinner for all of them. How she managed to do this I will never know. So it came to us as a great shock when she died suddenly on 1 August 1968. A terrible vacuum was left in all of our lives. It was difficult to accept that one so young, she was only 55, could die so quickly. My father was devastated and never really recovered.

My father was, like most men, a great provider. He loved all field sports. He also hunted in the winter and fished in the summer. If any situation could be improved he would be the first to volunteer. His financial assistance in helping to bring home my football colleagues from England in the late fifties was typical of the man. When Trinity College in Dublin founded their Gaelic football team they had no money to buy a set of jerseys. Dad agreed to buy them a set provided they chose the colours of his native county. That is why Trinity, to this day, still wear red and black gear.

In the years immediately after my mother's death, my father's general health gradually deteriorated. At the age of 72 he died in the month of April in 1973. Just before the removal of my father's remains from his home to the church for the funeral mass another poignant event occurred. The undertaker Michael Keenan, who was a lifelong family friend, died suddenly as he screwed the lid on my father's coffin.

When my mother died my eldest sister Eileen, who had been a nun for 18 years in South Africa, came home. Eventually she decided to leave the sisterhood and shortly afterwards took up a position as a primary teacher in Gilford school which was situated in Tullylish parish. Later she met and married Seamus Murphy from another region of the parish called Laurencetown. They have two sons, Sean and Seamus.

My second eldest sibling, Delia, qualified as a doctor and married another doctor, Felix McKnight from Killeavy in County Armagh. His older brother John played for Armagh in the 1953 All-Ireland final. John had been an excellent corner back who was selected on the *Irish Independent* Team of the Century in 1984. (This particular team was confined to players who had never won senior All-Ireland medals). The McKnight brothers, John, Michael and Felix, created their own piece of history in the late fifties. During the second half of an Ulster senior championship game against Tyrone, Felix was Armagh's full back and he was flanked on either side by Michael and John.

Originally Delia and Felix intended to emigrate to Australia for two years. Over 40 years later they are still in Perth. They have a family of four: Sharon, Felix, Ruairi and Orla. Some years ago Orla was the Perth representative in the annual International Rose of Tralee festival.

Dan married Nuala Dunne, a native of Dublin. They had one son, Mark, who was a member of the 1991 All-Ireland winning squad. Sadly, Nuala died several years ago. For over 35 years Dan had a dental practice in Belfast's Andersonstown district. One of the dentists he employed was a certain Greg Blaney who is now the proprietor. Dan is retired from work but both he and Mark are still involved with the Carryduff club in north Down.

Gay is the youngest of the family. She has always been a great football supporter and taught as a primary teacher in Belfast for many years. She is married to George Glynn who taught for sometime in St Malachy's secondary school in Castlewellan. George, of course, was a county footballer in his own right. He won a Connacht senior championship medal with Galway in 1960 before going on to captain UCG to Sigerson cup glory in 1960/61. He also won Down senior league and championship honours with Castlewellan in 1965 before crowning a great career with a senior All-Ireland medal with Down in 1968. The former British and Irish Universities heavyweight boxing champion also won Meath football championship medals with Kilbride in 1969, 1970 and 1971. Gay and George, who have two sons, Seoirse and Brian, moved to live in County Meath in 1969.

One spring day in 1966, in unusual circumstances, I first saw the person who was to become the love of my life. Marie Mulholland from the parish of Glenavy in south-west Antrim was at her uncle's funeral burial. When I spotted her, in that sad graveyard, I realised I wanted to see more of her. After a respectable length of time had elapsed and through the goodwill of a mutual friend I managed to obtain a contact number. She agreed to meet me and the rest is history. We were married on 5 September the following year. Coincidentally that was the same date that my parents got married. When we came home from our honeymoon my mother and father had moved to a different home a short distance away. Marie and I were now in charge of the farm and bar in Donacloney.

All our married life Marie has been the ever present solid rock who has bonded all the children and ourselves into a very happy family unit. As well as rearing the children, she ran the bar in a thoroughly efficient manner. Cleaning football boots and washing jerseys came second nature to her even though she consistently professed to have no interest in football. Her kind disposition is also reflected in the fact that she often made dinner for all the people in the bar. Her steadying influence, especially when community tensions ran high during the Troubles, helped us all to preserve our sanity.

Our five married ones come to visit us regularly with their children. Luckily kindness, loyalty and thoughtfulness are words that would describe all of them, including the unmarried Daniel and Eoin. Brian our eldest son is a pharmacist who lives and works in Dublin. He is married to Shirley Simmonson from Dublin and they have one daughter Simone. Brian won an All-Ireland minor medal at midfield in 1987 as well as obtaining honours at Mac Rory Cup, Hogan Cup and Sigerson Cup levels. He suffered a severe cruciate ligament injury when playing for the Down U 21 team. This setback effectively ended his blossoming football career. Later on he played for a time with St Sylvester's in Malahide in Dublin and actually made the Down senior panel in the mid-nineties. However the ill effects of that early injury meant that he could not replicate the form of his youth.

James is our second born. He is married to Linda McConville from Rostrevor and they live in Warrenpoint. James is a director and a civil engineer with the family quarry business. Linda and James have three sons, James, Cian and Matthew. As I have already mentioned James has won a lot of medals at every level including All-Irelands at minor and senior grades, Hogan Cup, Sigerson honours, and All-Star awards.

Delia qualified as a dentist and is married to Michael McCarron who is a native of Portstewart in county Derry. Michael was Irish triathlon champion in 2000. They have two children, Tara and Isa, and they live in Belfast. While at Queen's, Delia was a member of that college's first Ashbourne camogie winning panel of 1991. She also played camogie for Ballyvarley and is a big fan of Down football.

Charlie Pat is an accountant and is married to Sinead McKendry, a native of north Antrim. They have two children, Maille and Jessica. They also live in Belfast. Charlie Pat was a top class footballer and, in my opinion, was the man of the match in the 1993 MacRory Cup final for St Colman's. He has played at all levels for Down. While playing in a National League contest against Clare he also seriously damaged his cruciate ligament. That injury really finished him as a player. Perhaps if it had not occurred he would have made the Down side for the 1994 All-Ireland winning run.

Our youngest girl Maria by her own admission is not really a football fan. That did not prevent her from falling in love with a footballer! Her husband, Plunkett McConville from Hilltown, was a county midfielder for Down in the early years of this decade. He has also won a county senior championship medal with Clonduff. They have two children, Niamh and Caoimhe. Maria teaches in St Mark's secondary school in Warrenpoint. As she lives near us we usually have her and the family visiting us every Sunday.

Daniel, who is a dentist in Bessbrook in County Armagh, is planning to get married at the end of 2010. His fiancée, Gemma Collins, is from Camlough which is also situated in south Armagh. Daniel was captain of the Queen's University Sigerson Cup winning team in 2007. He served as chairman of Queen's GAA club as well as representing Down at all levels, including being the full back on Down's 2008 senior championship side and right corner back on the 2010 team.

Eoin is the youngest of the family and has represented the county in all grades. He is a fast skilful forward with a great eye for goal. Unfortunately a serious leg injury a few years ago has prevented him from advancing his senior intercounty career. Eoin, who also won a Sigerson medal with Queen's, is a pharmacist and is based in Belfast.

We also have another very good friend whom one could say qualifies for honorary citizenship in our household. In 1974 a close pal of mine Charles Patrick Byrne who was a publican in Lurgan died. In the same year his wife Peggy also passed away, leaving behind five children. Charles Patrick and I regularly attended All-Ireland finals together during the sixties and early seventies. We promised each other that in the year of the first of us to die, the other would miss that year's final as a mark of respect for our friendship. Thus, I missed the 1974 final between Dublin and Galway. Shortly afterwards, their son John came to live permanently with us. From that time, when he was a teenager, until the occasion of his marriage many years later John was an integral part of our family. He boarded in St Colman's College in Newry before going on to Queen's University in Belfast. Later he qualified as an accountant and today he is the proprietor of his own thriving accountancy practice in Lurgan. Married to Fiona McDonald, the happy couple have three children, Sarah, John and James. There is an ongoing wonderful bond of trust and friendship between our two families.

The extended family football connection is a riddle. My sister Delia is married to Felix McKnight. Felix's sister Mary (a real Armagh fan) is married to our first cousin Kevin O'Neill. Another of his sisters, Bridie, is married to my former playing colleague P.J. McElroy. Val and Damian (D.J. as he is popularly known) Kane's mother, Carrie, is a sister (and my first cousin!) of another first cousin, Seamus McCartan, who introduced me to Glenn GFC back in the 1950s. Seamus' wife Lelia is a sister of the late Sean Blaney, father of Greg who starred with Down in the 1990s. To complete the tongue twister, my sister Delia McKnight's nephew, Seamus Murphy, son of Eileen and Seamus, is married to her husband's niece, Orla McKnight, daughter of John McKnight.

Sean Blaney was the captain and star performer, at centre half forward, when Armagh won the 1949 All-Ireland minor title. To add spice to the merry-go-round, brothers]John and Michael McKnight were also members of that victorious All-Ireland panel. Some Armagh pundits maintain, to this day, that the course of GAA history would have been altered if Sean Blaney had lined out for Armagh in the 1953 All-Ireland senior final. (This is a reference to an internal dispute that occurred when Sean was playing for the Armagh senior side before this in the early 1950s. As a result of this altercation, the future Belfast-based chemist was destined never to play for the Orchard County again). If that scenario had unfolded, the more optimistic Armagh supporters would assert that the boys from the County Armagh would have been the first to bring the Sam Maguire Cup across the border. Thankfully the reality was somewhat different!

19

The Cream of the Crop

During the course of watching many great games and a host of wonderful players over the past 60 years, it is difficult to say which matches were the best and which players were outstanding. On an ideal team you have a commanding goalkeeper, a competent tight marking defence and an attacking half back line. Both midfielders should be good ball winners with one of them concentrating on defensive duties and the other being more attack conscious. All six forwards should be pacy, intelligent and able to score.

As I have said earlier, the Down and Derry Ulster championship clash in 1994 was probably the best game of football that I ever saw. Down emerged the victors in a truly enthralling game. That was probably the deciding factor in making this match my all time favourite. In a lifetime of witnessing many brilliant games, four others, in particular, stand out in my memory.

The first team to make an impression on me was the Galway side that defeated Cork in the 1956 All-Ireland final. That Galway team had a magnificent goalkeeper in their captain Jack Mangan, a very capable defence and a real industrious midfielder in Frank Evers. However, it was the scoring opportunism of Frank Stockwell and the empathy he enjoyed with Sean Purcell that I will never forget.

Since I started following Gaelic football I have seen many brilliant team exponents of the game. As well as Down, Galway, Cork, Dublin, Offaly, Meath, Derry, Donegal, Armagh and Tyrone have all won All-Irelands in style. The Galway side of the sixties, the Dublin team of the seventies and the Tyrone winners of the new millennium were especially gifted. However, the Kerry combination of the seventies and eighties was without doubt the greatest all round team ever to play Gaelic football. Their defence was superb, their midfielders dominant and the whole forward line exuded a splendid combination of skill, accuracy and determination. So it will come as no surprise that Kerry feature in all three of my remaining favourite matches.

The 1977 All-Ireland semi-final between the two leading teams of that era – Kerry and Dublin – is widely regarded as one of the best ever games of Gaelic football. This match was not a classic in the quality of its football, but for sheer excitement it could not be bettered.

The 1978 All-Ireland final between the same two contestants is my next port of call. Since the previous year's final, defeated Kerry manager Mick O'Dwyer had been under intense pressure from within his own county. O'Dwyer intensified his training schedule for 1978. So severe was it that many players got physically sick during the sessions, the number of which had also dramatically increased. For the fourth year in a row Dublin and Kerry faced each other in the championship. O'Dwyer's and Kerry's reputation were now on the line.

In this game Dublin began superbly. By the 20th minute they had eased into what appeared a very comfortable six points to one lead. Then a moment of hesitancy in the Dublin defence led to an excellent opportunist goal by Kerry's clever corner forward John Egan. Shortly before the interval, the ever alert Mike Sheehy chipped the ball over the head of Dublin goalkeeper Paddy Cullen from a quickly taken free kick for a sensational goal. Kerry had taken the lead and were, psychologically, in the driving seat.

In the second half, with Jack O'Shea lording the midfield exchanges, the awesome Kerry forward line tore the Dublin defence apart. New full forward, the towering Eoin Liston, proved to be an ideal target man when he notched three terrific goals in that period. Winning the encounter by 5-11 to 0-9 meant that no one could question either Kerry's greatness or, indeed, O'Dwyer's credentials.

Another encounter, which I really enjoyed, was the 1982 All-Ireland final between Offaly and Kerry. Over the previous five years Offaly, under the astute guidance of Eugene McGee, had improved gradually each year.

Thanks to a fantastic display against Dublin in the 1982 Leinster final and a win over Galway in the penultimate championship match, Offaly again reached the final. Once more they were destined to meet the men from Kerry. With all the media speculation focused on a possible "five in a row" for the Kingdom, Offaly were able to prepare calmly and diligently away from the spotlight of publicity. For me, this final will always be remembered, not only for its dramatic conclusion, but also for the high quality of football played throughout by two outstanding teams.

After an exciting first half, the interval score was Offaly 0-10 Kerry 0-9. In a rain soaked third quarter Kerry played brilliantly. However, a magnificent defensive performance by Offaly, including a wonderful penalty save by veteran goalkeeper Martin Furlong, meant that the Kingdom only led by two points as the game neared its end.

With two minutes left came one of the most amazing scores ever seen in an All-Ireland football final. Richie Connor got the ball in his own half back line and passed it to full back Liam O'Connor who had come running up the centre of the field. He floated a long diagonal kick into the left corner forward area. Kerry's Tommy Doyle jumped for the ball. Seamus Darby jumped behind him, appearing to nudge Doyle in the back before catching the ball cleanly. He turned swiftly and crashed a magnificent shot past the outstretched hand of goalkeeper Charlie Nelligan into the corner of the net. Whatever doubts there may have been about the goal's legality, its execution was worthy of any great occasion. The score now read Offaly 1-15, Kerry 0-17.

I would have to say that in terms of quality and drama, this was the best All-Ireland final that I ever witnessed.

MY PRE-1990 ALL-STARS

For the goalkeeping spot I would shortlist Jack Mangan, Johnny Geraghty, Martin Furlong, Billy Morgan and Charlie Nelligan. All of them were top class custodians but I think the quick reflexes and superb shot-stopping ability of Johnny Geraghty gives him the edge.

The best corner backs in this era were Willie Casey, Jerome O'Shea, Enda Colleran, Donie O'Sullivan, Robbie Kelleher, Paddy McCormack, Tom O'Hare and John Egan. The most prominent full backs were Paddy O'Brien, Noel Tierney, Greg Hughes and John O'Keeffe.

The consistently impeccable performances by Noel Tierney during Galway's three titles in a row during the 1960s swings the balance in his favour. Having observed both men at close quarters, during my playing days, I have no hesitation in plumping for the high-fielding Jerome O'Shea and the tenacious John Egan in the corner back positions.

My chief contenders for the wing half back places would be Sean Murphy, Stephen White, Tommy Drumm, Páidí Ó Sé, Jim McDonnell, Paudie Lynch and Ger Power. As far as I am concerned the four men vying for the pivotal centre half back position would be Gerry O'Malley, Paddy Holden, Nicholas Clavin and Kevin Moran.

No one could perform both his defensive duties and his offensive attacks as well as Paddy Holden. He was a perfect anchorman. I feel that the sheer skill and class of both Sean Murphy and Jim McDonnell would make this a perfect half back line.

The lynchpin for any successful team is a good midfield pairing. I have been privileged both to see and play against many of them. I would rate Jim McKeever, Mick O'Connell, Brian Mullins, Colm McAlarney, Jack O'Shea, Dermot Earley and Jody O'Neill as midfielders of the highest calibre.

There is no doubt in my mind but that Jim McKeever was the greatest midfielder of all. From a standing position he could leap skywards like a salmon to fetch the ball. He also had a phenomenal work rate. Similarly Jack O'Shea possessed the same type of skills and leadership qualities as McKeever. Technically speaking Mick O'Connell was probably the more naturally gifted player in terms of kicking and passing skills.

For centre half forward my choice is an automatic one. Sean Purcell really had no peers and was the greatest all-round footballer that I ever saw. For his vision and ball-playing skills he was simply the best.

The main contestants for the wing half forward places are Mickey Kearins, Sean O'Neill, Ger Power, Paddy Doherty, Packie McGarty and Pat Spillane. I give a very confident vote here to my two former teammates, Sean O'Neill and Paddy Doherty. O'Neill was the ultimate football purist and Doherty had an innate, intuitive ability to score from any angle.

For the full forward line there is a plethora of realistic candidates, many of whom could comfortably star in any of the three berths. Mikey Sheehy, John Egan, Matt Connor, Jimmy Barry-Murphy, Frank McGuigan, Eoin Liston, Jimmy Keaveney and Kevin Heffernan would hold their own in any company. Only for the serious injury that prematurely ended his career, at such a young age, I have no doubt but that Matt Connor would have developed into an all-time great. For the inventiveness of their play and their consistent threat to opposing defences I would put Sheehy and Heffernan in the corner forward spots. At full forward Eoin Liston, with his aerial ability and intelligent layoffs, would be an ideal target man. Thus my pre-1990 All-Stars would be as follows:

Johnny Geraghty
(Galway)

Jerome O'Shea   Noel Tierney   John Egan
(Kerry)   (Galway)   (Offaly)

Sean Murphy   Paddy Holden   Jim McDonnell
(Kerry)   (Dublin)   (Cavan)

Jim McKeever   Jack O'Shea
(Derry)   (Kerry)

Sean O'Neill   Sean Purcell   Paddy Doherty
(Down)   (Galway)   (Down)

Mikey Sheehy   Eoin Liston   Kevin Heffernan
(Kerry)   (Kerry)   (Dublin)

Substitutes

Jack Mangan (Galway), Paddy McCormack (Offaly), John O'Keeffe (Kerry), Páidí Ó Sé (Kerry), Kevin Moran (Dublin), Paudie Lynch (Kerry), Tommy Drumm (Dublin), Dermot Earley (Roscommon), Mick O'Connell (Kerry), Colm McAlarney (Down), Mickey Kearins (Sligo), Pat Spillane (Kerry), Matt Connor (Offaly), Jimmy Barry-Murphy (Cork), John Egan (Kerry)

MY POST-1990 ALL-STARS

I believe that the outstanding goalkeepers after 1990 were two Dubliners, John O'Leary and Stephen Cluxton, with Cork's John Kearns a close third. The fact that O'Leary won five All-Star awards between 1984 and 1995 certainly entitles him to be the number one choice.

Marc Ó Sé, Tony Scullion, Anthony Lynch, Martin O'Connell and Robbie O'Malley would be on my short list for the corner back places with a straight contest between Darren Fay and Seamus Moynihan for the number three jersey. For sheer consistency, over a prolonged period of time O'Malley and Scullion deserve corner back positions. The brilliant Moynihan, who could easily fill any of the six defensive jerseys, gets my nomination for full back.

For the half back line there is a talented group, many of whom would do justice either to the centre half or wing half vacancies. Paul Curran, Martin O'Connell, Henry Downey, Glen Ryan, Sean Óg De Paor, D.J. Kane, Tomás Ó Sé, Conor Gormley and Kieran McGeeney would all be worthy of consideration.

I love a centre half that can defend and attack. No one could do that better than Henry Downey. The playmaking ability of Paul Curran and Kieran McGeeney would complete a wonderful half back line.

The leading midfielders for the past 20 years have been John McDermott, Anthony Tohill, Darragh Ó Sé, Sean Cavanagh (though he often played in attack), Ciaran Whelan and Brian McGilligan. I think the natural athleticism of Anthony Tohill allied to the attacking talents of Sean Cavanagh would create a perfect launching pad for any forward line.

The main contenders for the half forward berths would be Michael Donnellan, Trevor Giles, Maurice Fitzgerald, Greg Blaney, Oisin McConville, Brian Dooher and Paul Galvin. For his outstanding vision and intelligent leadership I would select Greg Blaney at centre half forward. The enormous work rate of Dooher and the pace and skill of Donnellan would ensure a line of supreme quality.

Choosing the full forward line presents great difficulty as there are so many exceptionally talented individuals who must be considered. Men like Mickey Linden, Padraic Joyce, Colm O'Rourke, Brian Stafford, Bernard Flynn, Colm Cooper, Peter Canavan, Stephen McDonnell, Declan Browne, Ollie Murphy, Joe Brolly and Mattie Forde would be on any pundit's nomination papers. However none of these possessed the skill, poise and accuracy, especially under pressure, of Peter Canavan. He would be my selection for the number 14 jersey. Despite the vast repertoire of Colm Cooper's talents, I would opt for Stephen McDonnell at right corner forward. McDonnell has more mettle when the going gets tough. Owing to his consistently high standards, over such a lengthy period, I believe that Mickey Linden should be picked at left corner forward.

Therefore my post-1990 All-Stars would be as follows:

John O'Leary
(Dublin)

Robbie O'Malley	Seamus Moynihan	Tony Scullion
(Meath)	*(Kerry)*	*(Derry)*
Paul Curran	Henry Downey	Kieran McGeeney
(Dublin)	*(Derry)*	*(Armagh)*

Anthony Tohill   Sean Cavanagh
(Derry)   *(Tyrone)*

Brian Dooher	Greg Blaney	Michael Donnellan
(Tyrone)	*(Down)*	*(Galway)*
Stephen McDonnell	Peter Canavan	Mickey Linden
(Armagh)	*(Tyrone)*	*(Down)*

Substitutes

Stephen Cluxton (Dublin), Marc Ó Sé (Kerry), Darren Fay (Meath), Anthony Lynch (Cork), Tomas Ó Sé (Kerry), Glen Ryan (Kildare), Sean Óg De Paor (Galway), Darragh Ó Sé (Kerry), John McDermott (Meath), Padraic Joyce (Galway), Maurice Fitzgerald (Kerry), Colm Cooper (Kerry), Colm O'Rourke (Meath), Ollie Murphy (Meath) and Bernard Flynn (Meath).

20

Past Memories, Future Hopes

All of us who follow the GAA have a variety of opinions on changes that might improve the organisation. In my judgment the single most unfair system is the undemocratic and inequitable format of the current All-Ireland senior football championship. In recent years the traditional knockout provincial structures have been modified to include a backdoor qualifying arrangement, by which all teams get a second chance to progress. Whereas this is much better than what it replaced, it is still far from ideal as it depends primarily on a flawed provincial layout. If we are serious about creating a level playing field for each county, the current provincial system must be abolished. Let us examine some of the anomalies that now exist.

It is much easier for Connacht and Munster provincial winners to reach the present All-Ireland quarter-final knock out stages. Conversely, it is a lot harder for Leinster and Ulster champions to do so because they have 12 and nine counties respectively within their provinces as opposed to five and six in the others.

1992 was the only year since 1935 that either Cork or Kerry did not win the Munster title. That is over 75 years ago. Any system that tolerates this type of scenario is totally defective.

The vast majority of Connacht titles have been won by Mayo or Galway, with Roscommon a distant third. The other two counties, Sligo and Leitrim, have only obtained a total of six titles between them since Connacht finals began in 1892.

From the above we can see that it is virtually impossible for the "weaker" sides in Connacht and Munster to win a provincial title. In addition, a team like Limerick that have made tremendous strides in recent years have an added difficulty. It is nearly inconceivable for them to qualify directly for the quarter-final as they would always have to defeat one or two (Kerry and Cork) of the best teams in Ireland to do so.

Unfortunately some of these so called weaker counties, in every province, cling to the understandable though romantic and unrealistic notion of winning a provincial title. Consequently they remain powerful advocates of the current system that is curtailing their own development. Counties like Carlow, Fermanagh, Limerick, Leitrim, Longford, Kilkenny, Westmeath, Wicklow, Waterford and Sligo have only won a handful of provincial deciders between them in the last hundred years. Indeed Fermanagh and Wicklow have yet to gain a first title.

In both 2008 and 2009 the eventual All-Ireland senior football champions, Tyrone and Kerry respectively, did not win a single provincial match. That, in itself, speaks volumes for the current status of the provincial system that. In real terms, it is outdated and meaningless.

I believe that the only way to allow each county to develop its potential is to have a combined league and championship format. The best path for any side to improve, especially the weaker ones, is through the introduction of a more competitive and structured National League in which every county will do their utmost to win every game. No county will progress satisfactorily in a situation where players, officials and supporters, sometimes, have a mentality that tends to ignore the importance of the league and concentrates only on the championship. This thinking is contrary to all accepted norms in team sports of other codes.

Linking league performances to the championship structures would not only help the competitiveness of both competitions but would also give each side, in every division, an extra incentive to achieve their maximum potential. My proposals for the National League and the All-Ireland senior football championship would be divided into the following four phases.

Phase One

Run off the National Football League as at present with three divisions of eight teams and one of nine. In the event of any teams finishing level on points at the conclusion of the league, scoring differences/averages should determine final league positions. The team that accumulates the most points in any league deserves to be declared the winner. Furthermore, the elimination of league finals allows one more Sunday in the GAA calendar for club football in each county.

Phase Two

The final league positions should be linked to the All-Ireland senior football championship in the following manner. Eight groups (A-H) should be created with four teams in each section. Groups should be seeded as follows.

Each Division One side (qualifying positions) would be seeded as a number one ranking side in each of the new eight championship sections. Each Division

Two side (qualifying positions) would be seeded as a number two ranking side in each of the new eight championship sections. The same pattern would follow for Division Three and Division Four sides. If there were nine teams in Division Four the side which finished last would enter a new All-Ireland "B" championship.

There would be a round robin series of matches in each group, i.e. three games per team with scoring differences/averages again determining the final positions in the event of sides finishing on an equal number of points at the end of the series.

Phase Three

The top two sides in each section would then qualify for the last 16 of the All-Ireland senior football championship.

The bottom two sides in each section would qualify for a new, properly structured and intensely marketed All-Ireland "B" senior football championship. As there are five teams in my projected H group on the following pages, there would have to be a play-off between the bottom two to decide who qualified for the last place in the "B" championship.

Phase Four I

Last 16 teams for Sam Maguire Cup

The top eight sectional winners would be on one side of the draw and the eight second placed teams would be on the other side of this knock out phase. The winners would progress to the All-Ireland quarter-finals and the losers would be eliminated.

Phase Four II

16 teams for All-Ireland "B" championship

The eight sides that finished third in the round robin series would be on one side of the draw and the last placed sides would be on the other side for this knock out phase. The winners would progress to the All-Ireland "B" quarter-finals and the losers would be eliminated.

An open draw would then operate for both competitions at quarter-final and semi-final levels.

The advantages of this new system would be as follows:

- It is both fair and equitable and every county, in each province, is always treated the same.

- All counties have at least 11 meaningful competitive games (seven league and four championship) as opposed to the current nine (seven league and two championship).
- All 32 counties are given an opportunity to participate in the All-Ireland senior football championship.
- With the definite need for a co-ordinated, comprehensive marketing programme, a real meaningful "B" championship can be structured. This should be a huge incentive for the weaker counties to play in a major final in Croke Park.

These new structures should provide a greater variety of pairings on a consistent basis, in all phases.

With an imaginative use of playing appropriate "B" matches as curtain raisers to Sam Maguire Cup matches there is no reason that the last 16, quarter-finals and semi-final stages, in both competitions, could not be completed over ten weekends. This would mean that both the league and championships could comfortably be completed within a timeframe of 21 weekends. In 2009, for example, it took 25 weeks to finish the league and championship series.

From the above timetable, under my proposals, there would be a minimum of four additional weeks available to each county to schedule their own club and championship fixtures.

Based on the 2009 final league positions the seeded draw for an imaginary 2009 All-Ireland senior football championship would have looked like this:

(A)	(B)	(C)	(D)
Mayo	Derry	Galway	Tyrone
Laois	Meath	Tipperary	Armagh
Antrim	Sligo	Offaly	Fermanagh
Wicklow	Clare	Limerick	Carlow

(E)	(F)	(G)	(H)
Kerry	Dublin	Cork	Monaghan
Kildare	Down	Donegal	Westmeath
Louth	Cavan	Roscommon	Wexford
Longford	Leitrim	Waterford	Kilkenny/London

There is no greater sporting spectacle in the world than a top class hurling encounter. During my lifetime I have been privileged to see nine different counties claim the Liam McCarthy Cup on All-Ireland senior hurling final day. On each occasion all participants demonstrated the intrinsic artistic merit of this, the world's fastest field sport. Each final also had players of exquisite skill and exceptional determination.

During the 1980s when Galway had outstanding sides, they had several highly skilled hurlers. John Connolly was a hugely talented midfielder or full forward. They had tenacious defenders in Conor Hayes, Jimmy Cooney, Sylvie Linnane, Iggy Clarke, Tony Keady and Peter Finnerty. Joe Connolly, Joe Cooney and P.J. Molloy were forwards of the highest calibre.

Waterford, who have impressed me enormously in recent years without winning an All-Ireland, had many classic players in their successful side of 1959. Austin Flynn, Phil Grimes, Tom Cheasty, Frankie Walsh, John Barron and Seamus Power could hold their own in any company. When Clare secured their two famous Holy Grail wins in the 1990s no one displayed the full repertoire of hurling skills better than goalkeeper Davy Fitzgerald, full back Brian Lohan, centre half back Seanie McMahon, captain Anthony Daly and the versatile Jamesie O'Connor.

Though Limerick had been a dominant hurling force in the 1930s and early 1940s, it was not until 1973 that they won their next All-Ireland senior hurling title. On that team Pat Hartigan was a commanding full back and Eamon Cregan was equally at home in either defence or attack. Captain Eamon Grimes and Joe McKenna not only had great ball-winning ability but also were deadly accurate in front of goal.

For such a small county, no side has produced so many superb footballers and hurlers as Offaly. Their All-Ireland senior hurling triumphs in the 1980s and 1990s bear testimony to this, along with the footballers' successes in the 1970s and 1982. Eugene Coughlan, Pat Fleury, Pat Delaney, Brian Whelehan, Ger Coughlan, Padraig Horan and the three Dooley brothers all played significant roles in one or more of those thrilling days for Offaly hurling.

Wexford had magnificent All-Ireland achievements in the 1950s, 1960s and in 1996. The Rackard brothers, Bobby and Willie, were stupendous defenders and the third brother, Nicky, was a fabulous, opportunist, goalscoring full forward. In 1968, the talismanic and dynamic Tony Doran, who played at the top level for 26 years, was a powerful forward when the Slaneysiders deservedly annexed the 1968 All-Ireland. Goalkeepers Damian Fitzhenry and Art Foley, Jim English, Ned Wheeler, Tim Flood, Padge Keogh, Nick O'Donnell, Liam Dunne, Martin

Storey, Phil Wilson, Tom Neville and the Quigley brothers are just a sample of some of Wexford's marvellous hurlers.

Cork, along with Kilkenny and Tipperary, have been the most prominent sides at all levels, over the history of hurling. They have had a series of brilliant teams and outstanding individuals. Though I did not actually see him play very often, Christy Ring has to be at the top of any pundit's list. His skill levels were simply amazing and his determination, particularly in the face of adversity, was incredible. Gerald McCarthy, Denis Coughlan, Ray Cummins, John Fenton, John Horgan, Seanie O'Leary, Tom Cashman, Ger Cunningham, Brian Corcoran, Ben O'Connor, Con Roche, Jimmy Barry-Murphy and Joe Deane are but a cameo of so many fabulous wielders of the camán that I have enjoyed from the Rebel county.

No team has produced as many fine hurlers as Kilkenny. They continually have a conveyor belt of hurling aristocrats. Their side of recent times is undoubtedly the finest that I have seen. In each decade the Noresiders have supplied fantastic hurlers with an enthralling combination of skilled stick work, clever anticipation and deadly accuracy. Ollie Walsh and Noel Skehan were spectacular goalkeepers. Pat Henderson, Ger Henderson, Joe Hennessy, Fan Larkin and Tommy Walsh have been magnificent defenders. Pat Delaney and Frank Cummins were superb all-round hurlers. Eddie Keher and D.J. Carey were sporting icons that created a spontaneous buzz of excitement whenever they gained possession of the sliotar. Henry Shefflin's displays over the last ten years have been the most consistent of all. Skill, power, poise, determination and accuracy are just some of the more apparent characteristics this sensational exponent of the ash possesses. I think is only fair to emphasise that their inspirational manager Brian Cody has constantly reinvented the talent at his disposal so that the whole panel of players are always primed to put the interest of the team ahead of the individual. As a result of Brian's methodical approach, the team always delivers to its full potential.

Despite Kilkenny's justifiable claims to greatness, my favourite hurling team has always been the Tipperary side of the 1960s. Having watched them so often I got to know and appreciate their undoubted flair and their unyielding determination. I have never observed such a solid full back line as that of John Doyle, Michael Maher and Kieran Carey. Known as "Hell's Kitchen" they had a deserved reputation for taking no prisoners. Nevertheless, it must not be forgotten that they could hurl as well. Tony Wall was a terrific centre half back and Mick Roche was arguably the most superb stylist of all the midfielders during my time watching the game. Jimmy Doyle was a pure hurling artist and a brilliant marksman who won six All-

Ireland senior medals and six National League titles in a lengthy career between 1957 and 1973. His forward colleagues Donie Nealon and Liam Devaney, as well as midfielder Theo English, were other players whose exciting play thrilled so many of us in that era.

In latter years Nicholas English, Johnny Leahy and goalkeeper Brendan Cummins have illuminated many a dull spring afternoon with fantastic individual displays. However, in spite of all of the realistic claims of so many of the above, I would nominate Michael "Babs" Keating, of that Tipperary team of the 1960s and 1970s, as my favourite hurler of all time. In my opinion the mark of any truly great sportsman is his ability to perform to the maximum of his ability when the odds are against him. No one did that any better than the Ballybacon/Grange man. Whether it was playing for Munster in a competitive Railway Cup football match, where I first got to know him, or in a pulsating All-Ireland senior hurling final, he always retained that fierce innate will to win mentality. More significantly, he had the composure to score a match-winning point or goal in such difficult circumstances.

Aside from the occasional references of reservation that I have expressed about and to some of its officials, the GAA is a remarkable organisation. It is, nevertheless, too large a body to retain any negative rules within its ranks. I welcomed the abolition of the ban on "foreign games" in 1971, having been a recipient not only of its unfairness but also its discriminatory application. I was also delighted that Croke Park was made available for the playing of soccer and rugby internationals for the past number of years.

What is wrong with Ireland today is that some extreme unionists are still living in 1690 and some extreme nationalists are living in 1916. If we are to progress as an association we have to revolutionise the current democratic structures, abolish the stagnant mindsets of the past and let the young people play a more meaningful role. The youth of today are very forward thinking and fair minded. To enable the GAA to spread its wings to all the people of Ireland, in a tangible way, all of our politicians, in both political jurisdictions, must do their utmost to have Gaelic games as an integral part of our schools' curricula.

During my lifetime I have come to understand the immense value of the voluntary contribution of so many people to the development of the GAA. It would be accurate to state that I have not always agreed with the decisions and attitudes of a few officials at club, county and provincial levels. Notwithstanding that, I have always respected the vast majority of administrators who have been responsible for making the GAA the most powerful force for good in this country. Amongst the latter grouping are two Down men who have considerably enhanced the creativity and image of the GAA, not only in the Mournes but also throughout the country. Both have always shown a sense of balance and an aptitude for hard work. Blessed with plenty of ability they have continually striven to maximise the positive influence of the Association in our society. Dan McCartan (no relation) from Saval and Danny Murphy from Burren are respected throughout the 32 counties for making the rules and facilities of our games more relevant and beneficial to the whole GAA family.

When we left Donacloney, on that January day in 2002, we moved to a house that we had purchased in the parish of Saval with a few acres of land attached; it is an oasis of peace and tranquillity. Marie and myself have gradually adapted to a more relaxed approach to life. Collecting items of old tractor and horse farm machinery occupies much of my time now. I enjoy refurbishing the relics of my farming years to their former beauty and painting them in my favourite colours of red and black! Occasionally when some workmen in Tullyraine Quarries are absent, either through illness or on holiday, I don my working clothes again. I then get into a van and cheerfully traverse the undulating roads of Down, Armagh, Louth or Meath where most of our surfacing contracts are undertaken. Otherwise, I happily meander through every day with just my innermost thoughts and pleasant memories for company. Marie, as ever, is always extremely busy, whether it is joyfully hosting the many welcome visits of our increasing number of grandchildren or voluntarily helping out in the community.

Sport, in its many facets, still intrigues me but mostly, I must admit, from the less tense environment of a comfortable armchair. As I enter the autumn of life's journey I really appreciate the fact that I have been lucky to have such a wonderful wife in Marie and such a caring, healthy family. Our expanded clan of grandchildren, siblings, nephews, nieces, cousins, assorted in-laws and many friends complete our intimate circle of friendship and good humour.

Outside of God and my family, the GAA has been the greatest gift that I have received. Participating in and following Gaelic games has been one long rollercoaster ride of passion, pride, excitement and total fulfilment for the last 60 years. Nothing for me summarises the innate affinity of the GAA more than the following story that I have selected from a host of golden memories.

In the early 1980s I fulfilled a lifetime ambition when I attended my first Munster senior football final. The best team that I ever saw, Kerry, were at the peak of their considerable powers and they were scheduled to play their great rivals Cork. So, on the Saturday afternoon before the game two carloads of excited Down supporters left the Mourne County to travel to Cork where the game was being held on the Sunday.

After we had been watered and fed in a city hotel we discovered that tickets for the game were totally sold out. It was now midnight. In sheer desperation I rang a Kerry friend who happened to be a member of the Munster GAA Council and I informed him of our predicament.

"Be at Gate B at half past twelve tomorrow," he advised me. We dutifully and gratefully obeyed and at 12.35 p.m. there were seven staunch and proud Down men wearing stewards' uniforms. With the word "Maor" written across the front and back of their official bibs, they vigilantly patrolled, in military fashion, the sidelines at a Munster football final. From the stern look on our faces there was not much chance of any other ticketless fans escaping our clutches! This was a spontaneous and unique GAA solution to an apparently insoluble GAA problem. For me that anecdote epitomises the all-embracing camaraderie of the GAA. From Antrim to Waterford and from Galway to Dublin, we are all the one. To me there is no better kindred spirit in Irish society than the extended GAA family.

It can definitely be said that I would not have written this book but for the fact that I was honoured to be part of a fabulous Down team which created Gaelic football history. It is only as I have grown older that I have fully understood and appreciated the enormity of that achievement over 50 years ago. In 1995 a former Newry Mitchel's player, Nicky Barry, who also played for Down in the 1960s, wrote a fascinating article in the *Down GAA Yearbook*. In it he brilliantly articulated both the national mood and the overwhelming implications of and joyous reaction to Down's extraordinary accomplishment. Referring to that first All-Ireland senior success the Killarney based talented pianist, teacher and RTÉ radio journalist wrote:

> *For the people of Down this was much more than a football match. This was a cultural maturing. No longer on the outside, we really did belong in the heart of things. This was the high altar for high stakes and the high priest, Michael O'Hehir, knew all our heroes and all about us. Within the hour the names of mountainy townlands and hitherto insignificant parishes would be ringing out over Radio Brazzaville, and half way round the world ... At half time the Mourne men led by two*

points. Northern supporters were ecstatic and exhausted by tension. Was it a dream? If it was, Down's two second half goals turned the reverie into a nightmare for Kerry. To this day an abiding image in my mind is that of Barney Carr, in a belted gaberdine coat, signalling to the players that there were only two minutes left on the clock.

After sixty minutes of passion and fury it was all over. The mighty had fallen and Sam Maguire was heading north and crossing the border for the first time. A citadel had been breached. That fourth Sunday, in September 1960, was a momentous day. All Ulster rejoiced as County Down took its first tentative steps into the pages of history.

Not a day, in the meantime, has passed without me privately reminiscing about those days of days in 1960 and 1961. Thankfully others have added more glorious chapters to the unfolding story of the men in red and black. Still, one recollection above all the rest is constantly and affectionately recalled from within the deep recesses of my mind. Remembering my father on Jones' Road, so radiant with sheer happiness and beaming with unbridled joy, on that red-letter day for Down football, has been an eternal source of continual, personal satisfaction. It has sustained me, daily, for over half a century. I do not intend to let it go now.

James McCartan – Fact File

Playing Honours

    All-Ireland Senior Football Championship (2) 1960, 1961

    National Football League (2) 1960, 1962

    Ulster Senior Football Championship (5) 1959, 1960–61,1963, 1966

    Lagan Cup (4) 1959, 1961–63

    McKenna Cup (3) 1959, 1961, 1964

    St Brendan Cup (Down v New York) 1960

    Wembley Tournament (3) 1959–61

    Ulster Junior Football Championship 1958

    Texaco Player of the Year (2) 1960–61

    Ireland v Combined Universities (Captain) 1961

    Railway Cup (3) 1963–64, 1966 (Captain)

    Down Team of the Millennium

    Irish Farmer's Association "Telecom Farmer 15" 2008

    Corn na nÓg with St Colman's College, Newry 1951

    Down Senior Football Championship (3) with Glenn 1959, 1962–63

    Down Division One League (2) with Glenn 1954, 1958

    Down Junior Football Championship with Tullylish 1968

    Down Division One League with Tullylish 1973

    Down Division Two League with Tullylish 1971

    Down Division Three League with Tullylish 1970

    Down Winter League (Fr Tony Davies Shield) (3) with Tullylish 1970–72

Managerial Honours

    Ulster Senior Football Championship 1978

    National Football League Division One 1983

    National Football League Division Two 1978

    All-Ireland Under 21 Football Championship 1979

    Ulster Under 21 Football Championship (3) 1977–79.

Tributes from Famous Opponents

"Down were by far the best team that I encountered during my playing career. They were really skilful and moved the ball with purpose, precision and exceptional speed. They brought Gaelic football into a new era of unprecedented attainment. Their all-round brilliance was embellished by the absolute genius of Sean O'Neill and the remarkably talented Paddy Doherty. O'Neill was just pure class in every game he played. Doherty on the other hand, in my opinion, was the greatest left-footed player ever to play Gaelic football. However, it was the power and strength of James McCartan on the 40 which co-ordinated the team's full potential. I have never seen another player whose leadership qualities could spur on both his team mates and supporters to such high levels of anticipation and expectation."

> **Former Ulster and Cavan star James Brady (1955–1963)** who played in three provincial finals (he was successful in the 1962 decider) as well as a National League decider against Down. In 1960 he won a Railway Cup medal and captained UCD when he won his fourth Sigerson Cup souvenir. The veterinary surgeon lives in Offaly where he and his family have been involved with the Gracefield club.

"Down were very lucky to get a penalty against us in 1960 and we were decidedly unfortunate not to be awarded a penalty in 1961. Still, that should not take away from the many magnificent displays of a really great team. They were years ahead of their time in terms of overall team preparation and tactical ability. I remember the 1961 final vividly. James McCartan was wearing a cap because it was a very sunny day. Once he grabbed the ball and came storming up the field. He then brilliantly dummied an Offaly defender by throwing his cap at him as he continued his penetrating run into the heart of our defence! I have told him many times since he would not have done that to me! We have become great friends over the years through our mutual interest in greyhounds."

> **1972 All-Star and legendary Offaly defender Paddy McCormack (1958–1972)** who played against Down in those famous titanic battles of 1960 and 1961. Known as the Iron Man from Rhode he was the only Offaly player to be a member of their first Leinster winning side of 1960 and their two All-Ireland senior winning teams of 1971 and 1972.

The very mention of the name James McCartan conjures up only the most magical of memories for an older generation of football followers.

I had the privilege of lining out against himself and his brother Dan, also their cousins Sean and Kevin O'Neill and Val Kane, on numerous occasions and while Kerry could not beat Down in a knockout championship game over a span of eight years, we never begrudged them any of their victories.

That was primarily because we recognised them for what they were, a gifted group of people who had brought a special dimension to Gaelic football and elevated the code on to a new plateau of excellence.

Foremost among them was James McCartan, the heartbeat of the team, and the man who more than anybody else personified the unconquerable spirit of Down in the 1960s.

> **Gaelic football's greatest manager and four times All-Ireland senior medal winner Kerry's Mick O'Dwyer (1956–1974).** He played against Down in all of their many fantastic contests of the 1960s. Mick holds the unique distinction of managing his native county to eight senior All-Ireland titles as well as having successful spells as manager of Kildare, Laois and Wicklow.

Epilogue

Twice All-Ireland winning manager Peter McGrath was the Down senior team supremo until he retired in 2002. He was replaced by the captain of the victorious 1991 All-Ireland team, Paddy O'Rourke. In 2006 a management team led by his former playing colleagues and All-Ireland winners – Ross Carr and D.J. Kane – succeeded Paddy. When they were not reappointed in 2009 there was much speculation as to who would be selected. Eventually our second son James Junior, or "Wee" James as he is affectionately known, was chosen. Former Donegal National League winning manager Brian McIver, victorious ex-Tyrone All-Ireland trainer Paddy Tally and Down man Jerome Johnston, from Kilcoo, became his selectors.

Many supporters and indeed some county board officials have unrealistic expectations of what a manager can accomplish. They want instant success and unless this is achieved within a short timeframe the manager is deemed a failure. So, it was with some trepidation that I looked forward to James assuming the managerial reins of Down. However, he had been very successful in guiding Queen's University, Belfast, to four successive Sigerson Cup finals, winning the 2007 decider. He had also managed St Gall's of Antrim to a senior championship title in 2008 as well as being in charge of Down club, Burren, and Derry side, Ballinderry. On the football field James never shirked a physical or mental challenge. Similarly I knew that if he got a decent run of luck he would maximise the potential of all the players under his command.

Down possessed many quality footballers. Men such as midfielders Ambrose Rogers and Dan Gordon, as well as innovative forwards like Benny Coulter and Danny Hughes, would grace any of Ireland's top county teams. What made the prospects of 2010 more attractive was the homecoming from Australia of 2005 All-Ireland star minor Martin Clarke. The An Ríocht clubman's versatility was shown when he was signed in 2005 for AFL side, Collingwood. Despite his potentially lucrative professional career Martin yearned to play Gaelic football for his native county. So, in September 2009, he retired from the AFL and returned home. His immediate availability was a great boost to all associated with Down football. James and his management team were especially delighted.

In an impressive 2010 Division Two league campaign Down won all their games except for a drawn outing against Tipperary. This qualified them to meet neighbouring rivals Armagh in the Division Two final. Though they lost by two points to the Orchard County, the Mourne men had been promoted to Division One of the league. That was a very promising start both for players and management.

In the first round of the Ulster championship they eventually, after extra time, defeated Donegal by two points. Nevertheless, in the Ulster semi-final, they succumbed to a terribly disappointing four-point defeat to Tyrone. Down were now out of the Ulster championship. The only way to make further progress was through the qualifiers. The team gradually improved as they beat Longford, Offaly and Sligo, in successive weeks, to qualify for the All-Ireland quarter-final.

This match was against Kerry. Down had beaten them in each of their four previous championship engagements in 1960, 1961, 1968 and 1991. The game had everything: sheer excitement, controversial scores, a sending-off, and most of all, brilliant football – especially from Down. At the final whistle Down had recorded another momentous victory over Kerry on a score of 1-16 to 1-10. It was a great morale-boosting triumph with every player showing tremendous commitment and no little flair. Down were back in an All-Ireland semi-final for the first time in 16 years, and more importantly they were beginning to show the confidence and consistency traditionally associated with all good Down teams. Besides, we were starting to dream of what might happen in the future.

In the All-Ireland semi-final Down were pitted against a Kildare team that had featured regularly at the quarter-final stage in recent years. Ironically both sides had to field without their midfield anchormen for similar reasons. Kildare's Dermot Earley had a long-term cruciate knee injury problem. Down's inspirational captain Ambrose Rogers had also injured his knee in a club match after the Kerry game. In another intriguing encounter, in which controversial decisions and non-decisions played a part, Down again performed exceptionally well.

Deep into injury time Kildare were awarded a 13-metre free. Down were leading by two points. A goal now would win it for Kildare. The referee told the free taker that this was to be the last kick of the game. The tension throughout the stadium was unbearable. When Kildare substitute Robert Kelly prepared to take the kick the whole of Down and Kildare seemed to be in what we used to call the parallelogram. Would Down hold on or would Kildare snatch a sensational win literally with the last kick of the game? That was the question on everyone's lips. Kelly struck the ball hard and accurately. It was heading towards the underside of the crossbar and thus a dramatic one-point victory for Kildare appeared imminent. Suddenly and bravely the raised hand of Down midfielder Kalum King instinctively palmed the ball against the crossbar and it spun to safety. The full time whistle sounded. The last action of a truly memorable Gaelic football match had just concluded. It was for moments like this that we first laced

Epilogue

a pair of football boots and trained for countless hours in mucky fields or just travelled hundreds of miles to see our neighbours play for parish or county glory.

When Marie and I drove home from Croke Park, on that semi-final day, it took us a long time to fully realise that, after all these years, Down were in another senior All-Ireland football final. Not in my wildest dreams – especially after the Tyrone and Offaly games – did I think that would occur again in my lifetime. It was also a deep personal honour to know that two of our sons would be amongst the Down players and officials that would grace Croke Park on one of the greatest days in Irish sport. Just to be part of it would be a wonderful privilege. Anything else would be an unexpected bonus.

On Sunday 19 September 2010, Down met an experienced Cork team in the All-Ireland final. Down started somewhat nervously but then played some superb combination football to open up a five-point lead. However, Cork started to dominate in the middle third and when the sides retired at the interval they had reduced the deficit to three points. The introduction of Cork's injured but influential captain Graham Canty and the veteran Nicholas Murphy for the second half crystallised Cork's increasing supremacy. Though each Down player continued to fight heroically for every ball Cork were definitely worthy one-point winners in the end, on a score of 0-16 to 0-15.

This was Cork's third final in four years and they, too, had suffered the heartbreak of defeat in 2007 and 2009. As for Down, every player had played his part in recapturing the glorious days of a proud footballing past. On a personal level we were exceedingly happy that Daniel, the team's regular corner back, had capably played his role in the revival of Down's footballing fortunes. Amongst pundits and supporters alike, it is also generally accepted that James and his management team maximised the individual and collective potential of the Down side. All things being equal, there will, hopefully, be many more great days ahead for this group of talented players and the current management team.

Just before the senior All-Ireland football final of 2010 my brother Dan and myself, along with all our colleagues from the 1960 and 1961 winning teams, had the unique distinction of being presented to President Mary McAleese and the 82,000 supporters that thronged Croke Park. Their spontaneous applause as they recognised our historic achievements of 50 years earlier was a truly humbling experience. For all of us it was a beautifully symbolic emotional reaction that rekindled in our hearts the tremendous achievements of bygone years. As we waved to the crowd, we sincerely hoped that other Down players in the future would be able to share one day in a similar type of appreciation.

Index

A
Andrews, Davy 158
Anne, Princess 161
Austin, Liam 124, 125, 128–129, 130, 131, 132, 133, 135, 137, 140, 141

B
Bagnall, Gerry 110, 111
Barron, John 192
Barry, Aidan 142, 159
Barry-Murphy, Jimmy 184, 185, 193
Barry, Nicky 196
Barry, Peadar 101
Barry, Peter 163
Barton, Damian 138
Beamon, Bob 140
Bell, Donal 131, 133
Bernard, Denis 52
Blaney, Greg 19, 24, 129, 133, 135, 136, 137, 138, 140, 141, 142, 145–146, 146, 147, 152, 176, 179, 186
Blaney, Lelia 179
Blaney, Sean 19, 179, 180
Bloomfield, Sir Kenneth 108
Bowyer, Brendan 93
Boyle, Fabian 95
Brady, Aidan 54
Brady, Bernard 82
Brady, James 7, 8, 40, 199
Bratten, Jack 29
Breen, Barry 138, 140, 141, 142, 145, 147
Breen, Patsy 32
Brereton, Sean 42, 43, 44, 54, 64
Brolly, Joe 137, 146, 186
Browne, Declan 186
Browne, Mickey 159
Brown, Gerry 121, 130
Brown, John 114
Burke, Tom 60, 61
Burns, Brian 149, 151
Burns, Eamon 115, 145, 146
Burns, Eamonn 140, 142, 147, 150
Burns, Eddie 99
Butterfield, Gerry 72
Byrne, Billy 115
Byrne, Charles Patrick 179
Byrne, Hugh 70
Byrne, James 179
Byrne, Joe 115, 125
Byrne, John 179
Byrne, Peggy 179
Byrne, Sarah 179

C
Cahill, Sean 151
Cairns, Gerry 160, 167
Cairns, Rory 160, 167
Caldwell, John 53
Campbell, Pat 57
Campbell, Plunkett 115
Canavan, Brian 131
Canavan, Peter 149, 186
Carey, D.J. 193
Carey, Jarlath 2, 5, 7, 8, 29, 38–39, 41, 47, 52, 55, 56, 57, 61, 63, 64, 68, 91–92, 106
Carey, Kieran 193
Carey, Martin 91
Carey, Nuala 92
Carley, Mick 55
Carr, Barney 3, 7, 9, 47, 48, 51, 70, 74, 86, 99, 103, 104, 106, 114, 127, 128, 197
Carr, Charlie 71, 105
Carroll, Anton 82
Carr, Ross 137, 140, 140–141, 141, 142, 144, 149
Casey, Mick 63
Casey, Willie 183
Cashman, Tom 193
Cassidy, Damian 145
Caulfield, Finbar 25
Cavanagh, Michael 70, 73
Cavanagh, Sean 186
Cheasty, Tom 192
Clarke, Iggy 192
Clavin, Nicholas 184
Clements, Eamon 96
Cluxton, Stephen 185, 187
Cody, Brian 193
Cogley, Michael 89
Coleman, Gary 138
Cole, Mickey 118, 119, 121
Colleran, Enda 183
Collins, Gemma 178
Collins, Mayor 71
Collins, Neil 138, 142, 151
Conlon, Aidan 110
Conlon, Ciaran 110, 111, 112
Conlon, Fergus 111, 112
Conlon, Fr Fergus 111, 113
Connolly, Fr Hugh 19
Connolly, Joe 192
Connolly, John 192
Connor, Matt 184, 185
Connor, Richie 183
Convery, Harry 115
Convery, Paddy 159
Cooney, Jimmy 192
Cooney, Joe 192
Cooper, Colm 186, 187
Copeland, Roy 16
Corcoran, Brian 193
Corkery, Colin 150
Corvan, John 131, 132
Coughlan, Denis 193
Coughlan, Eugene 192
Coughlan, Ger 192
Crawford, Benny 128
Crawford, Nigel 128
Cregan, Eamon 192
Crothers, Master 16
Crowley, D.J. 121
Cullen, Paddy 182
Cullen, Tom 44, 64
Culloty, Johnny 47, 48, 61, 119–120, 120
Cummins, Brendan 194
Cummins, Danny 94

Cummins, Frank *193*
Cummins, Ray *193*
Cunningham, Ger *193*
Cunningham, Mickey *124, 125*
Cunningham, Tom *43*
Curley, Cathal *156*
Curran, Paul *150, 185, 186*
Cusack, Michael *26*
Cush, Adrian *149*
Cushing, Cardinal *71*

D

Daly, Anthony *192*
Daly, Peter *63*
Darby, Seamus *183*
Davies, Fr Anthony *110*
Deane, Joe *193*
Deegan, Conor *142, 147, 149, 150*
de Gaulle, General Charles *12*
Delaney, Pat *192, 193*
Denvir, Brian *3, 80, 82, 99, 101, 104, 106*
Denvir, James *99*
Denvir, Kieran *6, 8, 29, 31, 33, 41, 44, 47, 95, 99*
de Valera, Eamonn *50*
Devaney, Liam *68, 194*
Diamond, Karl *147*
Digney, Cathal *125*
Digney, Jarlath *125, 129*
Doherty, Harry *132*
Doherty, Paddy *4, 5, 6, 7, 8, 29, 31, 33, 37, 39, 40, 41, 42, 43, 45, 46, 48, 49, 52, 54, 55, 56, 57, 58, 59, 60, 61, 63, 64, 67, 68, 69, 77, 80, 81, 82, 83, 90, 92–93, 103, 105, 112, 118, 119, 120, 120–121, 121, 132, 184, 185, 199*
Donnan, Patrick *24*
Donnan, Peter *130*
Donnellan, Michael *25, 186*
Donnelly, Frankie *34*
Donnelly, Har *42, 43, 44, 63, 64, 65*
Dooher, Brian *186*
Dooley brothers *192*
Doran, Paddy *159*

Doran, Tony *192*
Dowling, John *48, 59*
Downey, Charlie *73*
Downey, Henry *146, 185, 186*
Downey, Paddy *87*
Doyle, Jimmy *193*
Doyle, John *193*
Doyle, Seamus *81*
Doyle, Tommy *183*
Doyle, Willie *81*
Drumm, Tommy *183, 185*
Duggan, Larry *24*
Dunne, Liam *192*
Dunne, Mick *37, 71*
Dunne, Nuala *176*

E

Earley, Dermot *184, 185*
Egan, John *54, 62, 182, 183, 184, 185*
Egan, Ron *115*
English, Jim *192*
English, Nicholas *194*
English, Theo *194*
Evers, Frank *1, 181*

F

Fagan, Joe *160*
Farrell, Aidan *150, 151*
Farrell, Dessie *151*
Farrelly, Des *82, 121*
Fay, Darren *185, 187*
Fearon, Padraig "Poppy" *174*
Fearon, Tony *25*
Feeney, John Michael *160*
Feeney, Patsy *160*
Fegan, Tom *24*
Fenian McCartans, The *163*
Fenton, John *193*
Ferris, Richard *145*
Ferriter, Sean *82*
Finnerty, Peter *192*
Fitsimmons, Jackie *81*
Fitzgerald, Davy *192*
Fitzgerald, Maurice *186, 187*
Fitzhenry, Damian *192*

Fitzpatrick, James *31, 99*
Fitzpatrick, Seamus *49*
Fitzsimmons, Jackie *123*
Fitzsimons, Pat *97*
Fleury, Pat *192*
Flood, P.J. *82*
Flood, Tim *192*
Flynn, Austin *192*
Flynn, Bernard *186, 187*
Flynn, Cathal *55*
Flynn, Danny *3, 9, 74*
Foley, Art *192*
Foley, Lar *69*
Forde, Mattie *186*
Fortune, Michael *157*
Fox, Bernadette *157*
Fox, Des *154, 156, 157*
Furlong, Martin *183*

G

Gallagher, Brian *7, 8*
Gallagher, Charlie *7, 8, 37, 40, 79, 81, 119*
Gallagher, Sean *110, 112*
Galvin, Paul *186*
Garrett, Mick *4*
Geddes, Alderman William *122*
Geraghty, Johnny *183, 185*
Giles, Trevor *186*
Glynn, Brian *177*
Glynn, George *39, 54, 81, 120, 121, 122, 141, 177*
Glynn, Seoirse *177*
Gormley, Conor *185*
Gormley, Enda *145, 146*
Gormley, Patsy *32, 33*
Graham, Mrs *16*
Greene, Tommy *42, 45, 64*
Gribbin, Hugh Francis *32*
Griffin, Pat *120*
Grimes, Eamon *192*
Grimes, Phil *192*

H

Hackett, Fr *24*

Index

Hadden, Tony *2, 5, 6, 7, 8, 9, 29, 31, 34, 36, 40, 41, 42, 43, 44, 46, 47, 48, 52, 55, 56, 60, 61, 64, 65, 68, 76, 93–94, 103, 106, 107*
Halpenny, Kevin *57*
Hamill, Robert *168*
Hamill, Ronan *25*
Hamilton, Canon Michael *101, 104*
Hartigan, Pat *192*
Haughey, Fr James *22*
Haughian, John *97, 106*
Hayes, Conor *192*
Hayes, Dr Maurice *3, 29, 32, 69, 74, 84, 97, 99, 100, 100–107, 101, 102, 103, 104, 105, 106, 106–108, 114, 175*
Heaney, Dermot *145*
Heffernan, Kevin *99, 184, 185*
Henderson, Ger *193*
Henderson, Pat *193*
Hendron Brothers *97*
Hennessy, Joe *193*
Hickey, John D *9, 38, 57, 62, 71, 80*
Higgins, Charlie "Chuck" *33*
Higgins, Mick *118*
Higgins, Paul *142, 145, 152*
Hocks, Jimmy *23*
Holden, Paddy *184, 185*
Horan, Padraig *192*
Horgan, John *193*
Howard, Con *71*
Hoy, Harry *20*
Hughes, Greg *62, 64, 106, 183*
Hughes, Sammy *16*
Hume, John *171*
Hurley, Paddy *113*
Hurley, Pat *111*
Hyland, John Sydney *16*
Hylands, Columba *49*

J

Jennings, Mick *110, 111*
Johnston, Brian *78, 81, 83*
Jones, Jimmy *175*
Joyce, Padraic *25, 186, 187*

Judd, Mrs *162*

K

Kane, D.J. *137, 138, 141, 142, 146, 147, 149, 151, 152, 179, 185*
Kane, Val *78, 81, 111, 122, 123, 131, 141, 179, 199*
Keady, Tony *192*
Kearins, Mickey *184, 185*
Kearns, John *185*
Keating, Michael "Babs" *194*
Keaveney, Jimmy *184*
Keenan, John *119*
Keenan, Michael *176*
Keher, Eddie *193*
Kelleher, Robbie *183*
Kelly, Barry *26*
Kelly, Danny *118, 119*
Kelly, Gabriel *7*
Kelly, Gerry *142*
Kelly, John *138, 142, 144, 145*
Kelly, Paul *81, 82*
Kennedy, Hugh *111, 112*
Kennedy, Paddy *124, 129, 131, 133*
Kennedy, Seamus *99, 110, 111, 112*
Keogh, Padge *192*
Kernan, Joe *131*
Kerrigan, Jimmy *130*
Kevin O'Neill *179*
Kielty, John *91*
Kielty, Patrick *91*
Kierans, Patsy *20*
King, Mickey *74*
King, Ned *129, 132*
Knox, Gary *159*

L

Langan, Bobby *9, 10*
Larkin, Fan *193*
Larkin, Gene *57*
Larkin, Jimmy *115*
Lavery, George (Geordie) *29, 32, 37, 46, 47, 59, 60, 62, 65, 76, 78, 79, 86, 121*

Lawlor, John *52, 71*
Leahy, Johnny *194*
Lennon, Joe *5, 6, 7, 9, 20, 29, 41, 42, 44, 47, 50, 55, 56, 57, 61, 62, 64, 78, 80, 82, 90, 91, 94, 96, 98, 105, 106, 119, 120, 121, 130, 131*
Lennon, John *111*
Linden, Mickey *133, 135, 138, 140, 142, 146, 147, 149, 150, 151, 152, 186*
Linnane, Sylvie *192*
Liston, Eoin *124, 133, 182, 184, 185*
Loftus, Mick *121*
Lohan, Brian *192*
Long, Tom *107*
Lundy, Eamon *31, 98*
Lynch, Anthony *185, 187*
Lynch, Brendan *120, 121*
Lynch, Paudie *183, 185*
Lyne, Tadhgie *47, 48*
Lyons, Mick *140, 142*
Lyons, Tim "Tiger" *48, 93*

M

MacFlynn, Paddy *74, 114, 116*
Magee, Pat *128*
Magill, Micheal *149, 151, 152*
Maguire, Liam *63*
Maguire, Tom *7, 8, 110, 113*
Maher, Michael *193*
Mahon, Jack *1, 2*
Mallon, Seamus *159*
Mangan, Jack *181, 183, 185*
Marsden, Diarmaid *25*
Martin, Jimmy *61, 63*
Mason, Brendan *131, 133*
Mason, Gary *140, 142, 144, 149, 149–150, 150*
Matthews, Alfie *44*
McAlarney, Colm *82, 118, 119, 120, 121, 124, 125, 130, 184, 185*
McAlinden, Brian *131*
McAlinden, Patrick *74*
McAlinden, Patsy *78, 122*
McArdle, Michael *7, 44, 63*

Index

McAteer, Pat *72*
McAuley, John *99*
McAuliffe, Dan *36, 60*
McCabe, Ciaran *147*
McCarron, Isa *178*
McCarron, Michael *178*
McCarron, Tara *178*
McCartan, Brian *24, 115, 135, 142, 161, 163, 173, 177*
McCartan, Brian (Briney) *10, 12, 38, 74, 105, 174*
McCartan, Carrie *179*
McCartan, Charlie *12, 158*
McCartan, Charlie Pat *24, 25, 115, 142, 163, 178*
McCartan, Cian *178*
McCartan, Dan *6, 8, 12, 13, 16, 17, 18, 22, 23, 40, 41, 45, 47, 49, 60, 61, 62, 67, 68, 69, 79, 80, 82, 89, 105, 110, 111, 114, 115, 118, 120, 121, 123, 132, 138, 141, 176, 199*
McCartan, Daniel *115, 142, 170, 177, 178*
McCartan, Dan (Saval) *123, 131, 195*
McCartan, Delia *12, 58, 142, 155, 161, 163, 176, 178, 179*
McCartan, Dominic *109, 110, 111, 112, 123*
McCartan, Eileen *12, 176*
McCartan, Eoin *115, 142, 168–170, 177, 179*
McCartan, Fr Daniel *109*
McCartan, Gay *12, 122, 177*
McCartan, Gervase *109, 111, 112*
McCartan, Greg *115*
McCartan, Gregory *147, 149, 151, 152*
McCartan, James *9, 12, 13, 23, 24, 51, 53, 54, 62, 114, 124, 158, 178, 199*
McCartan, James (Junior) *24, 115, 135, 136, 138, 140, 140–141, 141–142, 144, 145–147, 147, 149–152, 158, 161, 163, 167, 175, 178*
McCartan, Jessica *178*
McCartan, John *23, 24, 26, 124, 129, 130, 131, 158*

McCartan, Maille *178*
McCartan, Maria *142, 163, 178*
McCartan, Marie Angelique *12*
McCartan, Mark *89, 138, 141, 176*
McCartan, Matthew *178*
McCartan (nee Mulholland), Marie *84, 142, 154, 155, 159, 161, 162, 164, 165, 166–173, 177, 195*
McCartan, Seamus *23, 26, 28, 38, 49, 109, 124, 158, 159, 179*
McCartan, Shay *26*
McCartan, Simone *177*
McCartan, Xavier *158*
McCarthy, Cathal *154*
McCarthy, Gerald *193*
McCashin, Gerry *76, 98–99*
McClorey, Jimmy *158*
McConville, Caoimhe *178*
McConville, Linda *178*
McConville, Niamh *178*
McConville, Oisin *186*
McConville, Plunkett *178*
McConville, Ray *117, 118, 121*
McCormack, Paddy *42, 54, 62, 183, 185, 199*
McCorry, Liam *19*
McCrory, Fr *24*
McCusker, Damian *138*
McCusker, Eamon *159*
McCusker, Fergal *137, 146*
McCusker, Geraldine *159*
McDermott, John *186, 187*
McDermott, Peter *43, 44, 46*
McDonagh, Mattie *54*
McDonald, Fiona *179*
McDonald, Michael *23*
McDonald, Mickey *131, 132*
McDonnell, Jim *7, 40, 41, 183, 184, 185*
McDonnell, Stephen *186*
McElroy, P.J. *19, 20, 21, 29, 36, 37, 38–39, 41, 42, 44, 59, 60, 62, 64, 95, 96, 105, 106, 110, 111, 112, 179*
McEniff, Brian *82*
McEvoy, Eamon *26*

McEvoy, Leo *115*
McEvoy, Pat *115*
McFeely, Frankie *82*
McGarrity, Joe *73*
McGarty, Packie *184*
McGeary, John *57, 58*
McGee, Eugene *182*
McGeeney, Kieran *185, 186*
McGilligan, Brian *145, 146, 186*
McGinnity, Peter *133*
McGivern, Aidan *24, 25*
McGlennon, Tom *114*
McGovern, Brendan *133*
McGovern, Fr Bertie *19*
McGovern, Tommy *124, 130*
McGowan, Barry *138*
McGrath, Hilary *122*
McGrath, Peter *24, 135, 136, 138, 139, 139–140, 140, 141, 142, 145, 146, 147, 150*
McGuigan, Frank *134, 184*
McGuigan, Gerry *111*
McGuinness, Malachy *20*
McKay, Eamon *85*
McKay, Eddie *5, 6, 8, 36, 37, 38–39, 40, 47, 55, 57, 58, 62, 63, 76, 85, 96, 98*
McKeever, Denis *56*
McKeever, Jim *29, 32, 33, 34, 53, 57, 66, 83, 91, 184, 185*
McKeever, Kieran *146*
McKendry, Sinead *178*
McKenna, Ger *155*
McKenna, Joe *192*
McKernan, Brendan *140, 142*
McKnight, Bridie *179*
McKnight, Delia *179*
McKnight, Felix *54, 58, 74, 111, 176, 179*
McKnight, Fr James *73, 74*
McKnight, John *58, 74, 176, 179*
McKnight, Mary *179*
McKnight, Michael *74, 176, 179*
McKnight, Orla *176, 179*
McKnight, Ruairi *176*
McKnight, Sharon *176*
McLoone, Mickey *82*
McMahon, Bryan *107*

Index

McMahon, Gary *37, 107*
McMahon, Seanie *192*
McNally, Gerry *113*
McNeill, Des *89*
McNeill, Mark *24*
McQuaid, Declan *159*
McQuaid, Mick *58*
McVerry, Michael *25*
Meade, Sean *2*
Milligan, Jim *119*
Molloy, P.J. *192*
Mooney, Sean *114*
Moore, Ronnie *33*
Moran, Kevin *184, 185*
Moran, Ogie *124*
Morgan, Billy *183*
Morgan, Brian *2, 6, 7, 8, 25, 29, 37, 38, 39, 41, 42, 45, 47, 55, 61, 64, 65, 68, 81, 95, 110*
Morgan, Dan *95*
Morgan, Declan *25*
Morgan, Ray *23, 25, 26, 81, 95*
Morgan, Tom *81*
Moriarty, Ando *153–156, 157*
Moriarty, Ando Jr *156*
Moriarty, Margaret *156*
Moriarty, Mary *156*
Moriarty, Paddy *131, 156*
Moriarty, Peggy *156*
Moynihan, Seamus *185, 186*
Mr X *164–166*
Mulcahy, Ger *130*
Mulholland, Colm *32*
Mullan, Brian *159*
Mullins, Brian *184*
Murdock, Hugh *51*
Murdock, Sean *128, 131*
Murphy, Con *115, 127, 128*
Murphy, Danny *131, 132, 195*
Murphy, Delia *12*
Murphy, Dickie *122*
Murphy, Eileen *179*
Murphy, Joey *158*
Murphy, John *118, 120, 121, 139*
Murphy, Kevin *115*

Murphy, Leo *2, 3, 4, 6, 8, 31, 33, 37, 39, 43, 45, 46, 47, 54, 56, 63, 68, 79, 80, 83, 87*
Murphy, Mick *113*
Murphy, Ollie *186, 187*
Murphy, Seamus *48, 107, 115, 119, 176, 179*
Murphy, Seamus Jr *176*
Murphy, Sean *53, 114, 176, 183, 184, 185*
Murphy, T.P. *74, 107, 114, 121, 123, 127, 134*
Murray, Alf *53, 54*
Murray, Brendan *33*
Murray, Cathal *24, 26*
Murray, Jimmy *18*
Murtagh, Harry *110, 112*
Murtagh, James *110*
Mussen, Damien *88*
Mussen, Dan *88*
Mussen, Declan *26*
Mussen, Fintan *26*
Mussen, George *88*
Mussen, Kevin *2, 8, 9, 19, 20, 26, 29, 34, 38, 40, 41, 42, 46, 47, 48, 49, 51, 56, 57, 59, 61, 62, 69, 76, 88, 94, 105, 110*
Mussen, Liam *26*

N

Nealon, Donie *194*
Nelligan, Charlie *124, 183*
Neville, Tom *193*
Nic an Ultaigh, Sighle *85, 173, 174*
Nolan, Willie *42, 44, 45*

O

Oakes, Alfie *101*
O'Brien, Danny *39*
O'Brien, Paddy *183*
O'Caoimh, Padraig *103*
O'Connell, Martin *185*
O'Connell, Mick *47, 48, 49, 55, 60, 106, 119, 120, 184, 185*
O'Connell, Sean *32, 34, 118*
O'Connor, Ben *193*
O'Connor, Jamesie *192*

O'Connor, Liam *183*
O'Donnell, Joe *112*
O'Donnell, Nick *52, 192*
O'Donoghue, Hugh Barney *40*
O'Donoghue, Paddy *104, 121*
O'Dowd, Barry *160, 162*
O'Dowd, Declan *160, 162*
O'Dowd family *161, 167*
O'Dowd, Joseph *160, 162*
O'Dowd, Seamus *161*
O'Dowd, Teddy *60*
O'Dwyer, Mick *49, 54, 60, 99, 119–120, 120–121, 182, 199–200*
Óg De Paor, Sean *185, 187*
O'Hagan, Brendan *94*
O'Hagan, Fr Joe *15*
O'Hagan, Patsy *2, 4, 5, 6, 7, 8, 20, 24, 31, 32, 37, 38, 39, 41, 42, 44, 45, 47, 51, 54, 56, 57, 59, 61, 67, 79, 80, 82, 94, 110*
O'Hara, Paddy *80, 82*
O'Hare, Gervase *129*
O'Hare, John *101*
O'Hare, Pat *146*
O'Hare, Tom *79, 81, 83, 118, 119, 120, 132, 183*
O'Hehir, Michael *18, 45, 46, 70, 71*
O'Keeffe, John *183, 185*
O'Leary, John *185, 186*
O'Leary, Seanie *193*
O'Loan, Nuala *108*
O'Malley, Gerry *184*
O'Malley, Robbie *185, 186*
O'Neill, Captain Terence *148*
O'Neill, Gerry *23, 33*
O'Neill, Jody *7, 81, 184*
O'Neill, Kevin *6, 13, 14, 18, 31, 32, 41, 44, 46, 49, 52, 56, 59, 61, 62, 65, 67, 76, 89–90, 105, 141, 172*
O'Neill, Leo *33, 57*
O'Neill, Martin *23, 33*

Index

O'Neill, Sean *2, 4, 5, 7, 8, 13, 18, 32, 33, 34, 36, 37, 38, 38–39, 39, 40, 41, 44, 45, 46, 48, 49, 54, 56, 60, 61, 63, 64, 65, 68, 69, 71, 72, 76, 78, 80, 81, 82, 89, 92, 94, 97, 105, 107, 112, 117, 118, 119–121, 141, 172, 184, 185, 199*
O'Reilly, Noel *7*
O'Rourke, Colm *140, 141, 186, 187*
O'Rourke, Paddy *124, 129, 130, 131, 136, 142, 143, 144*
Ó Sé, Darragh *186, 187*
Ó Sé, Marc *185, 187*
Ó Sé, Páidí *183, 185*
Ó Sé, Tomás *185, 187*
O'Shea, Jack *124, 136, 139, 182, 184, 185*
O'Shea, Jerome *183, 185*
O'Sullivan, Donie *183*
O'Sullivan, Dr Eamon *59*
O'Sullivan, Timmy *60*
Owens, Paddy *156*

P

Paisley, Eileen *122*
Paisley, Ian *122*
Pettit, Fr Joseph *22, 102*
Powell, Larry *81, 120, 122*
Power, Ger *184*
Power, Seamus *192*
Pritchard, Peter *79*
Pudlowski, Walt *73*
Purcell, Sean *1, 2, 4, 181, 184, 185*
Purdy, Dan *114, 115*
Purdy, John *114, 115, 118, 121*

Q

Quigley brothers *193*
Quigley, Felix *81*
Quinn, Fr Peter *72*

R

Rackard, Bobby *192*
Rackard, Nicky *192*
Rackard, Willie *192*

Redmond, Charlie *151*
Reel, Ollie *24*
Rehill, John *133*
Rice Bookmakers *153*
Rice, Hugh *114*
Rice, Pat *2, 29, 37, 38, 43, 65, 67, 68, 87*
Ring, Christy *193*
Robinson, Kevin *159*
Roche, Con *193*
Roche, Mick *193*
Rodgers, Ambrose *97, 124, 131, 132, 135, 141*
Rogers, Declan *23*
Rogers, Martin *24*
Rooney, Dan *121*
Rooney, Peter *118, 119, 120, 121, 124*
Roussakis, George *73*
Russell, Eugene *112*
Ryan, Glen *185, 187*
Ryan, Matt *154*
Ryan, Sean *42*

S

Sands, Sean *123*
Scullion, Tony *146, 185, 186*
Sheedy, Jack *151*
Sheehy, Mikey *133, 182, 184, 185*
Sheehy, Paudie *37, 107*
Shefflin, Henry *193*
Shields, Mr *70*
Simmonson, Shirley *177*
Sinnott, Fr John *115*
Skehan, Noel *193*
Skelton, Paul *24*
Sloan, Brendan *118, 121, 124, 125*
Smith, Con *41*
Smith, Henry *21*
Smith, John *59, 60, 61, 97*
Smith, Peter *32*
Smith, Raymond *90, 92*
Smyth, Con *40*
Smyth, Miss *16*
Spiers, Sean *73*
Spillane, Mick *124*

Spillane, Pat *133, 139, 184, 185*
Spillane, Tom *139*
Stafford, Brian *186*
Stafford, Jim *76*
Stevenson, Denis *131*
Stevenson, Fr *24*
Stockwell, Frankie *1, 181*
Storey, Martin *192*
Stuart, Phil *57, 85*
Sugrue, Tommy *151*

T

Tierney, Brendan *24*
Tierney, Noel *183, 185*
Tinnelly, George *74, 102, 109*
Tohill, Anthony *137, 145, 146, 186*
Toman, Joe *160*
Toner, Brendan *125, 131, 132*
Toner, Declan *25*
Trainor, Barney *139*
Treacy, P.T. *20, 81*
Treanor, Fr *23, 25*
Treanor, Fr John *19, 26*
Tunney, Brother *113*
Turbett, Thady *6*
Turley, Mark *125, 132*

W

Walker, Trevor *142, 159*
Wall, Tony *193*
Walsh, Dr Martin *3, 23, 50*
Walsh, Frankie *192*
Walsh, Ollie *193*
Walsh, Sean *124*
Walsh, Tommy *193*
Whan, Jimmy *57*
Wheeler, Ned *192*
Whelan, Ciaran *186*
Whelehan, Brian *192*
White, Stephen *183*
Wilson, Phil *193*
Withnall, Peter *136, 138–139, 139, 140, 142, 145*
Wray, Jim *114*
Wrenn, Charlie *44*
Wright, Mr *16*

Bibliography and Sources

I would like to gratefully acknowledge the following publications, clubs and individuals for providing me with background information. This was invaluable to me in the compilation of this book. The availability of so much primary data from so many sources made my research all the more simple.

All-Ireland Football Captains Brian Carthy, Wolfhound Press, 1993

An Dún – The GAA Story Sighle Nic an Ultaigh, Down GAA County Board, 1990

Armagh Observer

Belfast Celtic John Kennedy and Bill McKavanagh, Pretani Press, 1989

Castlewellan GAC

Down's Days of Glory Fabian Boyle, 1994

Down GAA Yearbooks

Dundrum GAC

Evening Press

Frontier Sentinel

Giants of Gaelic Football Seán Óg Ó Ceallacháin, Gill and Macmillan, 2007

Glenn GAC

History of Gaelic Football Jack Mahon, Gill and Macmillan, 2000

Hogan Stand Gaelic Football and Hurling Lynn Publications, 1993, 2005

Irish Greyhound Board, Orla Strumble and Dawn Quinn, Marketing Department, Limerick

Irish Independent

Irish News

Irish Press

Irish Times

Newry Shamrocks GAC

St Malachy's GAC Edendork

St Michael's GAC Magheralin

The All-Ireland Dream Seamus McRory, Wolfhound Press, 2005

The Evolution of the GAA Donal McAnallen, David Hassan and Roddy Hegarty, 2009

The Football Immortals Raymond Smith, Aherlow Publishers, 1983

The Kerryman

The Road to Croke Park Seamus McRory, Blackwater Press, 1999

The Sons of Sam Seamus Maloney, The Brehon Press, 2004

The Sunday Press

Tullylish GAC

Ulster Football and Hurling Jerome Quinn, Wolfhound Press, 1993

Nicky Barry, Killarney and Newry

John Byrne, Lurgan

Plunkett Campbell, Tullylish

Barney Carr in "Linesman" and many other guises!

Colm Fitzpatrick, Rostrevor

Michael Fortune, Dublin

Gay Glynn, Ashbourne

Martin Goss, St Colman's College, Newry

John Hanratty, Lurgan

Dr Maurice Hayes, Downpatrick

Dan McCartan, Tyrella

Sean McCartan

Dr Frank McCorry, Lurgan

James McGarvey, Lissan

Brendan McRory, Lissan

Raymond Morgan, Retired Head of PE Department, St Colman's College, Newry

Danny Murphy, Secretary to Ulster GAA Council

Fintan Mussen, Former PRO Down GAA County Board